3 4028 06888 0211
HARRIS COUNTY PUBLIC LIBRARY

636.108 Gre
Greene, Ann Norton
Horses at work : harnessing
   power in industrial
 America
                        $29.95
           ocn220100352
           01/14/2009

D0897952

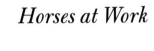

Horses at Work

Horses at Work

HARNESSING POWER IN INDUSTRIAL AMERICA

ANN NORTON GREENE

HARVARD UNIVERSITY PRESS

Cambridge, Massachusetts ★ London, England ★ 2008

Copyright © 2008 by the President and Fellows of Harvard College
All rights reserved
Printed in the United States of America

Library of Congress Cataloging-in-Publication Data

Greene, Ann Norton, 1952–
    Horses at work : harnessing power in industrial America /
Ann Norton Greene.—1st ed.
        p.   cm.
    Includes bibliographical references and index.
    ISBN 978-0-674-03129-6 (cloth : alk. paper)
1. Draft horses—United States—History—19th century.
2. Working animals—United States—History—19th century.
I. Title.
    SF311.3.U6G68 2008
    636.1'0886097309034—dc22   2008014745

For Bob, Liz, and Andy

CONTENTS

ILLUSTRATIONS

This book is about the draft horses found in the Northeast and Midwest during the nineteenth century and their role in the industrialization of the United States. Most books about horses end up being about the humans who write them, and this is probably no exception. Humans project their concerns onto horses; mine are with the meaning of work and energy. Horses, however, are largely indifferent to humans. They tolerate us in general, and they may like some of us in particular, but their interests lie elsewhere than with us. I have tried to keep horses at the center of this work by avoiding sentimentality and anthropomorphisms about them, and by not straying far beyond what I know of equine physiology and behavior.

Horses were nonetheless historical beings whose presence in large numbers affected how Americans lived and worked and how they perceived the world. Horses' historical agency lies in the substance of their existence, the physical power they produced, and the role of that power in shaping material and social arrangements. The material matters; nineteenth-century America would have been un-imaginably different without horses.

Writing this book took me on a journey through the pleasures and pitfalls of interdisciplinary work. The topic not only took me to the libraries and archives that are the usual workplaces for historians, but let me visit stables, veterinary clinics, urban carriage stands, horse shows, coaching parades, and Amish farms.

A small army of people made it possible for me to write this book. Funding from the University of Pennsylvania, grants from the Library Company of Philadelphia and the Hagley Museum and Library, and the Brooke Hindle Postdoctoral Fellowship from the Society for the History of Technology made research and writing possible. Seminar presentations at the University of Pennsylvania, University of Delaware, Rutgers University, Drexel University, the Massachusetts Institute of Technology, and at meetings of the American Historical Association, the American Society for Environmental History, the American Association for the History of Medicine, the Organization of American Historians, and the Society for the History of Technology provided feedback and discussion on many portions of this book. I have benefited from the assistance of librarians and archivists at the Adirondack Museum Research Library, the American Philosophical Society, the Civil War Museum, the Hagley Museum and Library, the Historical Society of New Hampshire, the Historical Society of Pennsylvania, the Library Company of Philadelphia, the National Archives, the University of Pennsylvania Archives, the University of Wisconsin libraries, and the Wisconsin Historical Society. In particular, I want to thank the staff of the Van Pelt Library at the University of Pennsylvania. Special thanks go to John Pollack and Lynne Farrington in the Rare Book and Manuscript Library for giving me the opportunity to curate an exhibit from the Fairman Rogers Collection of nineteenth-century horse books.

I have received a great deal of professional support for this project. I wish to thank Thomas Hughes for being my academic godfather and for supplying mentoring and regular glasses of wine. Drew Gilpin Faust supported this project in its beginnings, as it wobbled on spindly legs, and Thomas Sugrue guided it down the homestretch. Robert Kohler rescued me from more tangents than I care to remember, provided superb advice and badgerish friendship, and kept the project on course. Joel Tarr and Clay McShane generously shared their research as they wrote their own book on horses. Philip Teigen provided census statistics, research material, and conversation about animal history. Gary Gallagher, Steven Hahn, Susan Jones, Bruce Kuklick, Walter Licht, Stephanie McCurry, Walter McDougall, Eric Rau, Edmund Russell, Philip Scranton, Thomas Zeller, and Michael Zuckerman commented on portions of the manuscript. Thanks also go to Frank Abel, Brian Black, Alison Brooks, Laurie Carlson, Thomas Childers, Ruth Schwartz Cowan, Nathan Ensmenger, Gerald Fitzgerald, Katherine Grier, Richard Immerman, Richard John, Marily Langill, Nina Lerman, Alan Levy, Sue McConnell, Martin Melosi, Arwen Mohun, Bob Nelson, John Perkins, Gabriella Petrick, Rob Sigafoos, John L. Thomas, Bernard Unti, and Kristen Wood.

Many friends have cheered me on and tactfully refrained from asking me when the book would be ready: Gary and Mary Ellen Abrecht, Alison Brooks, Melissa Buckingham, LindaCarol Cherken, Eugenie Dieck, Kathryn Hellerstein, Pam Hill, Mary McConaghy, Linda Mellgren, John Payne, Victoria Sicks. My parents have provided both material and moral support; sadly, my father did not live to see the completion of this book, which had its origins in a world he loved and missed. I would not know what to do without the love and support of my brother, Howard Greene, and my sister, Elizabeth Greene.

It was my good fortune to have Joyce Seltzer as my editor. She is a great coach, insightful and incisive in her reading of manuscripts, and both firm and supportive about getting the writing done. I think better and write better because of her. Ann Hawthorne also did yeoman service laboring on the manuscript.

This book has spanned a large portion of my children's lives. If they minded, they did not tell me, and they have always cheered me on with a "Go, Mom!" My husband, Bob, deserves the most thanks of anyone; he has always supported me, and no more so than during the writing of this book. Bob has always shown me what love looks like, and I could not have done this without him.

In late October 1872 *The Nation* magazine published an article titled "The Position of the Horse in Modern Society." It was written
in the wake of an epidemic of horse influenza, which had swept
across the Northeast and incapacitated the horses there. In city after
city, and along the railroad lines and canals, daily life came to a halt.
As the epidemic waned and life returned to normal, *The Nation*
urged its readers to recognize "the importance of the part which
this animal has come to play in our commercial civilization and the
close relation there exists between [the horse's] physical condition
and *our* material interests." The article further expanded on why
horses had become an essential source of power:

> Our talk has been for so many years of the railroad and
> steamboat and telegraphy, as the great "agents of progress,"
> that we have come almost totally to overlook the fact that
> our dependence on the horse has grown almost *pari passu*
> with our dependence on steam. We have opened up great
> lines of steam communication all over the country, but they

have to be fed with goods and passengers by horses. We
have covered the ocean with great steamers, but they can
neither load nor discharge their cargoes without horses.

Popular excitement about steam engines had obscured the fact that
they made horses more important than ever. Horses and steam engines complemented each other as prime movers. City life underscored the significance of this relationship. Steam power concentrated industry and population in the industrial cities, but most of
urban life depended on power from horses.

We have collected at the mouths of our great rivers and
at the intersections of our railroads vast bodies of people,
covering miles on miles of area with their dwellings and
factories, but have left them wholly dependent for their in-
tramural travel and for their regular supplies of food and
clothing on horses. More than this, we have with the last
few years made horse labor an almost essential condition of
the protection of our great cities from fire.

Because horses were a traditional and familiar source of power,
many Americans failed to grasp that their reliance on horses had
been increasing for several decades. "This increase of our industrial
and commercial dependence on the horse has, however, been so
gradual, so quiet, and has issued so naturally from the state of things
prior to the introduction of steam, and has been so completely over-
shadowed by the great applications of science to industry and locomotion, that little or no thought has been bestowed upon its dangers."[1] Only when a crisis like the equine influenza epidemic
exposed the structure of the energy system was this symbiosis between steam and horses fully recognized.

The influenza had sickened the horses but killed very few. However, it raised the specter of what might happen if a deadly disease afflicted the nation's horses, "as plagues have broken out among men, which would sweep them away by the hundred or thousand every day, and which would momentarily baffle science." The energy crisis caused by such an epidemic "would totally disorganize our industry and our commerce, and would plunge social life into disorder." For this reason, the current horse epidemic was a blessing in disguise. By providing a graphic demonstration of society's reliance on horse power, it brought "public attention in a serious way to the necessity for some change in our treatment of horses" in order to avoid a catastrophe in the future.[2]

The cities suffered the worst effects of the epidemic, showing that urban conditions made horses as well as humans more vulnerable to disease. "Most of us have well-nigh forgotten that the horse was an animal like ourselves—liable to pains and aches and death. We had come think of him as a machine, on whose endurance we could calculate as on that of an engine and for whose mortality we could make ample allowance in our business under the head of 'wear and tear.'" Urban horses were exposed every day to "just those conditions from which the great pestilences among human beings have sprung." The combination of dense horse populations, hard work, and airless, fetid stables made every city "a hot-bed of horse disease."[3]

These conditions not only threatened economic prosperity but also called into question the nation's moral and cultural standing. "The condition of the horse among us is a disgrace to our civilization . . . worthy of the Dark Ages," not of a society that saw itself as being enlightened and progressive. Horses' living and working conditions should be as much of a concern to Americans as those of human workers. Just because horses were the property of private individuals and companies did not mean that their health and well-being was not a matter for public concern and involvement. "They are wheels in our great social machines, the stoppage of which means widespread injury to all classes and conditions of persons, injury to commerce, to agriculture, to trade, to social life."[4]

The Nation was far from alone in its perspective on horses. Many observers recognized that horses were a power technology of crucial importance. In the twenty-first century horses are often regarded as representing the very opposite of technology, but in the nineteenth century they were considered part of the "useful arts." This referred to the tools, techniques, and knowledge involved in making and doing things. It encompassed both art and science, combining the ideas of practical skills and scientific knowledge. Horses, as prime movers, were part of any discussion or manual of the useful arts. In the twentieth century the term "useful arts" disappeared, and "technology" came into wide use, in conjunction with the development of aeronautics, medical advances, weaponry, and computers. For many people, "technology" connoted large-scale, complex objects and systems, far removed from horses as organic creatures. In this context, horses became quaint vestiges of a preindustrial world.[5]

To many people, horses are symbols of nature, or the world of original things. They represent the idea of a place that is essential and timeless, the foundation of all things and diametrically different from an ever-changing human-built world. However, as much as people might like to think of horses as specimens of original nature, horses are one of the very oldest kinds of technology. More precisely, horses are biotechnology, or organisms altered for human use. Through the process of domestication, horses became living machines. For five millennia humans have been modifying horses by breeding them for size, strength, speed, temperament, and appearance so that they would be more useful in transportation, work, warfare, and sport. In addition, humans created the devices that make it possible to access horses' physical power and apply it to their purposes. Horseshoes, harness, vehicles, and machines are just some of the things that enabled humans to harness horse power, along with accumulated knowledge about horse care, training, riding, driving, breeding, behavior, and medicine. All these things are part of the technological network that horses represent.[6]

In human society, the utility and physical power of horses reinforced other kinds of power—aristocratic, military, political, sexual, religious. For many centuries, horses were primarily an elite animal. Of all the draft animals, horses were one of the most costly to use and maintain. If they became symbols of social status and ruling power, it was because leaders and ruling classes owned most of them. Horses were regarded as the natural aristocrats of the animal world that represented what the natural order of the human realm should be.[7]

The nineteenth century stands out because it was a time when horses were so widely used that they were not just elite animals, but the work animals for many Americans. Early in the century horse use began to increase noticeably, and this trend continued until the twentieth century was well underway and the use of horses began to decline. As a result, horses were ubiquitous in nineteenth-century society. By the end of the century, a bird's-eye view of the nation would show horses everywhere, working in cities, towns, and factories, on farms and frontiers, on streets and roads, alongside canals, around forts, ports, and railroad depots. Horses were particularly dense in and around the cities. Census returns would confirm the visible evidence that the horse population had grown substantially, and that Americans consumed more power from horses than from any other source.

Technologies never exist in isolation, but are always part of a network of usage. In this regard technologies are not unlike organisms, which always occupy a distinct niche in a larger ecosystem. Ecologists use the term niche to explain an organism's role. Charles Elton, a founder of the discipline, put it this way. "When an ecologist says, 'there goes a badger' he [includes] in his thoughts some definite idea of the animal's place in the community to which it belongs, just as if he has said, 'there goes the vicar.'" In nineteenth-century America, horses occupied the niche of fractional power, as highly mobile, versatile prime movers complementing the role of the steam engine, which had greater power but was less versatile. Without the motive power of horses, the role of steam power would have been far different. As steam power altered transportation and production, it created new jobs for horses in the interstices of these developing sectors. In the twentieth century, the role of horses would move from the center to the periphery of the industrial system, but for more than a century horses occupied a niche that no other prime mover could fill.[8]

Horses occupied this niche because in the early nineteenth century Americans tackled the problem of draft. Draft is the amount of power necessary to put an object into motion. It measures the resistance to motion in a mechanism or a vehicle. Calculated in pounds, it represents the working weight of a load or mechanism, not its weight at rest. For example, a load pulled in a wagon for a mile along a dry, level road has little draft and barely tires the horse, while the same load pulled for a mile along a road deep in mud and water has enormous draft and exhausts the horse quickly. Draft gauges energy cost.

In early nineteenth-century America reducing draft was a primary concern for those interested in commercial and industrial development. Poor roads meant high draft for horses and high transportation costs. These obstructed overland travel, funneled trade along water routes, curtailed economic development, and kept inland communities isolated. In a nation as large and as young as the United States, high draft was more than an economic issue; it had ramifications for national security and political stability. Americans addressed the problem by constructing roads and canals that would reduce the draft for horses so that they could be efficiently used for overland travel. An inevitable result is that the history of horses as prime movers is part of the history of American energy and technology.[9]

Energy history is environmental history; different kinds of energy transform the environment into different kinds of landscapes. Developments in transportation transformed the landscape, by rebuilding it into one where horses could be efficiently used, by promoting farming and manufacturing in newly accessible areas, and by facilitating the migration of populations of animals and plants—humans, horses, other domesticated animals, and the plants of crops and gardens—into new regions. As organic beings that are prime movers, horses challenge any conventional nature-technology divide.[10]

Technologies are considered to be labor-saving, but by streamlining or alleviating work for some tasks, technologies may increase work in other areas, create a new set of tasks, or trigger unintended consequences. Using a technology means accepting its demands, and, as living machines, horses made many demands on people. Their daily upkeep required a great deal of human work to produce a great deal of horse work. Horses were workers as well as machines that labored in partnership with humans. Horses were also residents, living alongside humans. As horse populations swelled, nineteenth-century America became more than a society that used horses; it became a society of horses and humans living and working together.[11]

One of the difficulties of animal history is a lack of understanding that animals change over time. There is a tendency to see them as static, in contrast with changes in human society. This circumstance relates to the equation of horses with a natural world traditionally assumed to be unchanging as well. Another difficulty is keeping the animals at the center of study. Much writing about animals is really about the meanings ascribed to them and the human interpretation of their actions.

Yet another problem is the question of animals as historical agents. "Agency," for humans, means the capacity to make and act on choices. It is associated with resistance, defiance, and intentionality. Clearly, it is inappropriate to impose a model of human agency upon another species, about whose cognition and consciousness we inevitably understand very little. In this context, it is also clear that historical agents do not require intentionality in order to affect the process of historical change. And without understanding the impact of horses on the social and material environment in the nineteenth century, it is impossible to understand the industrial transformation of American society.

The advent of the automobile did not eliminate the use of horses for power. Well into the twentieth century, the energy landscape of horse use remained an integral part of American society. The use of horses not only established lasting spatial arrangements but also established a set of expectations about energy abundance, personal autonomy, and mobility. Even today these continue to manifest themselves in ideas about time and space, travel and work, individuality and community, public space and private space. The resilience of horse power can be measured by the fact that it took three kinds of power to replace horses as prime movers. Steam engines replaced long-distance hauling, but with the consequence of dramatically increasing the number of horses used for short-distance haulage. Electric power replaced the use of horses in mass transit. Only the third one, automotive transport, came close to replicating the horse as a prime mover, by offering Americans not only more power, but power in the form of separate, self-propelled prime movers to which they had become accustomed.

Examining industrialization through the lens provided by the rise and fall of horse technology complicates the conventional narrative. Horse technology opens a window onto the material and social world of nineteenth-century America and directs our attention to aspects of American society assumed to be ancillary or marginal to industrial change. It points to how people use and think about technology, rather than to what was invented. Above all, it alerts us to the complexity of technological change.[12]

The rise and fall of horse power was in the end a product of American choices about economic growth. It took half a century before draft horses were replaced in most areas, but as living machines horses lost their niche in the cultural environment well before they lost it in the technological one. Carolyn Marvin has observed: "People often imagine that, like Michelangelo chipping away at the block of marble, new technologies will make the world more nearly what it was meant to be all along."[13] The use of horses fitted into a pattern of beliefs about technological change and economic growth that emerged in early nineteenth-century America, tying energy consumption to national prosperity and progress.[14] Americans were (and continue to be) firm believers in one best technology, one best kind of energy, one best way, and the notion that finding it would bring about not simply an improved society but a perfected society.

The nineteenth century was much more the age of horse power than the age of steam power. Horses, not steam engines, established the material environment and cultural values that have shaped energy use in the twentieth century. In our attitudes about transportation and mobility, in our relationships to automobiles, and in our language of movement and power, horses are still with us. Although they are no longer widely used as a source of energy, we must understand their role as the most important prime movers in the nineteenth century as we face the energy challenges of the twenty-first.

In 1819 the draft animal of the future was the ox, not the horse.

That at least was the opinion of former U.S. President James Madison, now president of the Albemarle County Agricultural Society. In a speech to that body, Madison asserted that it was "an error in our husbandry that oxen are too little used in favor of horses," for it was clear that oxen were the more practical choice. "Expence" favored oxen, said Madison, because unlike horses they were not were fed on Indian corn, "which requires the most labour and greatly exhausts the land." By using oxen, farmers both reduced their expenses and released acreage for more profitable uses; in addition, oxen produced not only power but also beef, tallow, and leather.[1]

Madison's speech was reprinted in *American Farmer*, where William Cobbett, a journalist and reformer who worked a farm on Long Island, echoed his sentiments. Cobbett saw oxen as the better choice of farm power. "Horses, if they are strong enough, are not so steady as oxen, which are more patient also . . . without any of the fretting and unequal pulling, or jerking, that you have to encounter with horses. And as to the slow pace of the ox, it is the old story of the tortoise and the hare." In addition to being easier to train and use, oxen were inexpensive, requiring little equipment or additional labor. "A single chain and the yoke, with no reins, no halters, no traces, no bridle, no driver ... an ox goes steadier than a horse, and will plough deeper without fretting and tearing; and he wants neither harness-makers nor groom." Cobbett firmly concluded, "I want no horses." When it came to making a success of farming, "all the food and manual labour required by such horses, ought to be considered as so much taken from the clear profits of the farm."[2]

Yet even as Madison and Cobbett argued the superiority of oxen, they revealed why horses were already taking greater hold as draft animals in an industrializing America. Cobbett admitted that he owned horses because his family objected to driving around behind oxen. "Horses may be kept for the purpose of going to church, or to meeting, or to pay visits ... This may be not only convenient, but necessary to a family. 'What!' the ladies will say, 'would you have us be shut up at home all our lives; or be dragged about by oxen?'" So, though Cobbett considered horses "neither convenient or necessary to a farm," he acceded to his family's wishes to be spared social isolation or public embarrassment. Oxen, clearly, had insufficient status. Madison had to concede that oxen were slower than horses, but he gamely asserted that a fine, young, well-matched yoke of oxen "may be kept to nearly as quick a step as the horse." Imagine the reaction of Cobbett's womenfolk to Madison's suggestion that oxen saved farmers so much money that they could hire someone to take their produce to market and never leave the farm at all.[3]

Madison and Cobbett were part of a generation committed to improvement, men with a vision of the destiny of the new nation, the belief that every decision was of utmost significance, and very specific ideas about how to turn the vision into a reality. Increasing the use of animal power for production and mobility fitted the kind of development they wanted for an agrarian and commercial republic.

Reformers like Cobbett often tried to set an example of best practices on their own farms. Discussions among reformers about the
relative merits of different kinds of draft animals were common
throughout the century at agricultural society meetings and in the
pages of the agricultural press. Convinced that there was one best
living machine to use, Americans debated, often passionately, which
animal was the right tool for the job.[4]

But Americans used more than economics and efficiency to
guide their choices of draft animals. They categorized draft animals
much as they categorized themselves, projecting identities of race,
class, gender, wealth, region, nationality, civilization, morality, and
character onto horses, oxen, mules, and other animals. Cobbett believed that horses were luxury items to be purchased only after the
farm was turning a clear profit. For Madison, advocating oxen was
as much a statement about the moral order of the political economy
and society he envisioned as it was about energy choice alone. The
desire to own an impressive, quick-stepping team of spirited horses
smacked of a desire for status and material luxury contrary to the
spirit of republican simplicity and virtue represented by the practical, phlegmatic, plodding ox, over and above the fact that horses
were more expensive to use. However, over the next half-century
horses would become increasingly cost-effective to use, and much
less of a luxury animal. In this sense, widening horse use in the nineteenth century reflected the rambunctious democracy, social mobility, and economic development that characterized the American
style of industrialization.[5]

That there were horses to use at all in nineteenth-century America was a contingency, not an inevitability, that arose from the inter-
section of national history and natural history. None of the draft animals Americans used were indigenous to the continent. Although
horses had originally evolved in North America, migrating over land
bridges to inhabit grasslands around the world, they became extinct

in North America more than 10,000 years before European settlement, during the Pleistocene period, most likely because of encroaching glaciers, climate changes, and human hunting. Horses returned with Spanish colonizers in the sixteenth century. There were no indigenous draft animals. All American draft animals—primarily oxen and horses and, to a lesser extent, donkeys and mules—were foreign imports rather than domestic models.

That Americans or anyone else could even entertain the idea of using horses for work resulted from the natural history of horses as domesticated animals. Of all human-animal relations, domestication is one of the most specialized, especially between humans and large animals. It is also one of the most misunderstood. Nineteenth-century anthropologists and archeologists saw domestication as one of the major stages of cultural development, a self-conscious and prescient act in which humans selected the animals that would be the most useful.

However, horses are one of only fourteen large (over 100 pounds) domesticated animals in the world, the others being camels, llamas/alpacas, reindeer, yak, asses (donkeys), pigs, sheep, goats, and several kinds of cattle (including water buffalo). Only three of these—horses, donkeys, and cattle—are used worldwide. All of them share the same set of characteristics. All of them are large enough to be useful for work or food, but not too large to control. None are carnivores that might view humans as lunch. All are herd animals with stable, sociable dispositions, accustomed to living in hierarchical social groups and fitting comfortably into the hierarchy of human society. They breed easily in captivity and have gestation periods of less than a year. They have nicely balanced fight-flight instincts, neither too aggressive nor confrontational, nor flighty and inclined to panic and stampede. In addition, they are not territorial, do not engage in elaborate mating rituals requiring lots of space or specific places, and do not have diets dependent on particular places or plants. They have manageable sizes—horses, for example, average four to six feet in height, six to eight feet in length, and a half-ton to a ton in weight.[6]

These characteristics eliminate most of the large animals in the world. Hippopotamuses, or "river horses," grow to nearly seven feet in height, thirteen feet in length, and over three tons in weight. They are extraordinarily aggressive and dangerous animals, responsible for a significant number of human deaths each year on the African continent. Rhinoceroses are relatives of horses (both are odd-toed ungulates, or single-hoofed) but unlike horses are solitary animals. They are taller and longer, twice as heavy, and famously ill-tempered and aggressive. Zebras are members of the horse family, though smaller and lighter, but as a group have never been successfully bred and employed for work, though there have been individual cases of success. On the North American continent moose are a manageable size (six to seven feet in height and around half a ton in weight) but are solitary and irritable in disposition, and not herd animals. Deer and antelope are too flighty to be easily herded or harnessed. Finally, elephants are an example of use without domestication. Though elephants have been used in Asia for centuries in work and warfare, and tamed and used for work when young, as they mature elephants grow to between six and thirteen feet in height and three to six tons in weight, and become not only too large but too aggressive to control. In addition, they have a lengthy gestation period of twenty-two months, twice that of horses, and do not breed well in captivity.

Though horses do not have the greatest strength, speed, size, or stamina available in the animal world, they do possess all the characteristics necessary for domestication: nonterritorial herd animals, easy reproduction, sociable disposition, and manageable size. In nineteenth-century America the confluence of natural history and national history provided both a natural and a social environment strongly conducive to their use. Horses were integral components of the "second nature" that Americans built during the industrial era, a transformed environment that quickly became "naturalized" until it seemed original and not constructed.

In the second nature of industrializing America, horses were living machines. Nineteenth-century Americans were enthralled with machinery of all sorts, flocking to factories and fairs to witness the latest mechanical marvels. The machine and its terminology was the dominant metaphor of society, much as the computer and its terminology are today. The idea of the machine encompassed a specific (often powerful) device and a set of relationships governed by discernible laws. Machines might be powerful and complicated, but they were ultimately comprehensible and predictable. As Governor Edward Everett of Massachusetts said, "The mechanician, not the magician, is now the master of life."[7] Machine analogies were used to describe all aspects of the social and physical world, and horses were no exception.

Analogies between animals and machines were already well established in Western culture. The mechanical clocks of the thirteenth century and the mechanical philosophy of René Descartes in the sixteenth century promoted a new view of the relationship between living creatures and their environment. Descartes argued that animals were not simply like machines, but were machines, and their actions could all be explained mechanically. By the nineteenth century, the Enlightenment concept of a mechanistic nature governed by universal laws seemed fulfilled in a world of growing mechanization, where human artifice could replicate and improve upon the machinery of the natural world. Important new machinery and sources of power received animal names—the locomotive was an iron horse, the spinning machine was a mule, the power of steam engines was expressed in horsepower—to signify the achievement of replicating the power of animals, and to express the exuberance of invention and a growing sense of mastery over nature.

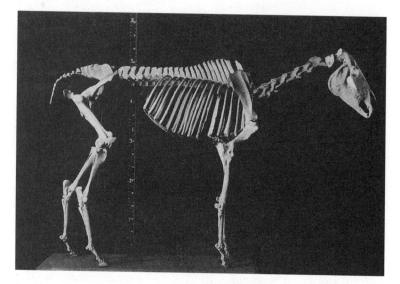

Equine skeleton (English racehorse Eclipse, 1764–1789). Source: Theodore Cook, *Eclipse and OKelly* (New York, 1907). Fairman Rogers Collection, University of Pennsylvania.

If machines were described as animals, animals were also described as machines. Nineteenth-century people often analyzed horses and other animals in mechanical terms. They used machine analogies to describe, decipher, and compare the operation of animal bodies and the production of power, and to express the results in scientific language. "It is only by acquaintance with, and a study of the structure of the horse, that we can put him to the best uses; not necessarily a scientific knowledge of his structure, but so far, at least as to comprehend the nature of the machine—for such the horse is."[8]

Most writing about horse motion analyzed it in terms of simple mechanics, seeing the equine body as a combination of levers (bones) put in motion by pulleys (muscles). A horse's legs were hinged levers swinging back and forth. A horse's long neck and heavy head functioned as a weighted lever whose momentum could help the animal increase speed or augment pulling. People knew that there was a tradeoff between speed and power in the equine engine. Just how the horse produced its power and exactly what kind of machine it was remained unsettled questions.

Twentieth-century knowledge about animal locomotion and energy efficiency has expanded the mechanical understanding of the nineteenth century. The horse's gifts as a prime mover lie in how the body structure facilitates motion and energy efficiency. A horse has four long, fragile-looking legs that hold the body well above the ground, giving it a long stride that contributes to its speed. The center of gravity is forward, so that approximately 65 percent of the horse's weight rests on the forelegs. The forelegs provide most of the traction, while the hind legs provide the driving power.

The entire leg, fore or hind, works as a pendulum, with the bone levers and muscle pulleys facilitating its back-and-forth motion. The heavy muscle is concentrated around the shoulder and hip joints, leaving the lower legs very light, little more than slender bone covered with ligaments, tendons, and skin, except for the hoofed foot on the end. As these upper muscles act on the upper leg bone to swing it forward, the lightly built, jointed lever of the lower leg begins to snap like a whip, stretching the leg forward through the knee (or hock in the hind leg), lower leg, fetlock joint (equivalent to the human ankle), and the pastern or foot bones to the hoof. This whipping motion, aided by the weight of the hoof, moves the leg faster and extends it farther than the leg muscles could do alone. In addition, the knee joints of the forelegs lock when the front hooves hit the ground, then buckle forward as the knees pass under the forward-moving body. This sequence triggers the release of the elastic bicep (similar to that found in a grasshopper) that helps shoot the leg forward. At the same time, the joints, muscles, ligaments, and tendons act as springs, not only absorbing impact but also releasing kinetic energy that further enhances the pendulum effect.

The shoulder and hip joints also augment the pendulum motion by allowing the legs to move back-and-forth in only a single plane.

This restriction gives the horse maximum leg extension, not only lengthening its stride, one component of speed, but also, and just as important, shortening the stride interval, or the speed with which the leg snaps forward and is pulled/swings back. By maximizing the efficiency of this forward-and-back swing, the joint sacrifices lateral movement. To change course it is easier for a horse to back up and then go forward in a new direction than to sidestep. This shoulder/hip construction makes a sideways kick (cow-kick) virtually impossible but makes the back kick potentially lethal: a person is relatively safe next to a horse's leg (where s/he may be stepped on but not kicked) but in danger behind the hind legs.

In the nineteenth century people argued constantly about proper hoof care and horseshoeing in accordance with the adage "No foot, no horse." The equine foot is a complex and fascinating structure for absorbing impact and applying traction. The horse walks on a single toe, encased in a hard hoof. Every component in this structure works to absorb shock and release energy. Like the human foot, the equine foot is composed of multiple bones. From fetlock to hoof the long pastern bone is attached to the short pastern, which rests on the pedal bone inside the hoof wall. The arrangement of pedal and other small bones, cartilage, and other tissue provides a shock-absorbing structure for the end of the leg. The pedal bone and interior hoof wall are connected by a membrane of interlocking lamina that would stretch for hundreds of miles if laid end to end. A triangular pad of spongy horn called the frog extends across the heel and helps with traction, while the convex sole of the hoof protects the interior, distributes weight across its area, absorbs shock, and pumps blood through the leg as it flexes and expands.

A horse's spine is relatively rigid; unlike some animals, it cannot arch its back very much or easily bend to one side. Whereas felines or canines can produce a burst of speed by arching their spines, bringing their front and back legs together, and uncoiling to snap forward, horses cannot. Then again, the rigid equine spine mini-

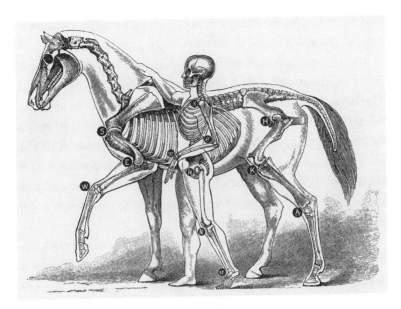

Corresponding joints in horse and man. Source: W. H. Flower, *The Horse: A Natural History* (New York, 1892). Fairman Rogers Collection, University of Pennsylvania.

mizes energy-sapping vertical motion. Thus, while a cheetah sprints faster than a horse, it wears out quickly. A horse can keep going for quite a long period, flexing its lower legs sharply to produce the greatest speed possible with the least loss of energy. The head and neck pump to provide momentum when the horse accelerates, but remain steady when the pace is even to conserve energy for forward motion.

People in the nineteenth century did not know how the horse's internal organs contribute to locomotion and efficiency. The horse's body rests in a thoracic sling that swings back and forth like a pendulum, gathering and releasing energy. The internal organs act like a piston within a cylinder, swinging forward to help compress the lungs from behind and expel as much air as possible, then swinging back to help expand the lungs. The horse has an enormous capacity for oxygen exchange, and is able to increase its blood oxygen more than thirty-five times during exercise. Getting as much air into the lungs as possible aids the transfer of oxygen into the blood.

Apart from knowing that forage was fuel, people in the nineteenth century did not understand how horses convert food into energy. The horse has a fast-working digestive system thanks to an organ called the cecum. The cecum breaks down food rapidly and makes the energy quickly available. A horse can literally eat and run. The price of this ability, however, is that a relatively low percentage of the available nutrition is extracted from the food. Consequently, a horse needs to eat a large amount every day in order to get enough nourishment.

Throughout the nineteenth century, people speculated endlessly about horses as a kind of engine, but not until the twentieth century did it become clear that they are essentially biochemical engines. Only then did biochemistry unravel the mysteries of ATP (adenosine triphosphate) metabolism, the chemical process of energy transfer that links digestion and locomotion in animal muscle. Through this process, "organisms have unrivaled intensities of energy conversions per unit of mass," surpassing the sun in power output. ATP metabolism begins as an anaerobic process to provide initial muscle action (like a starter engine), but ongoing ATP production is an aerobic, or oxygen-dependent, process. Consequently, the horse's ability to dramatically increase oxygen consumption during exertion gives it a huge advantage in ATP conversion. ATP triggers the contraction and release of muscles, and stamina depends on the ability to keep the cycle of ATP metabolism going as long as possible. Stamina is aided by good temperature regulation, by means of the skin and of veins just under the skin that cool the blood. In short, ATP is to animal muscle what gasoline is to an internal combustion engine.[9]

The horse's physical structure of bones and muscles and its physiological mechanisms of digestion, temperature regulation, and ATP conversion make it a very energy-efficient mechanism. Efficiency is the return in energy output in relation to energy input; the percentage is always less than 100 because energy is lost to heat in the conversion process. Equine efficiency is 15 to 20 percent, comparable to the efficiency of an internal combustion engine. In contrast, the steam locomotive had an efficiency of approximately 3 to 6 percent. That a horse is not as fast or strong as these prime movers does not mean it is inefficient, only that it is less fast or strong. That a horse cannot keep going indefinitely simply means that ATP metabolism is not a perpetual-motion device and eventually requires both rest and fuel (food). "The horse is in fact perfectly adapted to saving energy."[10]

In addition to its physical attributes, the horse was often described as "noble" or "sagacious," a perfect servant to man, because of its qualities of temperament. These are rooted in the nature of equine society. Though knowledge of equine behavior is still surprisingly limited, systematic observations of feral horses have established some baseline behaviors. Feral horses live in herds divided into family groups called harems, composed of one stallion, one or more mares, and their offspring. In addition to harems are groups of young males and young females who leave the harem at puberty. A young stallion acquires a harem either by challenging an older stallion for his or by abducting a mare or mares to begin one of his own. Within these groups horses form strong individual bonds with one or more other horses with whom they will graze, groom, play, watch over young, and stand head-to-tail for cooperative fly-switching. Between harems and groups of young males and females is a complicated politics of alliances, battles, and cooperative actions. For example, though harem stallions continually skirmish with other stallions, two stallions may take turns watching over both harems or, when the herd is threatened from the outside, all may work together, some skirmishing, some positioning themselves to attack, and some shepherding the mares and foals in case flight to safety is necessary. The same behaviors are evident among domesticated horses, and they work to human advantage. A group of unrelated domesticated horses will form a pecking order among themselves reinforced by dominance behaviors—bared teeth, lunging, biting, kicking, squealing—when going in and out of enclosures or getting food and water. Highly attuned to cues about hierarchy and power, they will accept humans at the top of their pecking order. Possessed of strong bonding instincts, they will bond with humans and with other animals, though their relationships with other horses always interest them more. Thus, the inherent behavioral attributes of horses suit them well to work with humans.[11]

Their cognitive abilities do so as well. Horses are usually regarded as intelligent, although what animal intelligence means is a topic of debate and conjecture that often slips into anthropomorphism. In part the horse is perceived as intelligent because it is good at many of the tasks that humans ask of it. In addition to being amenable to human direction and training, the horse has an excellent memory for patterns, and can memorize a work routine and perform it with little or no supervision. In logging operations, horses could be sent off with a load of logs to the depot, and sent back with an empty skid without needing a driver along the way. In milk delivery and trash collection, horses memorized the routes and knew when to move and stop on their own while the milkman carried bottles to the door or the trash man loaded garbage onto the wagon. Doctors' diaries describe their horses making their way home unguided after a late-night house call when the tired doctor had fallen asleep driving. In human terms, the horse is just smart enough to be a perfect worker who can follow directions without taking too much initiative.[12]

Although nineteenth-century Americans knew little in scientific terms about equine locomotion, physiology, and behavior, they had an enormous body of knowledge about how to use horses. Traditional horse culture was chiefly an oral culture. However, as the use

of horses expanded, with more jobs for horses and more people using horses, the traditional culture and the transmission of knowledge inevitably suffered disruption. As part of the proliferation of
printed material in the first half of the century, a growing body of
written work about horses appeared to augment the oral tradition.
The economic importance of horses attracted the attention of engineers, farriers, horse doctors, operators of stagecoach and express
companies, army officers, and others to the mechanics of horse
work.

Nineteenth-century Americans paid a great deal of attention to
the role of harness. A horse, however willing, cannot be used for
work without being attached to another device. A horse generates
power by using the muscles of its back and legs—driving with its
hind legs and supporting with its front legs—to push its hooves
against the ground for traction. The harness is a framework placed
around the horse for it to push against. The horse is the engine, and
the harness is the transmission that delivers the power. Secured
around the equine body without interfering with breathing or movement, the harness converts the horse's push against the ground into
forward motion.

There are many different types and styles of harness, but the fundamental components remain the same. The most important piece
is the padded collar. The collar should be fitted to rest properly on
the shoulders while leaving the throat and windpipe unobstructed.
The horse pushes against the collar to move the vehicle forward.
Hames, a pair of substantial, slightly curved wooden or metal strips,
are fastened securely around the collar and serve as the front end of
the harness. A pair of straps connected to the hames extends over
the back of the horse, running through a broad band encircling the
belly and reaching to the rump. At a junction on the rump another
arrangement of straps, called the spider, descends on each side, attaching by extended loops to a hip strap, which goes from the bellyband around the hips and under the tail. Together these form the

breeching, which helps to slow or brake a vehicle when the horse resists its motion or pushes back against it. Some harnesses have very heavy breeching, and some very little, depending on the vehicle and the job. Collar, bellyband, and breeching are all connected and counterbalance one another to provide a secure, safe, relatively flexible structure around the body.

The horse is attached to the vehicle by long leather straps called traces. Most commonly these run from the hames through looped straps on the breeching and are fastened directly to the vehicle or to a bar device behind the horse called a whiffletree, which is then hooked to the front of the vehicle. Altering the arrangement of and adding straps to this basic harness can increase the horse's safety and efficiency. If a single horse is used, it may be driven between shafts, which are attached by straps to the bellyband; a team is

Team of mules pulling a wagon in Alabama, ca. 1915. This photograph shows the major components of harness: collar, bellyband, breeching, and traces. Wisconsin Historical Society, image 44362.

driven with a pole between, which is attached to the collar by clips on a front yoke. Both the shafts and the pole serve as another device that the horse can resist or push against in order to slow or stop the vehicle.

All of the horse's power begins with traction—a horse might be called a living traction machine. Because traction is a function of weight, harness can act as a lever, with the horse's hind feet as the fulcrum between horse and load. The harness helps to shift weight onto or off of the horse's back and changes the difficulty of the work for the horse. It creates a line of draft that slants downward from the point on the collar where the traces begin and the front of the vehicle or machine where the traces are attached. This is where the lever of the harness and the lever of the vehicle (the axles are the fulcrums) connect. If a load pushes the front of the vehicle down too much, the harness lifts weight off the horse and reduces its traction. If a load pushes the front of the vehicle up, the harness levers weight onto the horse and increase its traction. Too much or too little traction for the circumstances of hauling makes the horse have to work harder. If the line slants downward too steeply, making too great an angle with ground, the harness levers the horse upward and reduces its traction and therefore its power. Thus harnessing the horse more loosely, away from the load, or more tightly, nearer the load, varies the line of draft. It also alters the spring effect of the harness and the ability of the horse to control the vehicle.

The horse powers the vehicle through the harness, but the bridle and reins provide the steering and brakes. The bridle is a framework of leather that fits around the head. A metal bit fits in the mouth, resting on top of the tongue and in a gap between the front and back teeth, to apply pressure to the sensitive nose and mouth. The reins are attached to each end of the bit, threaded through rings on the hames, and extend back to the driver. Reins enable the driver to stop the horse (by applying pressure), to start the horse (by applying temporary gentle pressure after an interval of release, often with a simultaneous voice command), and to turn the horse by bending its neck in the desired direction.

Driving horses required a set of mechanical skills involving harnessing, maneuvering vehicles and animals, using the brake correctly, and loading the vehicle properly; but these skills had to be combined with the social ability to establish a working relationship with horses. Drivers had to understand something about how horses related to and worked with each other.

For example, a team of four horses harnessed in pairs has two wheel horses, those closest to the vehicle, and two lead horses, those harnessed at the front of the team. Wheel horses have to be larger and stronger because they do the most pulling, and provide most of the braking on downhill grades, while lead horses have to be more agile, able to maneuver the vehicle without getting horses and harness tangled. The dominant horse of the team-herd, from which the other horses will take their cues, is not always a horse that is dominant in the pasture, and is usually not one of the lead horses, but is instead in the middle or at the wheel, where it can use its strength and leadership to keep the team balanced and together.

Drivers and horses were coworkers that formed a small horse-human herd in which drivers played the role of a dominant horse. Like player-coaches, drivers had to be able to observe and manage horses, taking their abilities and temperaments into account to use them most effectively. Horses learn to trust good drivers and to pay attention to their voices in much the same way that they trust and obey a the commands of a harem stallion. On a noisy city street, on a chaotic battlefield, or in any other difficult, dangerous, or frightening situation, the ability of horses to hear and respond to their drivers was of paramount importance. In the working relationship between humans and horses, the social temperament of the horse, its attention to hierarchy, and its responsiveness to humans con-

tributed to Americans' general preference for them as working
partners.

In the context of nineteenth-century industrialization, the physical
qualities of the equine machine, the social attributes of horses, and
the long history of horse-human relations acquired new value. The
conviction that American prosperity and democracy depended on
high energy consumption, together with the continuing importance
of animal power, increased the use of horses as prime movers. In addition, the fact that horses were status animals made them more attractive than other draft animals, even the useful ox.

What made oxen useful was that they were plentiful and cheap.
Oxen are not a breed or variety of cattle, but cattle used for draft.
Technically, they are mature castrated males. Males are preferable as
oxen because they tend to be larger and stronger, while females are
valuable for producing milk and calves. However, given the abundance of references to female oxen and ox calves, it is clear that people in the nineteenth century used the term broadly to refer to working cattle regardless of age, sex, or breed, the last varying according
to regional and occupational preferences.

The structural differences between horses and oxen are immediately apparent. A horse resembles a slender pod on long, thin legs;
an ox resembles a rectangular box on short, heavily built legs. Unlike even a large horse, an ox presents a solid wall of flesh and muscle. Oxen are built for power, not for speed. The joints of their
shoulders and hips are constructed for lateral as well as forward-
and-backward movement, a circumstance that lets them step or kick
to the side but restricts the longitudinal extension that gives a horse
its speed. Oxen move one-third to one-half as fast as horses at a
walk. They can gallop if necessary, but not for very long. Bovines
lack the efficient cooling mechanism of equines, so a steady, fast
pace is taxing, especially in warm weather.

Oxen deliver an estimated 40 percent less power than horses because power is a function of speed as well as force, and oxen are slow. However, they push more steadily and strongly against their neck yokes than horses. In the early days of settlement oxen were used far more than horses for jobs that required force without speed, such as breaking sod, extracting stumps, or pulling logs and rocks. Some farmers believed that oxen were less likely to break equipment by jerking and jolting it against rocks and trees. Their broad, cloven hooves maintained good traction in rough, wet, or boggy soil, and they could be shod like horses if necessary.[13]

Oxen are ruminants; their slow-moving four-stomach digestive system breaks down food thoroughly but slowly and regurgitates food to be further chewed (chewing the cud). Oxen extract a large percentage of the nutrition in their fodder, perhaps 30 percent more than horses, with the advantage of eating quickly and digesting later; if necessary, they can be fed once a day. The disadvantage is that the food does not release its energy until it is completely digested, so that oxen need time for rest and regurgitation. Consequently, oxen have less stamina than horses, which digest food 50 percent faster.

Differently configured from horses in the neck and shoulders, oxen could be harnessed with a neck yoke that on a horse would press on the windpipe. As Cobbett and others were quick to point out, oxen did not need complicated harness, and yokes were simple for farmers to make. Oxen are alert and agile, but have docile temperaments and are comparatively easy to train to voice commands. They are less likely than horses to shy, act out, or mind wet and weather. Farm letters and diaries often mention children managing oxen or being given a pair of calves to train. Overall, oxen were cheaper to acquire, train, and use than horses. Because they could be slaughtered for meat when no longer able to work, whereas Americans remained averse to eating horses, oxen "died on the right side of the ledger."[14]

In general, oxen were used wherever people needed cheap power but not speed, in regions with subsistence agriculture, little commerce, and poor roads, and for jobs requiring very grueling draft work. Farmers who could afford to own more than one or two draft animals sometimes kept a team of oxen to spare their higher-status horses from the most brutal work. For example, in 1864 the *American Agriculturist* advocated using oxen instead of horses to operate treadmills, because "the labor is not severe if continued for a moderate time; but it is cruel to work horses day after day in these treadmills."[15] Actually, because oxen cannot maintain a fast, unrelenting pace, working on a treadmill would be more cruel to an ox.

Oxen were easy and inexpensive to acquire because cattle were commonplace, and thus their status remained common as well. Outside New England they were rarely symbols of wealth and success, whatever advocates like Madison might say about them. Horses, ancient symbols of wealth, physical power, and social mastery, with their more exacting food and harness requirements and temperaments, remained markers of upward mobility and social status even as their use became more commonplace.

The expansion of horse use included a dramatic increase in the breeding and use of half-horses, or mules, during the antebellum years. Mules are hybrid animals produced by crossing horses with donkeys, specifically mares with jacks (crossing stallions with jennets creates an animal called a hinny). While using donkeys for draft was relatively uncommon in the United States—in contrast to Europe—many people regarded mules as a better choice than either horses or oxen. Mules are smaller and less powerful than horses, but hardy and strong. They have stocky legs, small, hard hooves, thick skin, and sturdy digestive systems. They tolerate heat, lack of water, and irregular forage better than horses. Mules mature more rapidly and can begin work at age two, in contrast to age four for horses, and they live longer. Though a mule usually cost more than a horse, it was a living machine that delivered power for longer and at less expense with fewer breakdowns.[16] Thus, mules would seem

to combine the best attributes of horses and oxen—hardy and economical, but also fast, alert, and powerful.

Just as there were different styles of working with horses and
oxen, so it was with mules. Although they are usually portrayed as
stubborn, it is more accurate to describe mules as tough-minded
animals deeply interested in self-preservation. Some people appre-
ciate mule temperament more than others do. Because they are
hardy and thick-skinned, people often treated mules much more
harshly than they did horses. The belief that mules were more resis-
tant to abuse probably made them more abused.[17]

Americans, especially in the North, expressed strong opinions
about mules. The *American Agriculturist* recommended using
mules instead of horses because they were more enduring and economical. In the *Rural New Yorker,* the author of "Morals and Mules"
disagreed, pointing to "mules' want of moral character" and describing them as "obstinate, mischievous and pugnacious." Mules
had to be worked constantly or would become "vicious," misbe-
have, attack other animals, and escape. He concluded, "This unless
it can be shown to have no general application proves the entire un-
fittedness of the mule for the uses of the farm."[18]

"Morals and Mules" elicited a rebuttal from C. J. J. of Cincinnati,
who argued that if as much care were taken in breeding and caring
for mules as horses, mules would have better temperaments and be
a match for horses as work animals. The *Rural New Yorker* reported
in 1857 that mules were replacing horses for use with the omnibuses
and express wagons of Cincinnati, located in the mule-breeding region of southern Ohio. "They are equally tractable, cost less by 20
or 40 per cent; they consume 40 per cent less food, are 33 per cent
more durable and move with a steady, unyielding celerity." Dr.
Fisher of Fitchburg, Massachusetts, concurred. His pair of mules,
which together weighed 1,400 pounds, "worked as hard and cost
less to keep than a pair of horses at 2200 pounds, and lived two to
three times as long."[19]

But despite those who sang the praises of mules, their use remained limited in the North. Even Dr. Fisher admitted, "It will be long before [mules] take the place which the horse now fills on our farms." The 1860 agricultural census noted that although "the prejudice against [mules] is not as great as formerly," in the North "it is very evident that mules are not a favorite working animal."[20] Americans projected more negative traits onto mules than they did onto horses and oxen. Horses were viewed as noble, spirited, willing, loyal, and sagacious; oxen as docile, patient, reliable, and hardworking; and mules as stubborn, unpredictable, cowardly, immoral, untrustworthy, and inclined to panic.

The intensity of opinion reflected the fascination and revulsion with which people in the nineteenth century viewed hybrid animals. The ability to create a new animal was a powerful example of human mastery over nature. "So great was the fascination exerted by hybrid creatures that many impossible mixes were reported as fact, or lingered over regretfully as persistent superstitions," such as the dog-tiger, lion-mastiff, deer-horse, raccoon-sheep, deer-sheep, and the possibility of creating unicorns.[21] At the same time, the existence of hybrid animals suggested that the boundaries between different kinds of animals were a great deal less absolute than people wanted to believe. and in nineteenth-century America such notions had disquieting implications concerning racial identity and miscegenation. Whether mules were more horse or donkey was unclear. They were usually sterile and could not reproduce themselves. This was a practical problem for farmers, who could not use good mules to breed even better mules; but for some it cast further doubt on the value of mules. The *Ohio Cultivator* wondered "why, if [mules] are as good and useful as many represent them to be, they were not in the list of good things that were created in the beginning, and why they were not made capable of propagating their own species."[22]

Despite the misgivings of some Americans, mule use became important in the United States as it had been for centuries in Europe and elsewhere. Mules were part of the second nature being created by American industrialization. The exuberance of reshaping and controlling nature was reflected in speculations about all the animals that could possibly be used for power. Americans pressed most of the traditional animals into service turning treadmills and pulling carts, such as dogs, goats, and sheep, but they continued to desire larger animals.

Since Americans generally believed that domestication was a simple matter of human will, some suggested domesticating the indigenous animals of the continent. In the U.S. government's agricultural report of 1851, one S. F. Baird surveyed the characteristics of caribou, elk, reindeer, moose, deer, mountain goats, musk oxen, and buffalo "with especial reference to the economic employment of several species, as beast of burden or draught, as furnishing food of excellent quality, or as yielding valuable materials for the useful arts. It is a little singular that . . . so little effort has been made to render them subservient to the uses of man. The experiments, when tried, have yielded satisfactory results."

In addition to the economic potential of domesticating these animals, Baird saw it as a technical solution to the social and political problems that resulted from American expansion into Indian territories. The difference between the nomadic pastoralism of Indian life and the extractive enterprises of white American life had led to ongoing conflict. Baird thought that if Indians could domesticate some of the indigenous species, they would start on the path of cultural progress; eventually they would adopt the ways and mores of white society and escape "the vicissitudes which are so rapidly sweeping off the Indians of the north and northeast of America . . . In this way these Indians might become a pastoral people, and possibly in time, as agricultural as the nature of the seasons would admit." Domestication could also facilitate further white settlement of the region. "Much of this continent, now desolate, and supporting a scanty and half-starved population, may become a populous region, filled with towns and villages and owing much of its prosperity to the employment of some of our own native animals in a state of domestication."[23]

Baird's optimistic vision of the future reflected the burgeoning confidence in improvement and progress characteristic of nineteenth-century Americans. Baird supplied little support for his claims that these animals could be domesticated, and was content merely to list them and speculate about their potential utility. None of these animals have characteristics that would enable them to be domesticated. Like the dog-tiger and the unicorn, domesticated mountain goats and caribou would remain no more than a beguiling fantasy. Domestication could not provide lucrative new animals, promote western settlement and development, or serve as a "technological fix" to make the problem of the Indians disappear.

A far more promising project than domesticating native animals was importing foreign animals already proven useful as products or sources of power. A number of crazes, "manias," and "fevers" for imported animals and plants swept the United States in the first half of the nineteenth century. There were fads for Saxony sheep, silkworms, Chinese mulberry trees (to feed the silkworms), rutabagas, Berkshire hogs, broom corn, and Rohan potatoes, not to mention the extensive merino sheep craze of the early century and the great "hen fever" of the 1850s. In addition, there were a number of individual experiments described in government agricultural reports during the 1850s, which attempted to introduce Asiatic buffalo, Brahmin cattle, Cashmere, Scinde, and Malta goats, and the "yak-ox" into various states and territories. As with the more widespread fads, it was promised that each of these animals would make individual farmers rich and increase the nation's prosperity and progress.[24]

The most sustained endeavor to utilize foreign draft animals occurred after the United States acquired some 500,000 square miles of territory as a result of the Mexican War (1846–1848). This was an arid region of plains, mountains, and deserts, popularly known as "the Great American Desert," which had to be organized, administered, policed, and settled. As they faced this challenge, some government officials thought that camels would be a useful asset. Thus was born the camel experiment of the 1850s.

The idea of using camels had originated among army officers who explored this region early in the century. After 1850 the army was responsible for maintaining forts and communication routes, controlling native inhabitants, and protecting white settlers in what is now California, Nevada, Utah, Arizona, and New Mexico. Carrying out these duties and military operations required moving freight over long distances and harsh terrain by pack animal and wagon train—brutally difficult work that took an enormous toll on the army's horses, mules, and oxen. If the army had to operate in "the Great American Desert," thought some officials, why not use camels?[25]

Americans were familiar with camels, which had featured regularly in traveling animal exhibitions since the early eighteenth century. Camels had religious significance to many Americans because of their association with the lands of the Bible. Known for being able to go for long periods without water, camels were objects of wonder and curiosity. They seemed like perfect candidates as draft animals for the West. "The camel is one of the most valuable gifts of Providence," declared one midcentury encyclopedia. "There is no creature more excellently adapted to its situation." As the sectional tensions of the 1850s intensified, people on both sides wanted to claim the territories if there was a schism in the Union, and army use of camels seemed to promise a solution to the problems of transportation, communication, and control that were essential to maintaining western loyalties. The U.S. agricultural report of 1853 described the acquisition of camels as "a matter of much national importance."[26]

The idea of using camels elicited enthusiasm from a widening circle, extending beyond army officers to include natural scientists, businessmen, diplomats, politicians, and government officials. In 1854 the distinguished natural scientist George Perkins Marsh delivered a series of influential lectures on the camel at the Smithsonian, which were later published as a book. A group of New York City businessmen solicited investment in the "American Camel Company" to import and use camels for western trade and travel.

Camel enthusiasts lobbied the government to take the initiative, gaining an important ally in Jefferson Davis, who became secretary of war under President Franklin Pierce in 1853. Davis was interested in securing the new territories of the Southwest, especially California, for the expansion of slavery. Trained at West Point, Davis had had a distinguished military career before entering politics. Drawing on examples from Middle Eastern and Asian history, he envisioned camels as "gunships of the desert," serving as gun platforms for artillery, carrying rapid-assault forces, and providing transportation and support for infantry. He also imagined a "camel express" for speedy communication across the West. In 1855 Davis persuaded Congress to establish the United States Camel Corps and to appropriate $30,000 for it. He immediately dispatched officers on a purchasing trip to the Middle East. In April 1856 the first shipload of thirty-four Arabian and Bactrian camels disembarked in Texas, followed by another forty-one camels in January of the following year.[27]

Both the one-humped Arabian camel and the two-humped Bactrian camel are larger, stronger, and faster than horses or oxen. They average seven feet at the hump, while horses average four to six feet at the shoulder. They can walk almost four miles per hour, which is 30 to 60 percent faster than a horse, and can maintain that speed for twenty to twenty-five miles at a stretch. They can carry at least 300 pounds on their backs, and some camels as much as 1,000 pounds, compared with 200 for a horse. Their carrying capacity eliminates the need for wagons, which are slow and subject to breakdown

Bactrian camels harnessed to an International Harvester mower in Russia, ca. 1910. Wisconsin Historical Society, image 9441.

or getting stuck in rugged terrain. Camels' two-toed feet need no shoeing, but have broad leathery pads suited to both sand and rocky terrain.

Camels can go without water for long periods because they are able to raise their body temperature by as much as eleven degrees Fahrenheit (six degrees Celsius), thus retaining more water by slowing evaporation. Camels can also tolerate substantial losses in body weight—up to 25 percent—from lack of food and water. As ruminants, they can digest very tough or poor forage and extract water from it. These characteristics enable them to tolerate the extreme temperatures of desert environments.[28]

Initial trials of the camels' abilities were promising. Edward Fitzgerald Beale, a former army officer who became leader of the Camel Corps, used them for a wagon-road survey in 1857 and reported: "[The camels] are exceedingly docile, easily managed, and I see, so far, no reason to doubt the success of the experiment." As hoped, the camels carried heavy loads, needed little water, ate "the herbs and boughs of bitter bushes, which all other animals reject," and traversed rugged terrain with apparent ease. Beale returned from this trip enthusiastic about "the economical and noble brute": "My admiration for the camels increases daily with my experience of them. The harder the test they are put to the more fully they seem to justify all that can be said of them . . . they are so perfectly docile and so admirably contented with whatever fate befalls them. No one could do justice to the merits or value in expeditions of this kind." *Scientific American* reported that the expedition demonstrated "a fair prospect of the Arabian camel becoming a regularly naturalized and valuable American citizen."[29]

These glowing reports glossed over some significant difficulties of working with camels. Some of the people involved with or witness to the camel experiment found that the idea of camels was better than the reality. According to some observers, camels smelled awful, developed unattractive skin conditions, spat foul-smelling cuds at unsuspecting humans, and produced a cacophony of sounds variously described as roaring, groaning, snoring, bleating, wheezing, and screaming. Although camels were as docile, patient, and intelligent as Beale reported, they could also be irritable and intractable, and at times so dangerously unpredictable that some people considered them malicious and vindictive.

When army teamsters accustomed to working with horses, mules, and oxen tried to handle camels, they found that their knowledge and skills in loading, driving, and handling conventional draft animals were useless. Working with camels required a different approach as well as new skills and equipment. Teamsters were not known for being gentle with their animals, and they were accustomed to receiving bites and kicks. Camels, however, were larger, more powerful, and aggressive animals that could rip a man's arm off. Only the "Turks" who came over with the camels from the Middle East could handle them and pack a camel load properly. Teamsters took masculine pride in their ability to handle and load draft animals. Not only did the camels frustrate them, but also dark-skinned foreigners in robes and turbans were showing them up.[30]

Army officers differed over the goals of the project. Even though camel enthusiasts had emphasized the military potential of the animal in order to get congressional funding, there were no actual plans for integrating camel use into the army. Neither Secretary of War Davis nor his successor, John B. Floyd, had support from Quartermaster Thomas Jesup, who was responsible for all army logistics and supply in the territories; Winfield Scott, general-in-chief of the U.S. Army; or Major General David E. Twiggs, the commander of the Department of Texas. In the end, there was no constituency in the army committed to using an exotic animal for a specialized military purpose in a recently acquired territory that was inhospitable and possibly uninhabitable. Without institutional or political support and lacking a clearly defined purpose, the camel experiment foundered. Distracted by the mounting sectional crisis, the War Department's interest in camels faded, and when civil war broke out in 1861, the Camel Corps was formally disbanded. The camels ended up in the unwilling hands of the Confederate government in Texas, where over the next few years most died of neglect, disease, and abuse. A few escaped, and for eighty years afterward there were tales of wild camels in the western deserts; occasional sightings occurred up through the 1930s.

The camel experiment was an attempt to find a technological fix for physical problems of western transportation and communication, but also for the political problems of the 1850s that erupted over issues of western development. But camels always remained objects of curiosity and derision, and were never seen as legitimate draft animals with a niche in the American environment. The response of horses and mules, which often panicked and bolted at their initial sight and smell of camels, seemed to provide prima facie evidence that camels were too alien to be assimilated into the American animal population.

There was an expansive extravagance and assurance about these antebellum enthusiasms for domesticating and importing new animals. American talk of domesticating the wild animals of North America and appropriating foreign animals for American use was a kind of zoological manifest destiny. As Mays Humphrey Stacey, a young man accompanying the Beale expedition, confidently wrote in his journal, "What are these camels the representation of? Not a high civilization exactly, but of the 'go-aheadness' of the American character, which subdues even nature by its energy and perseverance."[31] Other than the Camel Corps, these proposals never advanced beyond the rhetorical stage. Just as camel gunships never became part of the army, the Indians never domesticated antelope, mountain-goat wool did not replace the wool from Kashmir goats, the Great Plains were not covered with herds of yak, and ponies, not camels, carried express mail in the West.

The fate of the army's camels demonstrates the difficulties of displacing existing preferences for and uses of draft animals. A draft animal performed physical work, but it also did cultural work. Although camels seemed well suited to the physical environment of the American Southwest, the cultural environment of American society proved to be inhospitable to their use.

Despite enthusiastic dreams about the potential of new and different creatures, American draft animals consisted largely of horses, mules, and oxen throughout the nineteenth century. Their number increased through the decades, driven by the growing power demands of an industrializing economy and expanding nation. Statistics from federal census returns show changes in the size, configuration, and geographic distribution of the draft animal population. The census, like any other classification system, is a cultural artifact. Its categories reflect the distinctions that people choose to establish, the boundaries they want to maintain, and the things they consider important enough to count. Because animal power was such an important source of energy, changes in how draft animals were categorized and counted reflected changes in the social and material environment of nineteenth-century America.

Draft animals were first counted in the 1840 census, but only horses and mules were enumerated, and they were combined into one category. The 1850 census provided separate categories for horses and for "mules and asses," counting donkeys (asses) for the first time. This move reflected the growing importance of mule-breeding and the rapidly increasing mule population, and tried to take into account the relatively small number of donkeys whose primary use was for mule-breeding. The shift in the mule's classification from half-horse in 1840 to half-donkey in 1850 also reflected in part the ambivalent feelings that many Americans had about this hybrid animal. These were the decades in which a distinct racial ideology and an active proslavery defense emerged alongside an emphasis on democratic citizenship and equality. There was a disquieting jumble of ideas about the meaning of racial identity, especially white identity. The fact that mules were used on southern plantations associated them with enslaved blacks, who were often described as having "an affinity for mules," and cemented a link between the idea of mule and mulatto, a person half-black and half-white described by the Spanish word for mule. Just as mulattos were classified as more black than white, mules were classified as more donkey than horse. The species line, like the color line, did not easily include mixed identities.[32]

The 1840 census did not distinguish oxen (working cattle) from the tabulation of all cattle, but the 1850 census added them as a separate category. Oxen were included in the census only from 1850 to 1890, even though other evidence shows that they were still in use after that. Perhaps by the end of the century oxen were considered too marginal as prime movers to be worth counting, in somewhat the way that the census has often overlooked humans on the margins of society. And by then the American frontier had been "conquered", settled, and developed.

In 1840 there were 4.3 million horses and mules in the United States. By 1910 this figure had risen sixfold, to 27.5 million, nearly twice the rate of human population growth. In terms of changes in the material and social environment, there was one horse for every five humans in the nation in 1850, dropping to one horse for every three humans by century's end.[33]

The census also reveals regional differences. Most of the draft animals in northern states were horses. Oxen, which accounted for about a fifth of northern draft animals at midcentury, declined in overall numbers, but the oxen population shifted westward into newly settled areas, where they performed the grueling work of clearing land and breaking sod. In the trans-Mississippi West, freighting firms used oxen extensively. By 1860 the freighting firm of Russell, Majors and Waddell employed 4,000 people, 3,500 wagons, and 40,000 oxen, while the western freighting industry as a whole used 70,000 oxen. Settlers used oxen to haul their wagons and employed three to eight yokes of oxen for the enormous "breaking plows" to cut the tough prairie sod. However, this use was transitory. Paintings by Harvey Thomas Dunn and novels by Willa Cather, both of whom grew up in prairie settlements, detail the use of oxen in the initial work of clearing, plowing, hauling, and transportation, and the change to horses that occurred after the first work of settlement was complete. Oxen retained their niche as draft animals in logging regions such as Maine and northern New York and remained in wide use on New England farms into the twentieth century. Not only were oxen suited to the region's small rocky fields, compact settlements, and localized agriculture, but they were part of New England's cultural heritage, a symbol of the Yankee virtues of hard work, frugality, sobriety, simplicity, and tradition.

Meanwhile the use of mules in northern states remained minimal except for mining and for pulling canal boats. In the North a growth dynamic of transportation development, mechanized agriculture, commercial expansion, industrial production, and urban growth favored horses' versatility for many kinds of work. In southern regions draft animals were more specialized, and many more mules and oxen relative to horses. The South produced raw materials for a global industrial market, and its sparse network of roads, canals, and railroads, together with its labor-intensive, nonmechanized staple-crop agriculture used fewer horses and relied on mules and oxen. In addition, oxen use was prevalent among largely self-sufficient yeoman farmers during the antebellum period; when in the postbellum period these small farmers were drawn into market production of cotton, they often switched to mules.

The advent of war in 1861 imposed new energy demands and changed the value of the draft animal choices that Americans had made before it. As secession divided the country along the fissures of geography and politics, regional differences in draft animal populations would acquire new significance. As living machines, draft animals would have an important role throughout the Civil War.[34]

But even though horses were used less in some regions, they were always the most numerous draft animals. Their strength, speed, social temperament, and ability to bond with humans, together with their ability to provide individual, versatile, self-propelled power, remained unmatched. In the context of American society, horses were the best source of animal energy. As a result, horses were integral to the second nature created during the nineteenth century.

Anyone traveling by railroad from Washington, D.C., to New York City in 1860 used horses on every stage of the trip.

The journey began when travelers arrived at the Washington railroad depot by horse-drawn vehicle and departed for Baltimore on the Baltimore & Ohio Railroad. The B & O was the only railroad line into Washington. A single track connected Washington and Baltimore, without signals or sidings; only one train could travel between the cities at any given time. The train from Washington arrived at Camden Station in Baltimore. The next leg of the journey was on the Philadelphia, Wilmington, & Baltimore Railroad, which had its own depot on the other side of the city. Passengers and baggage got off the train at Camden Station and rode in horse-drawn streetcars along Pratt Street to the President Street terminal, where they got off the streetcar and boarded the PW & B train for Philadelphia to continue their journey.

North of Baltimore, the rails ended at Havre de Grace on the Susquehanna River. There was no bridge over the Susquehanna, so passengers and baggage left the train, and horse-drawn vehicles transported them to the ferry. Once across the river, horse-drawn vehicles conveyed passengers and baggage up to the station on the other bank, where they boarded the continuation of the PW & B train to Philadelphia. On the outskirts of Philadelphia the railroad cars were uncoupled from the locomotive, and horses pulled them along the streets to the Market Street depot in downtown Philadelphia.

From Philadelphia, travelers had a choice of routes, all of which began with taking a horse-drawn cab or an omnibus to the ferry dock at the end of Market Street. They could take a ferry across the Delaware River to Camden, New Jersey, transfer to the railroad station, and board a train to South Amboy. Or they could take a ferry across the Delaware to Bordentown, transfer to the railroad station and take a train to New Brunswick, and transfer again onto a train to Jersey City. At either South Amboy or Jersey City, passengers went from a train station to a ferry dock and boarded the steam ferry across the Hudson River to New York City. At the ferry dock on the Manhattan side, they took horse-drawn cabs or stages to their destination in the city. Or perhaps they boarded one of the new horse railways. If travelers were continuing their rail journey beyond New York, they would go to the railroad depot, from which horses would pull the railway cars to the city limits so the cars could be coupled to waiting locomotives.[1]

A "train trip" from Washington to New York at midcentury was also a horse trip. It took a lot of horses to fill in the gaps between the tracks of different railroad companies, and between railroads and other kinds of transportation. It is a reminder that horses were the indispensable prime movers of the nineteenth century. It further demonstrates that the "transportation revolution" that occurred between the American Revolution and the Civil War made horses even more important than before. Rapid construction of roads, canals, and railroads and the increasing use of steamboats provided the transportation infrastructure that stimulated rapid industrial development. Most of these improvements changed the landscape so that Americans could use more horses. The expanding network of roads and canals relied on horses as prime movers. The expanding railroad network did so as well. Horse-drawn transportation moved people, goods, and mail to and from the railroads, extending their influence beyond the narrow physical corridor of tracks. As prime movers, horses and steam engines complemented each other, each occupying an essential niche in the emerging industrial system. Directly and indirectly, the industrialization of transportation in nineteenth-century America centered on horses.[2]

At the beginning of the century, most travel in the young nation took place on water, contingent on winds, currents, tides, and water levels. Great distances, rough terrain, and rudimentary roads made overland travel by wagon team, pack train, stagecoach, or horseback slow, strenuous, and expensive. The high cost of transportation by horses under these conditions kept settlement and commerce concentrated along rivers and coasts, while backcountry areas were isolated from outside markets and government authority. Consequently, every plan for national development from the Revolution on emphasized transportation improvements, known as internal improvements, to lower the cost of overland transportation by constructing roads and canals. Since horses were the only source of power available for overland transportation, these improvements aimed at reducing draft. Internal improvements would reshape the natural landscape into one suitable for the use of animal power.

Roads allowed freight to move by wagon instead of by pack train. This was a much less costly use of horse energy, since horses can carry less weight than they can pull. A pack horse can carry about 200 pounds, which gives a pack train of twenty horses a freight capacity of about two tons, a load that two or four horses can easily pull in a wagon—if there is an adequate road to pull it on.

The central problem of horse-drawn transportation was how to make sure that when hooves and wheels met the road surface, there was sufficient traction but low resistance. Hooves and wheels had different requirements: whereas the optimal road surface for vehicles was hard and smooth so that wheels turned easily, the optimal surface for hooves was coarse and elastic to provide enough traction and resilience. A road surface that was too soft and wet sucked at hooves and wheels, absorbing too much of the horses' power and creating too much draft. A surface that was too smooth did not provide enough traction; one that was too hard left no resilience or spring effect to lessen draft.

Good roads for horses also needed other features. An ideal road would be as short and straight as possible, but straightness had to be sacrificed to follow the contours of the landscape and avoid grades that were too steep. Just one very steep grade on a road would require teamsters to bring along extra horses at additional expense. There was an ongoing debate in the nineteenth century about whether level roads or gently undulating roads were easier on horses. Some people thought that steady pulling on a level road was more fatiguing, and that going up and down alternated the muscles in use. Other people argued that horses did not have two sets of muscles, and "that in moderate ascents and descents, the periods of exertion and comparative repose on the single set of muscles, are not less trying than the continued and unvarying exertion that horses put forth on a level." Moderate curves were important draft-reducing features of good roads because it was hard for horses and vehicles to make sharp turns. Finally, the road surface was critical for reducing draft. By definition a good road for horses was an "artificial" road, an artifice of human design and craft, in contrast to a "natural" road that evolved from human and animal footpaths.[3]

Roads were few and good roads were fewer in the young nation because most were "natural" roads. The contours and features of the landscape determined the route. Natural roads were not graded, contoured, surfaced, or drained, and they quickly became a succession of ruts, mud holes, and washouts, often studded with tree stumps cut just below the height of most wagon axles so that teams had to navigate around them. Dusty, hard, and rutted in dry weather, in wet weather these roads became nearly impassable as slopes turned into waterfalls and level stretches into sloughs. Horse-drawn vehicles moved laboriously, if they could move at all; pack trains and travelers on horseback found their horses sinking up to their bellies in mud. On a tour of the northeastern states in 1799, Timothy Dwight encountered roads so bad near Utica, New York, that he had to dismount and walk his horse the last thirty miles into the town. A traveler in the 1840s described a road in the same area as "a series of deep and dangerous marshy holes covered with round boulders, large and small, which appeared frequently in such numbers that, when the wagon drove between them and the marshy ground, one expected to turn over at any moment, or that the wagon would break."[4]

In addition to their terrible conditions, many roads were so badly marked and hard to follow that travelers found themselves lost and floundering in woods or water. Those who left the road to get around an impassable stretch or cross a stream might be unable to find the road again. William Cobbett, traveling through Indiana, was following "a track which was marked out by slips of bark being stripped off the trees, once in about 40 yards . . . We soon lost all appearance of the track, however, and of the *"blazing"* of the trees . . . our only way was to keep straight on in the same direction, bring us where it would. Having no compass, this nearly cost us our sight, for it was just mid-day and we had to gaze at the sun a long time before we discovered what was our course." A lack of bridges forced travelers to find a ford or a ferry. Cobbett finally crossed a ferry in a canoe and got a ferryman to swim the horses across. Thomas Jefferson had to ford five out of eight streams he crossed when traveling from Monticello to Washington for his inauguration in 1801. A ford without low, firm banks, solid footing in the streambed, relatively shallow water, and a slow current could be hazardous as well. Traveling by stagecoach, Horace Greeley described how "the passengers were turned out . . . to lighten the coach, which was then driven cautiously through the steep banked ford, while the passengers severally let themselves down a perpendicular bank by clinging to a tree, and crossed a deep and whirling place above the ford, on the vilest log I ever attempted to walk." Fords were places where horses stumbled or fell or lost their footing in the current, vehicles overturned, spilling passengers and baggage into the water, and humans and horses could drown.[5]

Building artificial roads took engineering skill, which was in short supply in antebellum America. There were three acknowledged authorities on nineteenth-century road building, one French and two Scottish. Pierre-Marie-Jérôme Trésaguet (1716–1796), inspector general of roads in France from 1775 to 1785, was responsible for that nation's reputation for excellent roads. A Trésaguet road had a prepared dirt surface, a base built of large stones and mortar, and two layers of successively smaller stones, each hammered down and creating in the end a stone road almost a foot thick. In Great Britain, Scotsman Thomas Telford (1757–1834) built roads of similar design and additionally emphasized the importance of contouring the surface so that water would drain off. Perhaps the most influential person in terms of American road building was another Scottish engineer, John L. McAdam (1756–1836), the surveyor general for metropolitan roads in Britain. McAdam dispensed with the masonry foundation used in Trésaguet and Telford roads because he did not think it was necessary in order to support the weight of heavy wagon traffic. Instead, McAdam believed that the earth under the road would support the weight if it was kept dry. Packing successive layers of broken stone "into a firm, compact, impenetrable body" created a hard bonded surface six to ten inches thick (eventually giving rise to the term "macadam" to describe a road surface of stone bound with tar or asphalt) that shed water.[6]

Plank roads, which enjoyed some popularity in the 1840s and 1850s, also created smooth, hard surfaces. Plank roads were like inverted railroad tracks, with long rails of wood, called stringers, set into a dirt roadbed. The space between them was filled with dirt and then covered with planks set perpendicular to the stringers and pounded against each other and into the dirt to set them into place. Because of the abundance of timber in the United States and the relative lack of skilled labor, plank roads were thought to be less expensive and cheaper to maintain than stone roads. Plank roads were also said to provide an advantage in hilly areas because they reduced draft. The area between Syracuse and Albany soon had nearly 300 miles of plank roads either built or planned, and southern boosters were interested in their use for rural, hilly, and wooded regions.[7]

There were disagreements over the merits of dirt, gravel, macadam, paved, and plank roads. Some questioned whether plank roads offered enough traction, whether hooves and wheels wore down the surface too fast, and whether broken or shifting planks made them less safe. Plank enthusiasts claimed that horses and mules could pull twice as much on a plank road as on a macadamized road, with less wear to the road and the vehicle. The proprietor of a stagecoach line claimed that horses could travel ten miles on a plank road "with the same ease to themselves that they could perform six miles on a good summer road" and that there was "a slight elasticity which was highly favorable to the motion and ease of the horse." Others believed that plank roads were less elastic and caused horses to stiffen up; enthusiasts argued that it was horses' being driven too hard and fast, not the surface, that caused stiffness.[8]

The real problem, however, was not engineering or even draft, but money. Artificial roads were expensive to build, with Trésaguet and Telford roads costing the most, and the simpler macadam roads somewhat less. Perhaps more important, these roads were expensive to maintain.

Americans wanted good roads for the sake of economic development, but there was an ideological component as well. Good roads would be a sign that the United States belonged among the great civilizations and especially the classical republics of Greece and Rome. As one midcentury engineer put it:

> The roads of a country are accurate and certain tests of the degree of its civilization. Their construction is one of the first indications of the emergence of a people from the savage state; and their improvement keeps pace with the advances of the nation in numbers, wealth, industry, and science—all of which it is at once an element and an evidence. Roads are the veins and arteries of the body politic, for through them flow the agricultural productions and commercial supplies which are the lifeblood of the state . . . roads belong to that unappreciated class of blessings, of which the value and importance are not fully felt, because of the very greatness of their advantages, which are so manifold and indispensable, as to have rendered their extent almost universal and their origin forgotten.[9]

However, despite considerable rhetoric about the multifarious benefits of good roads, the reality was that Americans did not want to pay for them. They were even less willing to pay for the continued upkeep that public infrastructure required. It was a question of jurisdictions and taxes. While Americans complained about poor roads, they fought over who should build them, pay for them, and maintain them. Hence the peculiar paradox of American politics: Americans fought bitterly to get state and federal governments to foot the cost of building roads that benefited their localities, but they often fought just as bitterly against the expenditure of public monies to benefit other localities or other states.

Local governments built most roads. Farmers and others could supply tools, materials, draft animals, and their own labor for a few days of road building in lieu of paying cash taxes. Because few people were trained in road construction, road building often consisted of clearing and leveling a stretch of road, without doing any grading, contouring, surfacing, and draining. In addition, people might attend to the section of road adjacent to their farm but not to any others. Most roadwork took place during the winter because it was a slack time on farms, but it was a terrible season for building a road. Another practice was to build "summer roads" by smoothing and widening the shoulders in such a way that after the spring mud season they would dry even and hard for summer use. Although these bad roads were hard on horses and increased energy and transportation costs, the fact that the costs were borne by individuals appeared in the short term to be an advantage. The larger social costs and energy costs of bad roads were less concrete and harder to discern. Building a community of interest around the need for good roads was difficult in the face of chronic resistance to paying taxes for public services and works on which a taxpayer might see no immediate personal return.[10]

State and federal governments were in a better position to pay for roads without levying taxes. There was a flurry of turnpike building from the 1790s to the 1830s. One of the earliest and most successful was the Philadelphia-Lancaster turnpike, a sixty-two-mile road chartered by the General Assembly in 1792. This set the standard for a good horse road. The roadway was cleared to fifty feet in width, with a twenty-foot-wide roadbed of surfaced stone, flanked by ample shoulders. There were no fords—stone bridges spanned all streams—and the maximum gradient was 7 percent. In 1812 the New York–Philadelphia road across New Jersey was improved with stone surfacing. By the 1830s New York contained 4,000 miles of improved roads, and Pennsylvania 2,400 miles, which included features such as a mile-long covered bridge across the Susquehanna River at Harrisburg. Eighty percent of all turnpikes were in New York, Pennsylvania, Ohio, and New England, where a lacework of roads covered the landscape from Massachusetts to Lake Erie. Few were built west of Ohio or south of Virginia.

Road construction (and also construction of bridges, canals, and other infrastructure) was carried out by companies who obtained charters from state governments. These were corporations organized by investors interested in improvements that would attract commerce and increase land values in their locality. These proliferated during the nineteenth century for projects that ranged from single bridges to extensive roads and canals. The Ausable River Plank Road Company, chartered in New York in 1848, was a representative example. This company consisted of twenty-two men who invested from $500 to $5,000 apiece, raised another $23,000, and planned to capitalize the company for an additional $32,000 by selling 650 shares at $50 per share. They proposed building seventeen miles of toll road, from Ausable Forks to Port Kent on Lake Champlain, including at least one bridge. By the summer of 1849, three miles had been completed. By 1853 they had hired a man "to keep the Plank Road in order" and were collecting tolls at three gates.

However, expenses mounted while receipts and profits lagged. As so often happened with these companies, maintenance costs were far higher than expected, and toll receipts fell behind as travelers learned how to circumvent the tollgate. The company also incurred damage claims, although they refused to pay Odin Tiffs for his horse or William Martin and Joshua Hallock for their wagon, on the grounds that the breakdown of neither was due to the road. However, they did pay Ashley Ames for injuries his horse suffered from broken planking. In 1852 they asked the Albany government to levy an additional toll. In 1869 the company abandoned the portion of the road between Port Kent and Clintonville, and though the company limped on for a number of years, the road eventually reverted to the state.[11]

Yet financial failure was not the same thing as material failure. The turnpikes, though bankrupt or abandoned as business enterprises, often continued in use under local jurisdictions, improving transportation and becoming important feeders to waterways and main roads. By increasing horse efficiency and reducing draft, these roads shortened travel time and increased the volume of freighting and transportation. Freight moved the 90 miles between New York City and Philadelphia in three days, and the 290 miles between Philadelphia and Pittsburgh in thirteen days. Travelers frequently reported encountering large numbers of wagons on the turnpikes. For example, a traveler near Baltimore in 1827 counted 235 freight wagons in 35 miles. Since most wagons used four or even five horses, hitched two and two with the fifth in front, the growth in wagon traffic put hundreds of horses on the road. Thus road construction increased the use of horses by significantly reducing draft.[12]

On the national level, the issues of building and financing roads and other internal improvements became chronically contentious because of state rivalries, partisan differences, sectional conflicts, and constitutional questions. It figured in the outcomes of the elections of 1824 and 1828, the Maysville Road bill in 1832, and the Supreme Court decision in *Charles River Bridge* v. *Warren Bridge* in 1837. In 1806 Congress authorized funds for one national road from Cumberland, Maryland, to the Mississippi River. By 1838, with much starting and stopping, it had been completed as far as Vandalia, Illinois. However, the government encouraged road improvement indirectly by means of the Post Office Department, which was one of the earliest, largest, and best-developed government bureaucracies of the nineteenth century. Designating certain routes as post roads allowed the postal service to give mail contractors extra money to make road and bridge repairs. The department also encouraged road improvement and construction through subsidies to stagecoach lines in the form of contracts to carry the mail. The government also supported internal improvement in the western territories, which were directly under federal authority. Under the aegis of the army, the Quartermaster Department conducted surveys and constructed roads and bridges.[13]

However, underlying the contentious politics of internal improvement that often divided Americans along sectional and ideological lines was a politics of energy, which united Americans. Most Americans saw increased energy consumption as the solution to a wide range of issues, and they believed that applying energy to transportation and production would somehow mitigate political and social conflicts through economic growth. Their political disagreements focused on the role of government power, on who shouldered the costs, and on who received the benefits, but not over the use of energy or the role of energy in American society. In a country with ample land for pasture and crops, horses were one of America's most abundant energy resources. Provided with a material environment in which their power could be used effectively, horses were the engines of national development.

One of the consequences of road improvement was the expansion of stagecoach travel. Stagecoaches running on regular, reliable schedules were the latest in fast transportation. Drawn by four to six horses and loaded with luggage, a stage was an ensemble sixty feet or more in length. On improved roads, a regular stagecoach could travel ten miles per hour, and an express coach could cover as much as twelve miles per hour. This speed was astonishing in a world where humans walked two miles per hour and horses no more than three or four. There was no faster mode of overland travel.[14]

Stagecoach lines covered the eastern seaboard. Many stagecoach firms operated locally, providing service to two or three towns, as shown in the names of several New England enterprises: the Meredith and Dover Line; the Concord, Bristol and Haverhill; the Lowell, Derry and Concord, New Hampshire; and the Portland and

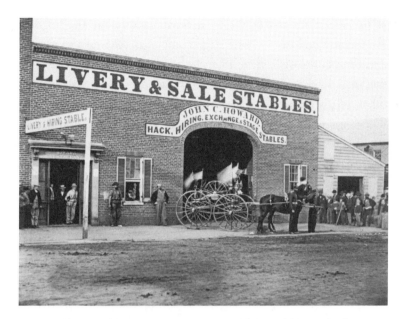

Livery stable in Washington, D.C., ca. 1865. In addition to hiring and selling horses, this establishment served as a waystation for stagecoaches and also housed a restaurant. Courtesy of the Library of Congress.

White Mountain Stage Company. At this level, it took relatively little capital to enter coaching. Local livery stables often operated coach services with their horses. Some of them had mail contracts that subsidized their operations.

There were also companies with extensive regional operations. The Eastern Stage Company in Boston owned 500 horses by the 1820s, and at its peak may have owned thousands. In addition, Eastern Stage owned stables and blacksmith shops and had financial interests in inns and hotels and wide investments in real estate and securities.[15] The same was true of other large stagecoach companies in the eastern part of the country, and of express and freight companies in the trans-Mississippi West.

Long-distance coaches made Boston, Philadelphia, Albany, and Baltimore important hubs for stagecoach traffic, New York City less so because it was well served by water transportation. In 1801 Boston already had twenty-four stage companies offering 100 arrivals and departures weekly; by 1826 the number had risen to seventy-five stage lines and 100 arrivals and departures daily. Sixteen lines offered daily return service to other cities. The corollary was an immense increase in the volume of travelers. In 1832, 14,000 people traveled between Boston and Worcester alone. By 1833 it was possible to go from Boston to New York in just over thirty-three hours without stopping overnight. In 1810 Philadelphia had thirty-eight stagecoach lines and over 400 arrivals and departures each week, rising to seventy lines and more than 1,000 arrivals and departures by 1819. These included routes across New Jersey and into New York City, to adjacent localities such as Germantown, Norristown, and West Chester, and into central and western Pennsylvania and Ohio. Competition for business was stiff on the most heavily traveled routes. Each line wanted to prove that its coaches were the fastest and most punctual, and sometimes ordered drivers to "make time or kill the horses."[16]

Stagecoach companies competed for postal subsidies, which accounted for as much as one-third of all passenger revenues. Because passengers preferred the punctuality of mail stages, stagecoach operators lobbied the Post Office Department intensively for the lucrative contracts that carried the right to include "and United States Mail" in the name of their stage line. Monitored by postal officials, mail stages were required to keep regular schedules to keep a contract. Obtaining or losing a contract could make or break a company. Thus the Postal Service, to all intents and purposes, shaped and regulated stagecoach service. Stagecoach lines served the eastern seaboard and reached into the South and the Midwest. By the 1850s stagecoach routes extended throughout the trans-Mississippi West, providing regular mail delivery in addition to passenger service.[17]

Galloping at ten miles an hour, coach horses needed to be relieved every fifteen to twenty miles, so stagecoach companies had stopping places to switch drivers and provide fresh horses. Inns housed and fed teams, drivers, and travelers, and sometimes provided the services such as horseshoeing. If they served drovers as well as coaches, they provided paddocks for livestock. On heavily traveled routes, inns specialized in drovers or coaches. Some were large enough to provide overnight accommodation for dozens of wagons and coaches, each with a team of two to eight animals.

Stage companies with long routes had to coordinate horses, vehicles, drivers, supplies, and services (such as horseshoeing and coach repairs) over the length of the route. For example, a six-horse stagecoach traveling a 100-mile route started with one team and needed four more teams, or thirty horses, waiting along the route and extra horses in case of injuries. Sometimes a coaching company would assemble a caravan of several coaches if there were more passengers or luggage than a single coach could carry. These trains would arrive at an inn, all calling for fresh horses and drivers, forage and stabling for tired horses, and food and lodging for tired passengers. Freight wagons, pulled by six to eight horses or by yokes of oxen, traveled in groups of as many as thirty, pulled by 200 or more animals. Some inns housed as many as fifty or sixty teams for a night.

Thus the expansion of the stagecoach network in turn created a network of small business hubs that served as collection points for passengers, mail, and freight and as centers of market activity. These locations were often determined by the distance that equine prime movers could travel before needing fuel and rest. As communities, their character was shaped by the needs of horses as workers, inhabitants, and consumers who required hay, oats, drivers, and horseshoes, and by the possibilities and limits of horse energy. Horses were a nonnative species that altered the environment of these hubs through what they ate, how they ate it, and how they lived upon the land. As an expanding horse-powered transportation system extended the market, farmers produced hay, oats, horses, livestock, and cash crops, altering the local ecology. Everything about the production and consumption of horse power shaped the material environment. The infrastructure of village, farm, and road that emerged within the stagecoach network was an energy landscape configured around horses as prime movers, and shaped by changing expectations about time, space, and energy consumption.

Stagecoach travelers knew this landscape through the bodily experience of travel. They saw the physical work of the horses in bulging muscles, glistening sweat, flecks of foam, flared nostrils, and heaving sides. In the rocking and pitching of the coach they felt the speed of the horses and the condition of the roads. Stagecoaches were notoriously uncomfortable, leaving passengers black and blue, and suffering from "stagecoach spine." One traveler recalled, "We had been sixteen hours traveling sixty-seven miles over a hard and rough road, without stopping to dine, and [were] bruised, tired and hungry." Traveling west from Buffalo, another traveler wrote, "There were none to hear the piteous groans every rut brought from me. I really expected my skin would be black and blue." When the coach hit a particularly deep rut the impact hurled the driver from his seat. As William Owen journeyed across New Jersey from New Brunswick to Trenton, he found the road "very bad though we sat on patent spring seats" and arrived at Trenton "prettily shaken." Charles Dickens described a road so rough that "at one time we were all flung together in a heap at the bottom of the coach, and at another we were crushing our heads against the roof. Now one side was down deep in the mire, and we were holding on to the other." Traveling in a half-empty coach, Frances Trollope soon yearned to be in one filled to capacity because she and her fellow passengers were "tossed about like a few potatoes in a wheelbarrow." A segment of her journey over a "corduroy" road of logs laid side by side left her feeling that "every joint was nearly dislocated."[18]

If roads were muddy, snow-covered, or icy, passengers had to get out of the coach to lighten the load for the horses, walking up and down hills even in inclement or severe weather. Bad weather could shut down land travel completely. A three-day snowstorm near Philadelphia in January 1831 stopped traffic for two weeks. Horses and riders were sent out in groups of twenty to break a trail through the snowdrifts, but stages still could not operate, "though dragged upon runners by six of the finest horses of the line, one of which perished from exhaustion."[19]

Breakdowns arising from broken coaches or broken horses were frequent. Wheels came off, axles snapped, harness gave way; horses lost shoes, injured legs and feet, or collapsed. If a coach got stuck in the mud or tipped over, everyone got out, and driver and passengers worked to free it or set it upright again. If they could not, they were stranded until help arrived. Accidents occurred from runaway horses, swaying top-heavy loads, collisions with rocks, logs, stumps, and potholes, snapped harness, and broken wheels and axles. Dickens described an accident on a downhill grade. "Immediately we began to descend the steep pitch, the driver pulling up with all his might, when the left rein of the leaders broke and the team was in a moment sheared out of the road and ran diagonally down the pitch. In a second, the wagon went over . . . the mules had been disengaged by the upset and were making good time across the prairie."[20] Sometimes drivers of rival coaches raced each other, galloping their teams full speed as their coaches swayed and bounced over narrow and rutted roads, or sometimes they tried to run each other off the road. Lawsuits against stagecoach companies for passenger injuries forced some of them to regulate driver conduct, and state laws were passed against racing, leaving the team of a loaded coach untended, and other dangerous behaviors.

The expansion of stagecoaching, freighting, and other horse-drawn traffic over extended and improved roads created a larger market for coaches, carriages, and wagons. It prompted innovations in the design and manufacture of vehicles to reduce draft and improve efficiency. It also encouraged the industrialization of vehicle manufacturing. Wagons became lighter, easier to maneuver, and more durable. One example was the development of the Conestoga wagon in Pennsylvania in the late eighteenth and early nineteenth centuries. This was a three-ton freight wagon pulled by six-horse teams. The wagon bed was curved like a boat to hold freight in place. Freight that was well balanced and did not shift around made a wagon easier to pull. The rear wheels of the Conestoga were very large to reduce wheel resistance, and the front wheels were smaller to make the wagon easier to turn. The Conestoga wagon could hold a larger amount of freight than other wagons without using more horses. It was perhaps the most efficient wagon of the period and the backbone of freight haulage until the construction of the railroads.

As better transportation made it possible to obtain a wide range of lumber from other regions, wagon and coach makers were able to obtain a variety of strong, light woods that reduced the weight of their vehicles. Using parts made of iron instead of wood to assemble the wagons and for the wagon fittings on wheels, shafts, and axles also made wagons lighter: wagon parts made of wood had to be large and heavy in order to be strong, but equal strength could be delivered by a much smaller and lighter iron part. Advances in metallurgy and in iron manufacturing—one of the central components of nineteenth-century industrialization—contributed to lighter wagons and the increased use of horses. For example, iron springs made travel both somewhat more comfortable for human passengers and easier on the horses. When a stagecoach hit a bump in the road, the spring created vertical lift that pulled the coach up and over the bump, at the same time absorbing the shock for the passengers.

The Abbot-Downing Company of Concord, New Hampshire, was known for its technical innovations in vehicle design and manufacture. Lewis Downing began building wagons and carriages for the local market in 1813, and was joined by Steven Abbot in 1827.

The company responded swiftly to growing market demand, and during the nineteenth century (the company stayed in business until 1925) acquired a national and international reputation for its wide array of well-built vehicles produced in its factory in Concord.

Abbot-Downing was perhaps best known for its custom-built stagecoaches, especially the "Concord Coach," first developed in 1827. The body of the Concord Coach was designed as an aerodynamic flat-topped oval. The company's artisans skillfully combined oak, ash, and other woods to make it both light and durable. By placing the baggage compartments under the driver's feet and at the back of the coach, they kept it from being top-heavy, and thus minimized the side draft, or side-to-side motion, that increased the work of the horses.

But the most important innovation of the Concord Coach was its suspension system. Instead of using iron springs (or, like some coaches, no springs at all) the Concord Coach was suspended on two leather devices called thoroughbraces. Each thoroughbrace consisted of six or more long straps of leather stacked vertically and bound together. These were attached to the front and the back of the coach frame and ran under the coach body on each side, suspending the coach body in a leather sling. The coach body had no direct attachment to the frame or the wheels, and the thoroughbraces let it move freely, providing a much less jolting ride for passengers. Additionally, the thoroughbraces created an upward motion that lightened the draft for the horses. "Dancing like a balloon" was how one person described it. Seasoned traveler Mark Twain called it "a cradle on wheels." The Concord Coach, built ruggedly yet lightly, came to be the classic stagecoach of the American West. Its reputation was such that Abbot-Downing began to market globally, filling orders from South Africa, Australia, South America, and Europe.[21]

Abbot-Downing benefited from the growing market for horse-drawn vehicles that resulted from internal improvements, and from the ways in which different kinds of power complemented each other. The company utilized waterpower and steam power to industrialize the production of horse-drawn vehicles. When the railroad came to Concord, it connected Abbot-Downing to the materials it needed, such as lumber, leather, iron parts, paint, and varnish, and expanded the company's market through finished vehicles to customers. At one point in 1868, for example, a train left the factory site with thirty Concord Coaches built for the Wells Fargo Company in Omaha, Nebraska.

In addition to vehicle design, wheel design provided a way of reducing draft through changes in diameter, width, and shape. Wheels transferred friction from the ground to the axle, where lubricants and ball bearings reduced it. Because wheel resistance diminishes in proportion to increases in wheel diameter, large wheels provided a mechanical advantage. On the other hand, wheels could not be so large that the axle of the vehicle was above the middle of the horses' chests, increasing draft by making them pull down toward the ground.

Wheel width not only determined the amount of friction produced; its efficiency also depended on road conditions. On a smooth, hard road, narrow rims result in less friction; on a soft road they create more. Wide-rimmed wheels sink less into wet and muddy roads, and they roll over ruts rather than into them, rather like the thick tires of a mountain bike on muddy ground versus the thin tires of a road racing bicycle. The shape of the wheel entailed a trade-off between low friction and durability. Wheels were the most vulnerable part of a horse-drawn vehicle, after the horses' legs and feet. A flat, or straight, wheel produces less friction than a dished wheel. Dishing the wheel involves making it slightly concave by angling the spokes off the rim and moving the hub out of the plane of the rim. A dished wheel resists moving straight forward because its moves in a circle rather than a straight line. But dished wheels are stronger, more resilient, and thus less likely to break on an uneven road. Differences in strength and effort among horses of a team could reduce its overall efficiency, but these could be evened out with modifications or additions to harness. One technological manual noted: "As such variations influence both the safety and efficiency of machines, it is necessary to provide against them by some appendage, which shall equalize either the supply or the distribution of the power." One device invented to handle these fluctuations was the whiffletree, a horizontal bar to which the lower ends of the traces are attached. It hangs behind a horse's heels and is attached by another strap or chain to the vehicle. A whiffletree acts as a spring between the horse and the vehicle. With the addition of other bars it can be expanded to accommodate the traces of several horses and equalize their efforts.[22] By allowing for harnessing abreast, it makes a team more powerful by giving the horses the same line of draft.

Roads remained the most immediate form of transportation access for most Americans, even if they were ambivalent about paying for them. But Americans were also interested in improving or extending the benefits of water transportation by building artificial rivers, or canals. These could link existing water routes, make rivers more navigable, provide power for manufacturing, reach inland resources and markets, and funnel commerce to towns and cities. Above all, canals would combine the reliability of animal power with the ease of water travel, freeing the latter from the vagaries of winds, currents, and tides. Americans built 3,326 miles of canals during a two-decade "canal boom" in the 1820s and 1830s.

Canals had long been the dream of many of the nation's improvers. Even before the nineteenth century many a joint-stock company tried to raise the necessary capital and lobbied the state or federal government for funds. In 1785 George Washington obtained char-

ters from the legislatures of Virginia and Maryland for the Patow-
mack Company to build canals around falls and rapids on the Potomac River. Few of these early dreams were achieved; by the second
decade of the nineteenth century there were only 100 miles of canals
in the United States. But the construction of the Erie Canal in 1817
changed everything.

The passage of almost two centuries has not lessened the sheer
audacity of the Erie Canal. It would be an enormous construction
project for the twenty-first century let alone for the nineteenth. The
Erie Canal traversed upstate New York from Buffalo to Albany and
connected with the Albany–New York City stretch of the Hudson
River. It took eight years to build the forty-foot-wide, four-foot-deep
ditch that crossed 363 miles of swamps, ridges, and rivers and used
eighty-four locks to manage elevation changes of 698 feet. At Rochester the canal crossed the Genesee River on an 802-foot aqueduct
supported by eleven stone arches. At the sharp change in elevation
at the geological formation called the Niagara Escarpment, the canal
made a three-mile-long "deep cut" through solid rock to a five-level
stack of locks. At it neared Albany, the canal threaded through the
Mohawk River gorge on two aqueducts, one of which was 1,188 feet
long, and via a groove cut into a cliff. No less a dreamer and technological enthusiast than Thomas Jefferson called it madness to join
the Great Lakes and the Hudson River, left so inconveniently
asunder.[23]

The completed canal was the newest, most modern thing in
America, and it relied entirely on horse power. It was a stunning financial success that slashed travel times and freight rates, and re-
couped the cost of construction in twelve years. It changed the
course of social and economic development, spurring settlement
and commercial development of upstate New York and the Midwest, and propelling New York City permanently ahead of its rival
seaboard cities in size and economic importance. It demonstrated
the centrality of horse power to industrial change. At least 2,000

horses worked alongside human laborers building the Erie Canal. Horses plowed ground to start excavation, pulled scrapers that carved out the canal bed, powered cranes that moved beams and stone blocks, hauled wagons of dirt, rock and lumber, and packed down its surface with their hooves to seal the canal bed.

Nineteenth-century canals were apparatuses designed to move boats and barges using horses and mules. "Canal horses" could mean either. The equines were the engines; the towpath along which they moved was the power line; the towrope was the transmission. Anything that obstructed the towpath or kept horses from moving brought canal traffic to a halt, so there were crossover bridges for horses to get to the opposite side if necessary, bridges for horses at the locks, and escape hatches cut into the banks of the canal so that tow animals that fell into the canal could clamber out again and resume work.[24]

Towing canal boats with horses was an efficient use of power, especially in comparison with land travel. Moving twenty miles a day, two packhorses could carry 200 pounds each, and a pair of horses pulling a wagon could haul a ton on a decent road; but two canal horses could tow a barge carrying fifty to eighty tons of freight. Line boats could cover forty miles per day if necessary, replacing four horses every fifteen to twenty miles; and express boats, or packets, covered eighty miles a day, changing four-horse teams every ten miles.

Canal boats changed people's ideas about speed and motion. For many it was an entirely new experience of travel. Wrote one traveler, "Commending my soul to God, and asking his defense from danger, I stepped on board the canal boat and was soon flying toward Utica." Since the average speed of a canal boat was four miles an hour, less than that of a stagecoach, it wasn't the speed that awed people, but the smoothness, the silence, and the sensation of effortless motion. The canal boat's gliding progress contrasted sharply with the teeth-rattling, bone-jarring, bruising experience of travel by stagecoach. Passengers could read, walk along the towpath, or just sit and watch the scenery scroll past; all they had to remember was to duck at the low bridges. The experience of canal travel suggested that the production of power could be separated from enjoyment of its use. The boat was separated from the horses by 250 feet of towrope that, like any harness, served as a spring that absorbed their motion.[25]

By midcentury there were more than 8,000 canal horses on the Erie alone. Some canal boat operators owned their own horses; others hired horses and drivers (often young boys) from public stables located at intervals along the canal. Some of the larger boat lines joined forces and established cooperative associations called towing companies that purchased animals and maintained them in large stables, sharing the expense by assessing a charge per horse-mile. One towing company supplied horses to a group of eight boat lines that had 157 boats. Three towing companies together supplied 1,400 horses.[26]

Steam power was never much of a factor on nineteenth-century canals, despite enormous interest in developing steam-powered canal boats. Steamboat wakes created waves that eroded and undercut the banks of the canal. Wakes not only threatened to sever the all-important towpath but also could breach the canal wall, empty the canal of water, and force its shutdown. An 1854 travelers' guide for Pennsylvania downplayed this issue:

> Several attempts have been made to introduce steam in the navigation of the Schuylkill [Canal], and though apparently attended with some success, have not led to any practical end, as yet. The only steamboats now plying on its waters are those between Fairmount and Manayunk. If coal could be used for fuel (of which, by the way, there can be no doubt,) and the machinery made sufficiently light to correspond with the tonnage of the boat, there would in-

deed, seem to be no practical reason why steam should not supersede horses. The splashing of the water against the banks of the canal, occasioned by the evolutions of the paddle-wheel, present the most potent objection;—yet this is but a trifle, and might readily be overcome, if sufficient attention were bestowed up on the subject.[27]

In 1857 *Scientific American* confidently stated that steam was soon to be "an established fact" on canals. In the 1860s the New York legislature offered a bounty to the inventor of a successful low-wake steam-powered canal boat. Each new entry in the competition inspired an enthusiastic announcement that the solution was now at hand. However, in 1872 the legislature was still offering a reward for "the profitable introduction of some motor for canal boats other than animal power."[28]

Pennsylvania planned to use both horses and steam on the 395-mile Main Line Canal between Philadelphia and Pittsburgh, capitalizing on the advantages of both in what they hoped would be a replication of the Erie's success. Unlike the Erie, the Main Line had to cut through a mountain chain, so segments of canals alternated with graded roads called inclined planes. Canal boats were floated onto railroad cars, and stationary engines at the top of each grade hauled them up railroad tracks using a cable. At the summit, gravity pulled the cars down the other side, where the boats were floated onto the next canal segment. Long sequences of inclined planes switchbacked up the mountains, with horses pulling the cars in between. Traveler Albert Koch described one of these, the thirty-seven-mile Portage Railroad. "We reached the mountain in various ways, sometimes by horses, sometimes by engines, sometimes by stationary steam engines operating cables, and finally the coach ran by itself 4 English miles down the mountain to the place where, for the second time, we went aboard a canal boat."[29] However, the Main Line canal, more audacious than the Erie, was a spectacular failure.

Pennsylvania's geography proved too much for this combination of animal power and steam power.

Steam canal boats had to operate for long stretches for their speed to offset their cost. Even if the problem of wake had been solved, growing traffic congestion on the Erie eliminated the speed advantage of steam engines and increased their energy costs. In 1870 an observer reported "a continuous line of boats . . . stretching in both directions." There were over 7,000 boats on the Erie, and long backups at the locks were common. Idling a steam engine was expensive, but so was shutting it down and having to take the time and fuel to fire it up again later. In these situations, equine engines simply recharged themselves by eating and resting along the banks. Furthermore, low water exacerbated the wake problem, so whenever water levels fell—a common occurrence in summer—steamboats became unusable. *Scientific American*, ever optimistic, suggested using road steamers, locomotives, underground cables, or electric engines to pull canal boats, none of which, except for locomotives, were even workable technologies.

Canal boats pulled by horses remained the least expensive way to haul bulky products such as lumber, stone, coal, and crops throughout the century, even after railroads diverted capital, passengers, and attention. They were an important link in the industrial transportation system. For example, the Black River Canal, which intersected the Erie at Rome, New York, opened in 1851 and stayed in operation for seventy-one years carrying lumber, potatoes, sand, and rock from the St. Lawrence River Valley. In the 1860s the Erie and its Champlain canal were still carrying one-third of east-west tonnage. Even as late as the 1880s fewer than 100 of the Erie's canal boats used steam power. Most canal boats used horses into the twentieth century because horses were still the most efficient and cost-effective prime movers.[30]

Like stagecoaches and roads, canals developed new energy land-

scapes through the consumption of horse power. They had enormous environmental impact, creating artificial "rivers," connecting
previously separate bodies of water, altering river levels and currents, and creating new bodies of water behind dams and locks.
Horses and mules were nonnative species that grazed the grasses,
plants, and bushes along the canals, trod towpaths into dust or mud,
dropped manure, scattered grain from their nosebags, and attracted
birds and rodents. The energy market of canals shaped land use,
crop choices, business development, and social arrangements by
concentrating human and animal populations on narrow strips of
land and water.

Whereas on canals horses moved boats by walking alongside the
water, on horse ferries, or "teamboats," they moved boats by walking on the water. This arrangement evolved for crossing bodies of
water lacking bridges or towpaths. Horse ferries used a capstan,
wheel, or treadmill set into the deck, and as the horses moved this
device the craft was propelled across the water. The earliest horse
ferryboats used capstans, which required the horses to walk in a
small circle around the hub. This arrangement caused the horses to
break down or to become lame and dizzy; some retired horses cir-
cled compulsively for the remainder of their lives. Horses' rigid
spines make it difficult for them to circle well in less than a forty-foot
diameter, but a forty-foot-diameter capstan would have been too
large for a ferry. Using upright wheel devices eliminated the problem of circling. A wheel was set with its uppermost portion flush
with the ferry deck. The horse could turn it by walking in a straight
line on the exposed surface. By the 1840s the upright wheel was replaced by a treadmill on the deck consisting of a belt of wooden
slats joined by leather strips or metal links and extending around
two cylinders to form a continuous, flexible walkway. The treadmill
was slightly inclined to move under the horse's weight and force it

to keep walking; railings or low walls on each side of the treadmill kept the animal on the straight and narrow. Traveler Albert Koch described such a ferry "set into motion by two horses, of which one on either side in a little house turned a wheel which was connected to a waterwheel. A single man managed the whole thing, for the horses were so trained that on command both started their march, and stood motionless immediately when the man rang a small bell." The treadmill was geared to the paddles driving the boat. As time went on, all horse ferryboats used the treadmill mechanism.[31]

The first commercially successful horse ferry began operation in 1814 between New York and Brooklyn. It used six to eight horses, carried over 200 passengers, and made the trip in less than twenty minutes. *Niles' Weekly Register* commented: "For short distances [the ferry] answers all the valuable purposes of steam boats. We congratulate the public on this cheap and important addition to their safety and comfort." By 1819 there were at least eight horse ferries operating from Manhattan, and *Niles'* noted the use of "many teamboats at different ferries in the United States." Horse ferries operated on the Hudson at Athens, Newburgh, and Albany. Harriet Martineau crossed the Hudson to Albany on a horse ferry in 1838, but found it "cruel as well as clumsy" and thought they should be done away with because "the strongest horses, however kept up with corn, rarely survive a year of this work." William Owen crossed the Hudson from Newburgh to Fishkill "in a teamboat drawn by seven horses and capable of containing several wagons and horses." Additionally there were horse ferries at Halifax, Philadelphia, Alexandria, Charleston, Cincinnati, Maysville, and along the upper St. Lawrence River. Richard Champion Rawlins saw one on Lake Canandaigua in about 1840, and they were used on Lake Champlain in the 1830s and 1840s. They operated on the Ohio and Tennessee Rivers until the Civil War, including one operating at Chattanooga during the Union army siege in 1863.[32]

Horse ferries were successful in their time because they were considered more reliable and safer than sailing ferries and steam ferries. As had been found with canal boats, steam power was not an economical choice for all ferries, especially those at narrow crossings or those used only occasionally or seasonally. Some ferry operators converted to steam, and then switched back to horses as a more economical source of power. Until the construction of bridges and the development of efficient steam engines, horse ferries were an important link in the transportation network. Horse ferries disappeared from use in the Northeast by midcentury, but they remained in use at river and lake crossings in less-developed areas across the South, Midwest, and West. There were three on the Columbia River in 1900, and some on the upper Mississippi, the Missouri, and the St. Lawrence into the twentieth century. The last known horse ferry operated on the Cumberland River in Tennessee until 1920.

Roads, canals, and ferries increased Americans' dependence on horses, but what secured the importance of the horse as an industrial prime mover was the expansion of the railroad system. Midcentury observers clearly understood that railroads reinforced and increased the use of horses. As Census Superintendent Joseph C. G. Kennedy wrote,

> The first impression made upon the popular mind by any great improvement in machinery or locomotion, after the admission of their beneficial effect, is that they will, in some way or other, diminish the demand for labor or for other machinery. There was an idea that [railroads] would result in diminishing the number of horses . . . the result, however, proves precisely the contrary. Horses have multiplied more rapidly since the introduction of locomotives than

they did before . . . Three-fourths of all the miles of railroad have been made since 1850; and we see that since then the increase of horses has been the greatest.

Census returns showed that horse populations had increased 12 percent between 1840 and 1850, and 51 percent between 1850 and 1860. In five western states—Ohio, Indiana, Illinois, Michigan, and Wisconsin—horse populations had grown 106 percent overall, while the growth in individual states ranged from 61 to 380 percent. The states with the most railroad miles also had the greatest increases in the horse population. "It seemed that railroads must diminish the number and importance of horses, but such was not the fact," observed Kennedy. "Railroads tend to increase their number and value. This is now an established principle."[33]

By the 1850s railroads had become a national obsession, dominating the American imagination with their explosive expansion accompanied by the rapid change they brought to many communities. In 1829 the Baltimore & Ohio Railroad opened the first 13 miles of track, with horses pulling the cars over the tracks. By 1860 the nation had 30,626 miles, two-thirds of which had been constructed in the preceding decade.[34] In three decades railroads shrank distances, flattened geography, altered political economy, and changed ideas about time and space.

Railroads coupled sheer physical power with dizzying potential to "annihilate space and time" in an enormous, undeveloped nation with a far-flung population and dreams of greatness. When Thomas Durant proposed building a railroad north from Saratoga into the Adirondack Mountains, the *New York Times* declared, "Within an easy day's ride of our great city, as steam teaches us to measure distance, is a tract of country fitted to make a Central Park for the world . . . with [the railroad's] completion, the Adirondack region will become a suburb of New York." Traveling thirty miles per hour or even more, trains were almost three times faster than a stagecoach, six or seven times faster than a canal boat, and ten times faster than a horse could walk.[35]

Despite the noise, smoke, and jolting speed of the steam locomotive and its cars, people compared the experience of railroad travel to flying. At first they likened the locomotive to a mythological creature of power and flame and called it a dragon.

> But this is the *Car of the People,*
> And before it shall bow all Kings:—
> Be they warned when they hear the shrieking
> Of the Dragon with Iron Wings![36]

Charles Dickens also described the rushing, diving, clattering, pell-mell passage of the train as "the mad dragon of an engine with its train of cars, scattering in all directions a shower of burning sparks from its wood fire; screeching, hissing, yelling, panting." But unlike a dragon, the locomotive was neither mythical nor untamed, but quite real, both made and controlled by humans. The metaphor more often invoked was the swiftest and most powerful animal they knew . The steam locomotive inspired countless poems in which equine imagery galloped unchecked, such as this one:

> But now a proud and mighty steed
> Whose nostrils breathe a living fire,
> High, rears aloft his smoking head
> And rushes with relentless ire.

An otherwise sober article with the unpromising title "Statistics and Speculations concerning the Pacific Railroad" concluded thus: "The Iron Horse, the earth-shaker, the fire-breather, which tramples down the hills, which outruns the laggard winds, which leaps over the rivers, which grinds the rocks to powder and breaks down the gates of the mountains . . . shall build an empire and an epic"

Horses pulling a locomotive overland for use in the Pine River and Stevens Point Railroad, Wisconsin, 1876. Wisconsin Historical Society, image 24557.

Even Henry David Thoreau, a profound critic of industrial society, succumbed to the image of equine power. "I hear the iron horse make the hills echo with his snort like thunder, shaking the earth with his feet, and breathing fire and smoke from his nostrils . . . I am awakened by his tramp and snort at midnight, when in some remote glen in the woods he fronts the elements . . . I hear him in his stable, blowing off the superfluous energy of the day."[37]

The sobriquet "iron horse" reflected the continuing importance of real horses and the persisting tendency to assess the success of inanimate machines in terms of living machines. Horses pulled the trains of the very first railroads, often spelled "rail-road" or "rail road" to distinguish them from dirt, plank, macadam, and other surfaces used by horse-drawn traffic. Putting wagons onto hard, smooth rails and providing a good surface for traction increased the amount of weight a horse could pull by at least a factor of eight. The first locomotives were too large and heavy for effective use, but as they became smaller and lighter as a result of improvements to high-pressure steam engines, they began to replace horses on the rails. Railroads continued to use horses in the 1830s because locomotives were not reliable and powerful enough. Sometimes they were supplemented by horses up steep grades, and often they were entirely replaced by horses during the winter months. Some very short railroads continued to use horses instead of locomotives into the 1840s, and some were even powered by horse treadmill devices, like those used for horse ferries, mounted on wheels.[38]

Horses remained essential to every aspect of railroad operation, beginning with construction. Just as horses built roads and canals, they built railroads, by hauling materials, grading roadbeds, powering cranes, pulling cars on completed sections, and transporting workers. The way in which railroads developed as businesses also made horses central to their success. Unlike roads and canals, from the beginning railroads were built as private rather than public enterprises. They began as quite small companies, usually composed of local investors using local capital, and this local context determined where the tracks were laid. Railroads were built not as mass-transit systems serving the public, but as moneymakers for individual investors. Their purpose was to channel commerce and control markets in a way that favored those investors and local business interests while excluding competitors. Creating an integrated system was not to their advantage. Economic returns came from preventing, not promoting, connections with other railroads.

For example, if there were several railroads in a city, they maintained separate depots; the concept of the "union" railroad station, where the tracks of different railroads intersect, lay in the future. Philadelphia had seven separate depots, Baltimore had three, and Richmond had five. This was also the case in Petersburg, Savannah,

Charleston, and Montgomery, where tracks were neither joined nor even adjacent. Railroads did not work together in any way. Each one kept its own clock, made its own timetables, and established its own time zones. Railroads did not coordinate their arrivals and departures, so passengers could not easily transfer from one to another to make through connections. Consequently, railway journeys over any considerable distance usually involved layovers. The fragmented structure of railroading meant that all travel used a variety of transportations, and that travelers were constantly moving between stations, from one form of transportation to another, or between lodgings and transportation. For all this movement, only one prime mover was available, and that was the horse.

Railroads were also fragmented because the technology was so new and unsettled. There was no consensus or industry standard as to the best equipment to use or the best way to design railroad infrastructure. Railroads did not use interchangeable cars, locomotives, or parts. Nor did they use a consistent track gauge, or width. From a purely technical standpoint there was no one gauge that was clearly optimal, so each railroad built its tracks using whatever gauge it wanted. Railroad companies could exploit this technologically open-ended situation as part of their strategy of protecting themselves from outside competition and maintaining control over local markets. Choosing a different gauge from that used by other railroads prevented rail connections. If locomotives and cars could not transfer from one line to another, railroads could not steal business from each other, nor could they abscond with a competitor's rolling stock by sequestering it somewhere on their own tracks. American railroads were a welter of gauges. What eventually became standard gauge (4'8½") was most widely used, but there were many gauges ranging between 4'8" and 6'. The rival New York Central and Erie Railroads used two different gauges, and Ohio railroads six different gauges. Between Philadelphia and Chicago there was one gauge change, but between Philadelphia and Charleston there were eight. Not until 1886 would gauges be standardized in most of the country.[39]

Local business interests were in favor of keeping railroads separate. The money to be made around railroading came from terminal trains; a through train could easily become a train that did not stop. The discontinuities in railroad travel generated a tremendous amount of ancillary business, so that railroad officials, teamsters, omnibus and horse railway companies, livery stable owners, stagecoach lines, ferryboat operators, proprietors of hotels and restaurants, and anyone else who profited from moving passengers and freight and from housing and feeding travelers during layovers had a vested interest in maintaining them. There was no continuous railroad "system," but instead a disjointed hodgepodge of companies with many interstices in which horse-related businesses flourished.

However, understanding why railroads increased the importance of horses means going beyond the business history of railroads to the physics of railroads. A railroad is an ensemble that cannot be disassembled. Rails, locomotives, and cars are made for each other and are bound together by one device. The rails are not accessible to any other vehicles, and locomotives and railroad cars can travel only on the gauged rails for which they are built. As a prime mover, the locomotive is permanently harnessed to its rails, and benefits from the reduced friction of hard, smooth wheels rolling over on hard, smooth rails. Low draft comes at the expense of flexibility. Railroads can go only where rails are laid. Routes, established during railroad construction, are locked in place. In contrast, horses are not harnessed to the road, nor must they be harnessed to only one kind of vehicle. They are self-propelled prime movers that can be ridden or driven, harnessed to any number of vehicles or machines, and used on many different surfaces. Local mobility came at the price of distance travel. Railroads expanded the national market, increased the volume of commerce, stimulated production, and triggered urban growth, but only horses could provide short-distance hauling to and from the railroads and between points not on the railroads. Railroads enhanced the value and volume of horse-drawn traffic on well-placed roads and canals that provided access to the railroads, but horses made the railroads useful in the first place.

The most important difference between locomotives and horses as prime movers in the nineteenth century was not between machines and animals or between different amounts of horse power. The critical difference lay in *how* and *where* each worked most efficiently, with living machines and steam machines each occupying a unique niche in nineteenth-century industrialization.

Another factor increasing the use of horses alongside advances in steam power technology was the complex of problems associated with the latter. Nineteenth-century sources understandably abounded with unbridled enthusiasm for steam. Steam was the first kind of power that seemed to be entirely at human command. Humans had to wait for favorable winds, tides, currents, and water levels, and for horses to be rested. But steam produced such immense, sustained power that it seemed to remove human limits and fulfill utopian dreams. Yet the adoption of steam power occurred slowly in the United States. Steam power had to compete with water power and animal power, both of which were plentiful and cheap. In addition, steam engines were not universally applicable to all kinds of work.

As sources of motive power, steam engines were useful on rails and water. Attempts to adapt steam to land travel were far less successful until the end of the century. Initially the success of the railroads led many to believe that it would be easy to put locomotives onto the roads. During the antebellum years the *Journal of the Franklin Institute* and other publications frequently reported on successful test runs of "traction engines" and soberly predicted that they would soon be used on the nation's roads and fields. However,

these experiments were usually conducted under optimal conditions that bore little or no resemblance to the conditions in which
they would actually be used. Prototypes were heavy and cumbersome, and though some achieved speeds of five to ten miles per
hour (less than a stagecoach) they consumed large amounts of fuel
relative to results. Given the nineteenth-century mania for steam,
there would have been a market for traction engines if they were at
all useful, but no one was going to use them just to use them, no
matter how much they loved steam engines. Although the experiments with traction engines were useful in the evolution of steam
technology, in the short run these engines were done in by their own
inefficiency and technical problems.[40]

Steam engines were powerful but not necessarily efficient. Efficiency is the ratio between energy in and power out, or between the
energy sources an engine consumes and how much it converts into
power. Locomotives seemed more efficient than horses because of
their speed and stamina. A "tired" engine needed more fuel, but
theoretically it did not need to cool down, rest, and recover. However, getting up steam and building pressure ate up time and fuel,
and frequent stopping and starting consumed a great deal of additional fuel relative to distance traveled. These factors reduced steam
efficiency substantially. Consequently, antebellum steam locomotives were more efficient than horses over long distances with infre-
quent stops, but over distances of less than fifteen miles that included stopping and starting, living machines were more efficient
than locomotives. Short-distance hauling by horses, operating at
better efficiency than antebellum locomotives, was an efficient use
of power. W. J. M. Rankine, one of the leading steam engineers of
the midnineteenth century, claimed that "animals acting as prime
movers have a higher efficiency than any inorganic machines."[41]

Steam engines were also unsafe. Steam engine explosions were
frequent throughout the century. Sometimes these resulted from
defects in the construction of the engine. But more often than not

they were caused by errors people made as they used a new, powerful, capricious technology—ignorant or incorrect operation, poor
maintenance, or cavalier attitudes about steam power in general.
Steamboat explosions were some of the most deadly, causing deaths
from the blast and from drowning. In 1824 the steamer *Aetna* exploded in New York harbor, killing more than a dozen people. By
1830 there had been nearly sixty such explosions and 300 hundred
casualties. After the disastrous explosion of the *Helen McGregor* at
New Orleans that year, Congress funded a six-year investigation at
the Franklin Institute of Philadelphia. On the basis of the institute's
report, Congress passed mild regulatory legislation in 1838, but
only after more than 150 people died when the *Moselle* exploded at
Cincinnati. Despite repeated congressional action, explosions continued to cause fatalities. In 1842 Charles Dickens found "it was ad-
visable to collect opinions in reference to the comparative safety of
the vessels" bound from Pittsburgh to Cincinnati. Locomotive engines also exploded, but they exacted fewer casualties because of
their isolated position at one end of the train, and because people
did not drown. The greater danger was that the explosion would set
fire to the wooden railway cars or surrounding buildings. Steam
boilers in factories exploded, causing fire and damage, especially in
urban locations. During the last thirty years of the century alone,
more than 6,000 steam explosions killed over 8,300 people.[42]

More dangerous than explosions were railroad collisions and de-
railments caused by excessive speed, bad driving, damaged track,
and lack of signals and sidings. Trains had head-on collisions or
rammed into slower or stopped trains from behind. Fragile wooden
cars splintered, telescoped into one another, or burst into flames.
Trains derailed with some frequency. If some Americans extolled
railroads as celestial horses or magnificent dragons, others excoriated them as hellish devils and wicked monsters. One victim of a
railway accident published a long poem about this experience with
the "foul fiend of fire" that read in part

Thou last invention of the D——!
Thou champion of the long dead level!
Thou prototype of Death's pale horse!
Strewing his track with many a corpse.[43]

Of course there were regular coach and wagon accidents involving horses, but horse-drawn vehicles did not explode, travel thirty miles an hour, or carry dozens of people. Steam locomotives were considered so dangerous that they were banned from many cities as fire hazards, forcing railroads to use horses to pull their cars from the city limits to downtown depots.

Even as Americans read sensational accounts of steamboat and railroad accidents or scanned the "disaster" columns that were a regular feature of many newspapers, they continued to extol the benefits of steam engines. Proponents of steam consistently overstated its beneficial effects, minimized its liabilities, and exaggerated the extent of its use. At the same time, critics of steam also exaggerated the proliferation of steam engines in order to strengthen their polemics against them. Consequently, "an energy mystique, part exaggeration, part misinformation, blurred the distinctions between what was desirable, what was possible, and what was happening." This mystique caused serious misperceptions about the adoption of steam power in nineteenth century, including a false impression of their efficiency. Most important, it obscured both the continuing importance of horse power and the symbiotic relationship that developed between the use of horses and the use of steam.[44]

By the middle of the nineteenth century the transportation revolution had transformed the landscapes of the Northeast and Midwest from the one Americans had first encountered into one with roads, canals, and railroads that were the foundation for expansion, settlement, and development. The evolution of this landscape was not whimsical or accidental. It was in part a cultural landscape, in part an economic landscape, and in part a political landscape. But most fundamentally it was an energy landscape. Everything about it, whether demographic patterns, land uses, human geography, cultural values, came from the kind of energy that Americans used for transportation. It was not just about using horses or about using steam engines, but about the complementary relationship between horse and steam powers that set the material terms of American life and from which everything else flowed. The pattern of American life that emerged—the energy landscape of horse power—became the basis for American expectations about energy abundance and the arrangement of society. The growing use of horses constituted the great energy transition of the first industrial revolution.

3   REMAKING HORSES

As the energy demands of industrialization increased Americans' dependence on horses, the horse population grew in size but began to alter in composition. Industrialization required more horses and created demand for a wider array of them. During the nineteenth century Americans' ideas about breeds and their approaches to horse breeding changed as they remade horses to fit the needs of industrial society. Industrialization transformed the bodies of horses as well as their uses.

Reshaping horses for human purposes through horse breeding is a very ancient form of biotechnology. American horse breeding reflected the spirit of improvement that permeated all aspects of nineteenth-century society. There was little that Americans did not try to perfect and little that they did not think they were capable of perfecting. Just as they transformed the natural landscape with internal improvements, they transformed horses. As one breeding enthusiast put it, "Such is [the horse's] pliability of physical structure and constitution, that man may mold him to the form and build best fitted for the particular service in which he is to be employed."[1] The industrialization of breeding was a part of the energy landscape of horse power.

Nineteenth-century horse breeding was a form of industrial production, in which manufacturers (the breeders) got their workers and machines (the horses) to reproduce themselves. It was oriented to an expanding market that demanded a widening array of specialized horses. What breeders needed was a form of mass production that could come up with brands of horses that had consistent characteristics and met the demands of a segmented market. These brands were what nineteenth-century Americans defined as breeds. The specifications for each breed formed a template or model for breeders to replicate. Even as specialized breeding diversified the American population, it was accompanied by the growing commodification of horses using breed designations.

Horse breeding became a form of production best described as batch production, in which producers turn out small groups of similar products for specific markets. But unlike producing clocks or locomotives, much about producing horses remained unknown and uncontrollable by horse breeders. They sought a reliable technology of horse breeding, but in the absence of scientific knowledge about reproduction and the transmission of characteristics, much of what they claimed as sound material practice was a set of social and cultural beliefs imposed on the unseen and mysterious process of heredity. Reliance on horses made horse breeding part of nineteenth-century energy production, but horse breeding was also a cultural politics of energy that connected the material use of horse power to the power structures of industrial society.

A person familiar with horses in 1900 who had been transported back to 1800 would have noticed immediately that the horse population looked different. The horse population at the beginning of the century was much more homogeneous in size and appearance than it was at the close of the century. Most horses around 1800 were of a "middling sort," about fifteen hands (sixty inches) high at the withers (the point where neck and back meet) and between 800 and 1,200 pounds in weight. Before the nineteenth century, the word "breed" in reference to horses meant a kind or type of horse found in a specific country or geographical region. Over the century "breed" came to refer to horses descended from a common sire and with specific hereditary traits. These horses were registered with a breed association that established breed standards and kept track of breed membership. Sometimes used interchangeably with "race" and "species," "breed" denoted a fixed and identifiable biological group.

There were no horse breeds in this sense in the United States until the middle of the nineteenth century, other than Thorough-breds. What people called breeds were types that had developed under the relatively localized conditions of animal breeding. "Breed" was a geographical rather than biological designation. Quartermaster accounts of Union horse purchases during the Civil War categorized horses according to state origin, for example, "Michigan horses."

One regional horse breed was the Conestoga, a strong wagon horse used in the six-horse Conestoga wagon teams on Pennsylva-nia turnpikes. Descriptions of these horses were variable: Cones-togas were portrayed as long-limbed and light-bodied horses of around 1,000 pounds, as heavy-set and strong-bodied horses weigh-ing 1,200 to 1,300 pounds, and as very heavy, fat horses weighing close to 1,800 pounds, of any color. There was much speculation about their origins, and people named German and Flemish horses, English cart horses, Suffolk Punches, Thoroughbreds, and Arabs as possible progenitors. Some accounts said they were descendents of a group of horses brought over by William Penn. Conestogas rep-resented the robust trade, prosperous agriculture, and stable society of southeastern and central Pennsylvania.[2]

Conestogas flourished from the late eighteenth century into the antebellum period, but when railroads replaced long-distance freighting on the turnpikes of Pennsylvania, they eliminated the market in slow, large, well-fleshed wagon horses for the time being. By the middle of the nineteenth century, Conestogas were said to have "disappeared." It is doubtful that the horses, whatever they looked like, actually vanished. But as the social and technological ecology of the turnpikes faded, the niche that Conestogas had occupied did indeed disappear, taking the horse's identity with it.

Another regional breed was the Morgan horse of New England. Civil War records called them "New England horses." Morgans were strong, sturdy, medium-sized horses, brown (bay) in color with strong, arched necks, deep chests, active leg movement, and steady temperaments, equally useful for farm work and road transportation. Descriptions of the Morgans' character make them sound like equine versions of the ideal Yankee farmer.

All Morgans were said to be descended from Justin Morgan, a small, brown, unprepossessing-looking stallion foaled in Vermont in the 1790s and owned by man named Justin Morgan from whom the horse got his name. Justin Morgan and four of the colts he was said to have sired—Revenge, Bulrush, the Sherman Morgan, and the Woodbury Morgan—had near-mythological status as foundational sires for the Morgan breed. However, actual documentation about these horses and their progeny was (and remains) scarce. The modern breed of Morgans was not established until 1893. But the history of Justin Morgan and his progeny was frequently and lovingly retold. As one author said, "The farmer's horse in New England is peculiar to himself, and is, moreover, peculiarly an American institution." Certainly a horse's value could be enhanced by a claim of Morgan ancestry. For most of the nineteenth century, if a horse looked like a Morgan, or like a person's idea of a Morgan, or was believed for any reason to be a Morgan, then for all practical purposes it was a Morgan. It provided both draft power and cultural power.[3]

Justin Morgan. Source: D. C. Linsley, *Morgan Horses: A Premium Essay*
(New York, 1857). Fairman Rogers Collection, University of Pennsylvania.

The relative insularity of most regions gave rise to these and
other regional breeds. In addition, nineteenth-century Americans
believed that external environments affected the physiology and
morphology of horse bodies, just as they thought there was a relationship between environment and human bodies. Norway's hilly
topography was said to produce surefooted horses, while Arabia's
dry climate resulted in fine-boned horses with no superfluous fat.
Moving animals from one part of the world to another could cause
bodily changes, even degeneration. For example, in 1861 army quartermaster Elias Smith wrote to the War Department that northern
horses were short-lived in Texas, almost half of them dying even after a year or more of rest and acclimation. He questioned whether

horses from one climate could be bred in a new location, saying, "It is quite reasonable to suppose that a material change in climate, or even in the mode of feeding may so derange the organs of reproduction as to cause partial or total loss of sexual power."[4]

As political conflict intensified at midcentury, regional horse identities became a way of expressing sectional differences. Many northerners subscribed to a romantic image of southerners as cavaliers riding the finest pure-blooded horses. If horses were military hardware and horsemanship was military software, many Americans believed that the Confederates were cutting-edge. At the beginning of the Civil War Union military leaders and many other northerners believed that the Union could not use cavalry as effectively as the Confederacy because both its horsemen and its horseflesh were inferior. As late as 1862 the *Atlantic Monthly* asserted: "So far in this contest, the South has possessed one great advantage. The planter's son . . . has been accustomed from childhood to the use of the horse and the rifle." *Wilkes' Spirit of the Times* urged the North to take up turf racing so that it could breed better horses for the war effort.[5]

The innovative and aggressive use of cavalry by J. E. B. "Jeb" Stuart, Nathan Bedford Forrest, Fitzhugh Lee, John Hunt Morgan, and Wade Hampton reinforced belief in the superior horses and horsemanship of southerners. No one exemplified the Confederate image quite like General Stuart. During the Peninsula Campaign in June 1862, Stuart and 1,200 troopers rode entirely around McClellan's army in Virginia, outwitting, eluding, and thoroughly embarrassing Union leaders. Four months later he did it again, this time entering Pennsylvania to raid and burn Chambersburg. Wearing his signature plumed hat and flamboyant cloak, staging elaborate pageants, and masterminding daring raids, Stuart seemed to have ridden straight out of the novels of Sir Walter Scott.[6]

Northerners' perceptions of southern horseflesh and horsemanship stemmed in part from the more specialized uses of animal power that had evolved in the South during the antebellum period. Mules and oxen did most of the farm work and accounted for nearly half the work animal population, and a larger proportion of horses were reserved for pleasure use by whites. Plantations were self-sufficient for many foodstuffs and implements, and yeoman farmers pursued a "safety-first" strategy that placed self-sufficiency above market-oriented production. A limited internal market generated little demand or need for good roads, and the railroads, built to connect cotton-growing regions to coastal ports, did not generate the kind of commerce and travel that they did in the North. Travelers through the South such as Frederick Law Olmsted found it very undeveloped and reported that settled areas were often connected by little more than a trail. With transportation infrastructure relatively limited, riding seems to have been more widespread in the South, along with activities such as hunting, racing, and militia exercises.[7] Although the successes of the Union cavalry in the final two years of the war overturned the notion of superior southern horsemanship and horseflesh, at the beginning of the conflict images of southern "thoroughbreds" versus northern "plow horses" mingled with sectional politics, military concerns, and beliefs about environment and breed.

By midcentury the idea of breed as something determined by environment was giving way to the idea of breed as a fixed, innate identity. This shift was accompanied by an emphasis on breeding purebred animals—animals that would "breed true," transmitting a group of fixed, predictable characteristics to their offspring. An important influence on the development of purebred breeding was the work attributed to Robert Bakewell, an eighteenth-century English farmer who developed improved varieties of cattle, sheep, and horses. Bakewell demonstrated that it was possible to bring about rapid change in horses and livestock through a deliberate and intense breeding program, and then, having produced the desired animal, to produce a set of animals that replicated and transmitted

those traits. Bakewell was regarded as the best authority on breeding in the Anglo-American world. He was credited with having created the Leicester sheep, and to a lesser extent Longhorn cattle
and Shire horses. A contributor to *American Agriculturist* in 1842
wrote that Bakewell "regarded the animals on his farm as wax in his
hands, out of which in good time he could mold any form that he
desired to create." More than two decades later another contributor
expressed the continuing admiration for Bakewell, describing him
as an "agricultural patriot" and asserting that his most famous principle, "like begets like," was "the only rule that can be pursued with
safety."[8]

Bakewell argued against the practice common among farmers of
selling the best-quality animals and breeding the rest. He wanted
farmers to reverse this practice and instead breed "the best to the
best." Bakewell carefully selected male and female candidates for
breeding, believing (unlike many breeders at the time) that both
parents were equally important in influencing the quality of offspring. He relied on "progeny testing," selecting his breeding stock
according to the extent to which they had transmitted desired characteristics. He even kept track of animals that he had sold. Bakewell
kept careful records of all his animals' lineages but never used pedigrees to make breeding decisions.

In order to "fix" desired characteristics to create a group of animals that would reliably transmit a set of traits from parent to offspring, Bakewell relied on two methods. The first was inbreeding,
also called breeding "in and in." Inbreeding paired very closely related horses—parents, offspring, and siblings. The other was line
breeding, which paired animals that were less closely related, but
still part of the same line of descent. Through intense inbreeding
or line breeding Bakewell found that he could improve animals
fairly quickly, within relatively few rounds of breeding. Less often,
he used outbreeding or crossbreeding with unrelated animals in order to introduce new desired characteristics. Using the principles of

"like begets like" and breeding "the best to the best," through in-breeding and line breeding Bakewell "established a recognizable procedure for making breeds."[9]

Thoroughbred breeding was another important influence on the development of purebred breeding practices at midcentury. Thoroughbreds had been developed in England during the seventeenth and eighteenth centuries by crossbreeding stallions from the Middle East with English mares to produce faster racehorses. The Thoroughbred became the first modern breed when the Jockey Club of England published the *General Stud Book* in 1791. This listed the pedigrees of thirty-one horses verified as descendents of three stallions brought from the Middle East before 1730, known as the Darley Arabian, the Godolphin Arabian, and the Byerly Turk. These stallions became the foundational sires of the breed. From then on, what made a horse a Thoroughbred was having documented descent from one of these three horses. Registration in the *Stud Book* was a combination of identification card and membership in an exclusive club; it confirmed a horse's identity and verified that it belonged to a select family of horses.

The Jockey Club took this action in response to fraudulent practices in both horse racing and the Thoroughbred market, where other horses were being passed off as Thoroughbreds, thus jeopardizing both the market value and the social cachet of these elite animals. The Jockey Club gained control of the market in racehorses by restricting the supply of pedigreed animals. Their action effectively drew a line around a specific group of horses and declared them a breed. This idea of having an institution serve as a public repository of pedigrees would have an enormous impact on American horse breeding.

Thoroughbred breeding was another step away from early environmental beliefs. The horses imported from the Middle East had bred "true," transmitting their traits to offspring despite being in a different part of the world. This palpable evidence suggested that

Thoroughbred foundation sires. *Above:* Darley Arabian. Source: Walter Gilbey, *Horses Past and Present* (London, 1900). *Below:* Godolphin Arabian. Source: John H. Wallace, *The Horse of America* (New York, 1897). Both from Fairman Rogers Collection, University of Pennsylvania.

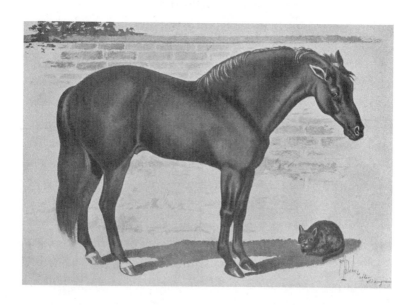

traits might be independent of environment, and something that humans could influence. There was a great deal of similarity between Thoroughbred breeding and Bakewell's practices. Both used careful selection of both parents, and progeny testing. In the case of Thoroughbreds, the progeny test was performance in racing. Thoroughbred breeders did not use in-and-in breeding, however.

Thoroughbred breeding was a rarefied and therefore expensive enterprise. It took a long time to see the results of production, usually at least three years from a foal's conception until the animal could be tested on the racecourse. Any business with a lengthy production process and delayed returns on investment required a great deal of wealth from other sources. However, although Thoroughbred breeding tended to be restricted to the wealthy, it was a source of improved horses for all horse breeders. Precisely because it was so rarefied, it could function as a laboratory for horse breeding, providing concrete evidence about the transmission of traits under controlled conditions. Thoroughbreds and Thoroughbred breeding became industry standards against which other breeds and other breeding methodologies were measured.[10] It was the highest form of technical practice. Thoroughbred breeding asserted that the boundary between bodies and the environment was impermeable; consequently heredity counted more than environment. Horse production could happen anywhere; what mattered was the capital, human and otherwise, invested in the process. Freed from location, the possibilities for producing different kinds of horses and ways to consume horse energy could be endless.[11]

As purebred breeding developed at midcentury, it adopted Bakewell's techniques of intensive inbreeding combined with progeny testing to create new animal varieties. But nineteenth-century breeders did not subscribe to Bakewell's notion that animal improvement was an ongoing process. They wanted to stop change at the point at which a breed was considered "pure." Instead of relying on progeny testing to select the best breeding stock and using pedigrees to track the results, nineteenth-century breeders upended Bakewell's methodology by relying on pedigrees to decide which animals to breed.

In purebred breeding equine bodies were regarded as malleable but equine identities as fixed. On the one hand, breeders believed they could wield the laws of nature to change horses and create breeds; on the other hand, they wanted to assert that pure breeds, once achieved, were essential categories of nature. Purebred breeding reflected the social thought of the late nineteenth century, which depicted the social structure as mutable but social position as immutable, using the new Darwinian ideas both to defend industrial change and to justify the status quo. As one animal husbandry expert said, "Natural selection can explain the survival of the fittest but it cannot explain the arrival of the fittest."[12]

Paradoxically, these beliefs and practices about horse breeding developed just as Darwin and other naturalists were beginning to question whether concepts of species, breed, and race had any material basis at all. In the popular mind, however, "breed" meant a group of animals distinguished from others by clearly defined biological boundaries. These boundaries had the authority of nature. But this was a classification system freighted with social and biological implications. People made so many distinctions within a single species as to call the species itself into question as a category. In the words of one breeder, "so great is the distinction [between cart horses and Thoroughbreds] they stand at the two extremes of the equine tribe" and were hard to imagine as members of the same species.[13] J. H. Sanders, founder and publisher of the *Breeder's Gazette,* explicitly extended breeding beliefs to the human world when he separated "rights before the law" from "physical moral and intellectual" equality based on the "value of pedigree in the human family." Hereditary principles were "the same throughout animal life . . . the human species furnish no exception to their operation."[14] Even as science moved away from formal definitions of breed and species,

breeders clung to the notion that these identities had a material basis. Shaping and wielding animal energy had social consequences.
Breeding beliefs naturalized both industrial society and the new
animal population of the energy landscape.

Mule breeding influenced the development of purebred breeding and ideas about the malleability and stability of animal identity.
Mules had been bred for centuries in Europe and the Middle East,
and in colonial America for the West Indies trade. In the antebellum
period mule breeding increased, though it had long been an interest
of agricultural leaders in the South. Mule breeding was a particular
interest of those who decried the backward state of southern agriculture, preached the necessity of agricultural improvement, exhorted farmers to adopt more scientific methods, experimented
with plants and animals, organized fairs and exhibitions, and disseminated information through agricultural societies and journals.
Through the highly specialized breeding needed to create an animal that would otherwise not exist, the southern elite associated
themselves with progressive agriculture and technical prowess. To
set an example, George Washington bred mules at Mount Vernon
with European jacks given to him by the king of Spain and the mar-
quis de Lafayette. Henry Clay's efforts helped develop the large
Mammoth jack stock in Kentucky. The mule population increased
sharply between 1840 and 1860 as mules were widely adopted in
the South as work animals. Ironically, most mules were bred outside
the Deep South, in Missouri, Kentucky, Tennessee, and Ohio.[15]

People found mules fascinating because they straddled the border between what in the popular mind were two separate species.
People found mules unsettling for the same reasons. Was a mule
more of horse or more of a donkey? Did it look like a horse with
donkey traits, or like a donkey with horse traits? Could a mule pass
as a horse or donkey? Could a mule be both a horse and a donkey at
the same time? Nineteenth-century people, with their love of classification, were disquieted by these border crossers who did not seem

to belong to either category. The use of the Spanish and Portuguese word *mulatto* (young mule) to describe a person of mixed race and the use of mules in plantation agriculture associated mules with blacks, and discussions of mules often became explicitly racial. As a cross between two species or "races" of equines, mules revealed that the boundary between races was permeable. White native-born Americans wanted the distinctions between themselves and African-Americans, Native Americans, and immigrants such as the Irish (who were not considered white) to be unambiguous. As Harriet Ritvo summarizes the situation, "The existence of hybrids or mongrels or crosses thus emphasized the existence of boundaries between groups and simultaneously obliterated them. The intensity of the aversion provided by mixed creatures suggested the importance of the divisions thus called into question."[16]

Because most mules are sterile, the best mules cannot be used to produce more mules. Thus mule production necessarily started afresh with each breeding, and there seemed no way to get around the fact that each mule was a genetic dead end. In order to improve the quality of mules—which in the nineteenth century meant producing the larger mules in demand for southern agriculture—breeders instead had to improve the quality of jacks and mares. Consequently, mule breeding encompassed both donkey breeding and horse breeding. It was further complicated by beliefs about jacks and mares that affected breeding choices. Some people maintained that once jacks were bred to mares they lost all sexual interest in jennets; others believed the same thing about mares bred to jacks. Some believed that mares bred to jacks could never be used for horse breeding again. Because of these beliefs, mule breeding involved six groups of animals: the jacks and jennets used to breed larger donkeys, the improved jacks used only for mule breeding, the stallions and mares used to breed larger mares, and the mares used only for mule breeding. Because mules could not reproduce themselves, mule breeding came closest to factory production. Even more than horse breeding, mule breeding was batch production of prime movers to meet a segment of market demand. As a way of producing energy it symbolized technological progress by creating new prime movers that were both natural and man-made. Yet, when it came to explaining inheritance, selecting horses for breeding, and controlling breeding outcomes, actual breeding knowledge had advanced little over the centuries. The physiological process of reproduction was poorly understood. Until Mendel's midcentury work on heredity was rediscovered in 1900, creating the modern science of genetics, there was little understanding about why some traits were passed on and not others, or why offspring might have traits not manifested in either parent. This complexity and unpredictability led one writer to observe: "Upon [horses'] conformations, a thousand influences, partly moral, and partly physical operate."[17] Nonetheless horse breeders still tried to come up with rules they could rely on. Debates over breeding reflected questions about about biotechnological change—its causes and control, the ethics of production and product, and the implications for society.

There was no absence of theories about heredity. For example, Charles Darwin (an avid breeder of dogs and fancy pigeons) suggested that there were tiny particles called "gemmules" transmitted from parent to offspring. In a foreshadowing of gene theory, he argued that resemblance of offspring to parents depended on how the gemmules were distributed among offspring (more relevant in breeding animals that produced litters than in horses, which mostly produce single offspring) and whether the gemmules were active or dormant in nature. Darwin's gemmule theory was of little use to breeders; it was explanatory, but it was not predictive. Even if the average farmer breeding horses knew about gemmules, that knowledge would not help him decide which animals to breed.[18] The fundamental guide was Bakewell's oft-quoted maxims of "like begets like" and "breed the best to the best"; but although this approach sounded simple, choosing what was like and best was more difficult in practice. Just how to make breeding decisions that accomplished the goals of purity and quality was a debate that mingled technical practices with cultural values.

By the midnineteenth century the method of breeding "in and in" was widely accepted in horse production as the way to effect rapid change, inculcate traits, predict outcomes, and maintain the purity of a breed. Yet it was a practice that often made people somewhat squeamish, as it involved what in human society would be classified as incest. People often saw the animal world as a mirror for human society, either by providing exemplary models of fidelity, kindness, diligence, duty, and other virtues in good animals, or by providing examples of cruel, savage, or immoral behavior in bad animals. Breeding in and in seemed to force incestuous behavior on horses, which were considered a moral and intelligent species. As a practice, it blurred the line between horses as products and horses as workers, and raised questions about the parallels and differences between the animal and human world. Many breeding manuals took great pains to explain just why inbreeding was not the same as incest, and to separate the operation of animal heredity from that of human heredity. As the author of one such manual put it: "Consanguineous unions amongst mankind as offensive to morality and law as they are disastrous in results do not appear to be so contrary to the natural decrees which govern the liaisons of the brute creation." Opponents of in-and-in breeding said it brought about "a speedy tendency to degeneracy." These were questions about method, not about the importance of breed purity.[19]

The antidote for too much inbreeding was crossbreeding, or "breeding out." This practice mated unrelated horses with different traits in order to introduce design changes into a line of horses. This might produce offspring with a unique combination of traits or even new traits not seen in either parent. Breeding out could also be used to halt the process of change once purity of line had been reached and animals were in danger of being overbred. But crossbreeding had dangers too. If horses were too different from each other, their union was called a "radical" or "violent" cross, the results of which were unpredictable. The first generation of offspring might possess the desired mix of characteristics but not the ability to transmit them to the next generation. There was always the danger that those offspring might revert to type and resemble one or the other of the original crossbred pair. Though mule breeding was an example of violent crossing, the fact that mules were almost entirely sterile avoided the problem that reversion to type posed to breeders. Their views reflected the racial context of the times. As late as 1897 John H. Wallace, secretary of the Iowa Board of Agriculture, editor of *Wallace's Monthly,* and author of *Wallace's American Stud Books,* wrote: "The most prolific and satisfactory sources of evidence in support of indirect or reversionary heredity are to be found in the crosses between the white and the black races . . . many a proud family has been humbled to the dust when the long-concealed 'black drop' makes its unexpected appearance . . . it is impossible to make even an approximation of the number of generations that would be required to wash out the stain."[20]

Breeders faced a production problem in trying to breed specific horses. At what point were two horses similar enough for inbreeding, different enough for crossbreeding, or so different that they constituted a violent cross? Where was the dividing line? Pedigree seemed to provide an answer. An 1843 contributor to *American Agriculturist* asserted: "Pedigree directs attention to all the outcrosses; or if inline bred, just how far; or if inbred, just the state." Outbreeding was more of a concern than inbreeding because, as the U.S. commissioner of patents put it in an 1854 government report, "heredity makes of every individual the sum or essence of that which has lived before him, and is essentially a conservative force."[21]

In addition to choosing the correct degree of relationship between two horses, breeders had to choose sires and dams carefully on the basis of the specific traits each would contribute. Stallions were usually considered prepotent, or having greater influence in the transmission of hereditary traits to offspring; thus it was more important for the stallion to be purebred than the mare. Breeders no longer considered the dam to be merely a container for the foal, but emphasized that she must be sound, well shaped, and, above all, feminine. "What is estimable in a mare is almost invariably a defect in the stallion," stated on author in 1894 as he stressed the importance of selecting a sire with "true masculine character." Some breeders believed that certain traits were linked to the sex of the parent, such as "blood from the sire and beauty from the dam" or "colts follow sires, fillies follow dams." But opinion varied on which specific traits came from sire or dam. It was said that sires influenced the foal's size, strength, and appearance, and dams the internal organs, or that the sire provided conformation and strength to the foal, the dam height and hindquarters, the sire the back and hindquarters, the dam the head and neck, the sire the "locomotive organs," the dam stamina and staying power.[22] In the end, even when sire and dam were considered equal contributors, descent was traced through the sire's line.

However, mares were thought to be highly impressionable and thus capable of modifying the sire's influence by imprinting the foal with erratic characteristics. Sometimes these came from the mare's physical surroundings, as when it was claimed a gray mare bred to a gray stallion gave birth to a chestnut foal after being stabled with chestnut horses during her pregnancy.[23] Others scoffed at such examples. "If it were true that visual impressions could be conveyed to the offspring, breeding would be chaos . . . calves conceived in summer would be green."[24]

Of more concern was the mare's personal history. Telegony was the belief that the characteristics of the first stallion to impregnate a filly were transmitted to offspring of subsequent pregnancies with different sires. The example cited *ad nauseam* throughout the century was that of Lord Morton's mare. Early in the century Lord Morton of East Anglia in England bred an Arabian filly to a striped, dun-colored zebra from South Africa called a quagga (now extinct). As expected, she gave birth to a half-quagga and half-Arabian foal. But when the mare was bred to a black Arabian stallion in each of the next two years, both foals allegedly bore "a striking resemblance to the Quagga," including having stripes and stiff zebralike manes. The conclusion was that impregnation had irrevocably altered the body of the mare and turned her into a different kind of animal.

According to Louis Agassiz, female horses were "hereafter so modified by the first act that later impregnations do not efface that first impression." Dr. James Law, dean of the Cornell Veterinary School, believed that the impregnated ovum impressed the maternal placenta with the sire's traits, which were then imprinted on all subsequent embryos. Dr. James McGillivrary, head of the Edinburgh Veterinary School, went even further and suggested that female horses lost their breed identity and henceforth were hybrid animals. "When a pure animal of any breed has been pregnant to an animal of a different breed, such pregnant animal is a cross ever after, the purity of her blood being lost in consequence of her connection with the foreign animal." The explanation for Lord Morton's mare was that she was no longer a purebred Arabian; sex with the zebra had stripped her of her purebred identity and turned her into an Arab-quagga hybrid who would always produce hybrid offspring. Impregnation was an environmental event that altered mare bodies and made the entire sexual history of the mare relevant. Similar arguments were made about mares bred to donkeys when it was said they could never again be used for horse breeding because their offspring would always be mules.[25]

Literature on breeding cited cases of human telegony as well. Stephen Goodale, secretary of the Maine Board of Agriculture and author of a midcentury book on breeding, wrote that "a young woman residing in Edinburgh, and born of white parents, but whose mother previous to her marriage bore a mulatto child by a negro man servant, exhibits distinct traces of the negro." This account combined moral, racial, social, sexual, and gender transgressions in its message that breeding, both animal and human, was a moral arena in which violations of the law were punished. Telegonic belief eventually faded, and in 1907 the early genetic scientist Eugene Davenport dismissed the story of Lord Morton's mare as "overworked" and proof of the "resistance of tradition" and the "extent of credulity" in breeding knowledge. "The many successive marriages of both colored and white women to men of opposite color should afford numerous examples . . . were [telegony] a consequential force in heredity."[26]

Belief in telegony resembled belief in inheritance of acquired characteristics, especially as expressed by French naturalist J. B. Lamarck (1744–1829). Lamarck's theory suggested that characteristics acquired by a horse during its lifetime could be inherited by its offspring. Some breeding manuals offered what they considered to be conclusive examples of how an injury or experience had been transmitted. Goodale said, "Horses marked during successive generations with red-hot irons in the same place, transmit visible traces of such marks to their colts." John Wallace claimed that the racehorse Lexington, who went blind after he gorged on oats and was run in a race, produced many offspring who subsequently went blind as well. Wallace concluded, "The horse world, and I might say, the whole animal kingdom under domestication, abounds in examples, seen and unseen, of unsoundness originating in injuries to the parents." However, Wallace believed that acquired characteristics might have less "adhesive strength" in heredity than ones fixed through inbreeding. Lamarckism blurred the boundary between acquired and inherited traits. Davenport rejected Lamarckism, but the problem was still that, as Davenport wrote, "The degree of development of an individual at maturity is not a complete index to his inherited characteristics. It is both something less and something more."[27]

The issues of telegony and acquired characteristics had technological implications because they raised questions about material and social change. How malleable was the world, how responsive to human endeavor? How much was determined by inheritance and history, and how much could change be accomplished and lead to more change? Within horse breeding, society and technology were mutually shaping. Telegony filled the lacuna in scientific knowledge about heredity by providing some kind of explanation. According to one writer, "there are many well-authenticated cases on record that cannot be satisfactorily explained on any other hypothesis."[28] Beliefs about women and sexual morality shaped breeding decisions; in turn, breeding outcomes were explained by beliefs about women and sexual morality; and so on. The technology of breeding showed how society and technological practices influenced each other when it came to producing horses for industrial society.

The focus of purebred breeding in the postbellum years was draft horses. Americans needed horses that were heavier and stronger than before. The adoption of mechanized equipment brought horses into agricultural production; as the machines grew heavier and more complex, they required more draft than before. The economies of the rapidly expanding cities created demand for medium and heavy horses for transportation and hauling. The magazine *Spirit of the Times* observed: "What is wanted in a draft horse is a combination of power, willingness, activity, soundness and constitution. We gain power as we secure size and weight, provided we have good form and willingness to exercise it."[29] The Gilded Age became the age of the heavy horse.

In the 1850s, as Americans began importing European draft breeds in order to produce heavier horses, one of the most important was the Percheron. This was a type of French draft horse, named for the La Perche region of eastern Normandy. In general,

Percherons were dapple gray or black, stood sixteen hands tall, and weighed close to a ton. They had solid, graceful bodies; smooth legs with no "feathers," or long hair, to catch debris; and active, powerful movement. The first Percherons arrived in the United States before the Civil War. In the postbellum years Percherons rapidly became one of the most popular draft horses for farm work and were also crossbred with large American mares. By the 1880s there were 50 breeders importing Percherons, mostly in the Midwest, and 1,634 by the end of the century. Percherons were widely used for farm work and haulage in the Midwest.[30]

Ongoing disagreements among breeders, importers, and buyers about the identity and designation of these horses illustrate how purebred breeding shaped the market in animal energy. Some of the French horses were referred to as Norman horses, a linguistic difference that developed into a several-decades-long conflict over the designation of the breed and the control of the import trade in these French horses. The first registry for these horses in 1876 referred to them as Norman Percherons. This designation was confusing because "Norman" didn't refer to any particular kind of horse at all in France. Furthermore, not all French horses were Percherons. There were other types of French draft horses, and indeed there were even two types of Percherons, light and heavy, the latter being preferred in the American market.[31]

Significantly, the French did not maintain a registry or define Percherons as a breed. In short, Americans importing a "Percheron" could not be sure that what they were getting was "really" a Percheron because no one knew what that meant, least of all the French, who did not define their horses that way. But the value of the American horses depended on the designation. The horses imported from France were expensive, and almost inevitably other French horses were labeled as Percherons and sold for high prices. In 1883 American breeders changed the name of their registry to Percheron (dropping the Norman) and, by threatening not to im-

Prize Percheron at the Wisconsin State Fair, ca. 1900. Wisconsin Historical Society, image 33797.

port any horses that were not registered, convinced French breeders to establish a stud book open only to horses from the La Perche region. Since the United States was the biggest market for Percherons, the French complied.[32]

Just as the French Percheron registry came into being, the situation was confused by the establishment of another registry in the United States for horses imported from France and referred to as Norman horses instead of Percherons. Making things even more bewildering, this group then changed its name from the Norman Association to the French Draft-Horse Breeders Association. As a result, starting in the 1880s American breeders, French breeders, and the French government were beset by different understandings of the meaning of "breed," different goals, fraudulent pedigrees, and the use of the name "Percheron" to refer to all French draft horses. Only in 1911 were these differences over the standards and stud-

books used for draft horses from France resolved with the establishment of the Percheron Society of America.

The experience with Percherons illustrated the biotechnological
implications of the pedigree system. It was one thing to agree that
breeds were "distinct types that bred truly."[33] But whereas Americans increasingly defined breed in terms of pedigree, the French did
not define their horses in that way and did not see the point of regis-
tering them. The power of the enormous U.S. energy market enabled Americans to impose their desires on the French breeders
and force them both to document the parentage of each horse and
to change their breeding choices accordingly. Pedigree guaranteed
market value, and market value validated the pedigrees.

Percheron breeding followed the model of Thoroughbred breeding in the eighteenth century, when the Jockey Club established the
stud book as a public registry of pedigrees to protect the market
value of Thoroughbred racehorses. Though purebred horse breeding had the aristocratic aura of luxury, quality, and a disregard for
profit making, the entire enterprise of purebred breeding rested on
the market value of the horses. Breed associations were established
for every kind of horse that was imported into the United States.
These associations, in the name of breed purity, controlled the market in their horses, restricting supply and keeping prices high by
means of the pedigree system. Breeds, like brand names, differentiated not only horses but also their market value.[34]

Another popular foreign import was the Shire horse from England, reputed to have been a favorite breed of Robert Bakewell's.
English breeders enjoyed a thriving export trade with the United
States in the decades before World War I. Shires are some of the
largest draft horses, standing over seventeen hands (sixty-eight
inches) at the shoulder and weighing over a ton. They are dark
brown and have feathered legs. Closely related to the Shire was the
Clydesdale, a breed originating in Scotland. It was nearly as tall and
heavy, with feathered legs, but with a rangier build and more active

movement. Because Shires and Clydesdales were interbred, and because of differences among American, Scottish, and English breeders about the meaning of breed, some of the same conflicts beset the
Shire and Clydesdale market as the Percheron market.[35]

Shires and Clydesdales were often used for the heaviest wagon
work in cities; according to one English writer, "Civilization has
converted [the Shire] into one of the principal factors and aids in
our modern commercial life."[36] Their powerful but ponderous bodies illustrate the trade-off between strength and speed in the equine
body. In the cities, speed was not a concern, because efficiency depended on the size of the load, and crowded streets necessarily kept
travel slow. Both breeds had feathered legs, which were very showy
for urban hauling but were not always popular with farmers. The
long leg hair acquired mud and added weight to the legs, it trapped
moisture and caused leg irritation, and it created a lot more work for
the farmers in grooming their horses.

Belgians became very popular with American farmers. Belgians
were smaller than the Shires and Clydesdales, perhaps fifteen or
sixteen hands, but equally heavy, with a blocky, compact body, un-
feathered legs, and a famously mild disposition. Americans also imported two other kinds of English draft horses, the Suffolk Punch
and the Cleveland Bay, but these were never as widely used in the
United States as Belgians, Percherons, Clydesdales, and Shires. The
physical differences among these horses, in addition to height,
weight, and leg hair, lay in the physical conformation of neck, shoulders, and legs—the power-producing parts of their bodies—and in
their "action," or movement. A turn-of-the-century breeding authority wrote, "While all the users of draft horses require many fundamental points in common their varying classes of service and
their dissimilar ideas of indications of efficiency and durability give
outlets for the array of good types represented in several breeds."[37]

Between 1860 and 1900, breed associations and public registries
were established for a variety of horses. In 1900 the Department of

Agriculture yearbook listed seventeen associations for horses and one for donkeys:

American Association of Importers and Breeders of
   Belgian Draft Horses
American Breeders' Association of Jacks and Jennets
American Cleveland Bay Breeders' Association
American Clydesdale Association
American Hackney Horse Association
American Morgan Register
American Percheron Horse Breeders' Association
American Saddle Horse Breeders' Association
American Shetland Pony Club
American Suffolk Punch Horse Association
American Thoroughbred Stud Book
American Trotting Registry Association
French Coach Horse Society of America
German, Hanoverian and Oldenburg Coach Horse
   Association of America
National French Draft Association
Oldenburg Coach Horse Association of America
Select Clydesdale Horse Society of America[38]

These included three for the disputed Percherons, two for Clydesdales, and two for Oldenburg coach horses, reflecting rivalries among breeders, disagreements over the rules of inclusion, and differences among Americans, the British, and Europeans over the identity of the animals and the meaning of breed. J. H. Sanders noted in 1885, "These divisions from first to last are more or less arbitrary ... in many cases it is impossible to locate the dividing line. This is especially true of breeds. We may assume any standards that our fancy may dictate ... and classifying with reference to the possession of any or these assumed peculiarities we may divide a species into breeds. Theoretically there is no limit to the extent to which this division of breeds might be carried."[39]

The appearance of rival associations would seem to demonstrate that horse breeds were not innate or natural groups, but the proliferation of groups had the opposite effect of underscoring distinctions among horses and strengthening the popular notion that there were innate physical differences at the core of these conflicts. Many people who wrote about horses and breeding bolstered this notion by asserting the ancient lineage of various breeds even as they described their recent improvement. The Percheron was given a lineage back to the "great horses" of the Middle Ages or even further to Arab horses at the time of Charles Martel in the eighth century. The Shire, wrote an English author, was "no upstart but had existed in greater or less degree for at least some 2000 years," and breeders should preserve "the original purity of the race." He moved the origin of the Thoroughbred back by 500 years. Yet he also wrote that breeds "are more or less the creation of the breeders, having been brought into existence through the requirements of the times and the advance of civilization."[40]

The breeding of draft horses imported from Britain and Europe centered in the established agricultural region of the Upper Midwest. The goal of importing was first to make these horses available for farming and urban work. But there was also the goal of improving the general quality of American workhorses through crossbreeding, especially the horses used by farmers. Farm horses had to be lighter, all-purpose animals, or "chunks," not the very heavy specimens used in the cities. "Strength was not the sole requisite . . . the horse that plows must also draw the wagon upon the road," stated *American Agriculturist*. The new ideal was a strong, fast walker of middling size and weight, heavier than the 800-to-1,000-pound horses than had previously constituted most of the chunks.[41] As a consequence of crossbreeding and improvements in nutrition, the average size of draft horses, especially in the cities, increased by possibly as much as 75 percent in the second half of the century.[42]

Despite the presence of larger-scale specialized breeding operations, such as Dillon Brothers in Illinois, most horse production was carried out by thousands of farmers and small breeders. Many farmers bred horses occasionally for extra income. Consequently, farmers became the targets of directives about breeding, ranging from British and American books concerned with breed purity and aesthetics to the agricultural press, which urged them to breed specifically for the market. Like agricultural reformers of previous generations, breeding authorities extolled farmers' importance, excoriated them for bad practices, and exhorted them to be modern, scientific, and market oriented. "To raise better horses is a long step toward better farming, and better farming means easier work, more profit and more of the comforts and civilizing influences of life," proclaimed *American Agriculturist* in 1891.[43]

The agricultural press and publications from the Department of Agriculture continually urged farmers to breed horses in the 1,200–1,600 pound range and to pay attention to pedigree as a way of improving the physical and market quality of their animals. They complained that too often farmers used local stallions for reasons of convenience rather than seeking out purebred stallions to improve the quality of their horses. *National Livestock Journal* referred to "the long fight we have gone through . . . urging such a course of breeding as would result in giving increased size to the horse stock of our country," only to find farmers still breeding their mares to "worthless little trappy so-called trotting-bred stallions." It urged farmers to breed Percheron and Clydesdale stallions to other powerful, heavy horses to produce "a race of horses which are now so scarce," and promised a sure profit to those who did. *American Agriculturist* printed "The Science of Breeding," telling farmers:

Breed only to pedigreed stock. What is pedigree? Simply genealogy; but by this we determine the value of the ancestors. We must reject where, from any cause, they are deficient in the lines it is desired to breed for . . . It must be understood that all animals of any values as breeding sock are recorded in the books of record established for the respective breeds. By reference to these we may ascertain the exact status of an animal . . . It is never safe to take anyone's word, "that animal is just as good." But, with an authentic pedigree, we can trace it out and know.[44]

Through the 1870s and 1880s agricultural magazines depicted purebred draft stallions on their covers, often Percherons, Shires, and Clydesdales. These were accompanied by a physical description, the horse's merits as an individual, his pedigree, a record of his progeny, and information about the breeder. These periodicals also carried advertisements for other breeding operations that pictured or named their pedigreed stallions. Pedigreed stock were regarded as a reservoir of quality traits on which farmers could draw to breed improved horses. They were the means of technological transfer between purebred breeding and general-purpose breeding.

Horse breeding as a form of production resembled two kinds of mass production common in manufacturing: custom production and batch production. Breeding was custom production when its goals were the most specialized, focused on a specific sire. At its most rarefied, custom breeding produced individual racing or sporting horses from specific sires and dams. Breeding was batch production when a breeder had the goal of producing a batch of horses from one or more sires, whose common characteristics could be identified and advertised. Apart from the most elite breeding, which needed high market value for its horses but did not depend on profits, most breeders had to respond to the market. Just what constituted that market was not always clear, and it was further complicated by the inelasticity in the supply of particular kinds of horses in response to changes in demand.[45]

The discussion about what horses farmers should be breeding revealed the ways in which class differences and market perception shaped the path of technological transfer or diffusion, the technology in this case being purebred horses. Breeding discourse was dominated by elite writers, whose books were aimed at the monied and upwardly mobile classes, or by breeders and importers, or by officials in the U.S. Department of Agriculture (USDA) trying to predict or create markets.

Farmers were bombarded with conflicting advice about what kinds of horses they should be breeding and how. They were told to produce general-utility horses for the market and criticized for trying to breed specialized or pedigreed horses. They were criticized for breeding general-utility horses when the market was in specialized horses. They were told to use pedigreed sires and dams, pedigreed sires only, or progeny testing to evaluate the quality of local stallions. They were told that the business of breeding heavy horses was "a safe and profitable one for years to come." They were told to breed light mares to heavy stallions, heavy mares to light stallions, or heavy to heavy and light to light because crossbreeding was unpredictable.[46]

There was much discussion about the need for an all-purpose horse, but a lot of questions remained about whether there was such a thing. The all-purpose horse was one of the perennial "holy grails" of the breeding literature. Sanders wrote, "I do not believe it is possible that a horse can be bred combining all the desirable qualities. The horse-of-all-work is a myth that can not be realized." But farmers continued to get advice about how to produce such a horse. Percherons would become the basis for general-purpose horses. Or French Coach Horses "when crossed on the native mares of the country ... produce a grade which comes as near as anything can to answering the call for a general purpose horse." Or, trotters provided a basis for breeding "the best of all general purpose horses . . . [the trotter] was the greatest all purpose road horse and work horse suitable to the vast continent." What farmers said about all this is less clear. They seemed to have produced the horses they needed, but apparently there was not much of a market for them outside agriculture. There was a gap between what farmers, as the primary users of horse technology, wanted and bred in the way of horses, and what breeding authorities, as technological designers, thought farmers should breed and use, and what the market should want.[47]

Trotting or harness horse breeding reflected the tension between function and pedigree in horse breeding. Harness racing was the most popular form of horse racing in the nineteenth century. Especially in northern states, harness races were a traditional fixture at fairs and exhibitions, and when their popularity spread to urban areas harness racing became the first mass spectator sport in America. A good "roadster" (a carriage or buggy horse) was a prized possession, and informal races were an ongoing ritual of country and suburban life. It was not just the demands of mechanized farm equipment that called for horses with a good strong trot. Breeding trotting horses became a popular pastime for the first generation of the new monied class, who often went into the breeding of horses for harness racing rather than flat racing. Fancy horses were a traditional status symbol, and horse breeding, with its requirements of lavish investment and low return, was an important entrée into the upper echelons of society and a signal of social arrival.[48]

Unlike Thoroughbred racing, where participation required a pedigree, in harness racing participation could earn a pedigree. The trotting horse registry used tests of performance, progeny testing, and inheritance. According to the 1879 standards of the National Association of Trotting Horse Breeders, any mare or gelding able to trot a mile in 2 minutes 30 seconds (2:30) or less could be registered as a Standardbred (the term for a trotting horse that met the standards set by the association). Any stallion with this speed could be registered if it produced a horse with a speed of 2:40 or better or two with a speed of 2:30 or better, or if one of its parents or grandparents was a Standardbred. A mare producing a horse with a speed of 2:30 could be registered. The progeny of a Standardbred sire and dam or of a dam with one Standardbred parent could be registered. The trotting registry was open to talent displayed on the racecourse, which many Americans regarded as a democratic test of ability. As Oliver Wendell Holmes said, "Horse-racing is not a republican institution; horse-trotting is."[49]

Sanders called the trotter "the creation of an American fancy—the result of a fashion that has demanded the fastest and stoutest trotting horses in the world for driving on the road; and to this end we have selected and bred until our horses surpass all others in this particular." The standards of registration encouraged crossbreeding. Pedigrees were valuable only if ratified by speed on the track. Wallace believed that American trotters were descendants of the horse Messenger, who "founded a family of trotters—something which no other English horse had ever been able to take the first step toward accomplishing." The success of Hambletonian, a great-great-great-grandson of Messenger, was a progeny test. However, Wallace believed that Messenger had been unique in his abilities and prepotency, and he challenged those who thought that crossbreeding with Thoroughbreds would automatically improve trotters.[50]

The trotter was a symbol simultaneously of social status and of democratic values. Those who bred trotting horses on lavish breeding farms could claim to be producing horses of social and economic utility even as they reproduced the social hierarchy of the Gilded Age. They continued in the tradition of American elites, who argued that elite or specialized breeding—which only they could afford to do—was an important contribution to national progress. The *American Agriculturist* stated in 1883 that the breeding of good trotting horses had improved the quality of American horses in general. "Fast trotting in itself, with much that surrounds the trials, is unworthy of our civilization, but the effect of careful breeding of trotters has been of untold value to our country. The needs of our modern methods of business require quick roadsters and there is not doubt that the latest development in horse-flesh, the trotter, is the best."[51]

In the 1890s photographs of champion trotters began to replace the pictures of pedigreed draft stallions on the covers of agricultural magazines. Trotting was a genuinely popular spectator sport, and people liked to see pictures of these equine celebrities. For example, an 1894 *American Agriculturist* began with a several-page photographic feature on Leland Stanford's enormous ranch in Palo Alto, California, where he bred trotters. By then the depression of 1893 had caused the entire horse market to collapse, but the market for the light and general-utility horses bred by many farmers was particularly hard hit. Because any horse could become a trotter if fast enough, the showcasing of trotters in farmers' magazines implied that farmers could breed such horses and hinted at a "rags to riches" scenario in which a trotting champion would be discovered on a humble American farm. This suggestion minimized the investment in breeding, time, and care necessary to cultivate successful racehorses, one greater than many farmers could afford to risk. The photographs and descriptions of the Stanford ranch sent a conflicting message, keeping farmers in their place socially yet suggesting that they should nonetheless try to breed winning trotters.[52]

Even though the biological understanding of breeding changed little during the nineteenth century, a great deal of practical knowledge accumulated. Horse breeding was aided by improvements in transportation and communication that improved access to a wider variety of horses, and by an expanding market that demanded not only more horses but also specialized breeds. The holy grail of being able to design horses and guarantee breeding outcomes remained elusive. Many horse breeders joined the American Breeders' Association, hopeful that "the wonderful potencies in what we are wont to call heredity may in part be placed under the control and direction of man."

> For example, methods wrought out by plant breeders may show how to produce a fertile race of mules, in which are combined the size of the draft horse with the toughness, longevity and small food requirements of the donkey. It possibly may be proven . . . that a third species, fertile with both the horse and the donkey, or with only one, may serve as an intermediary through which the desirable blood mixture may be made. The modern, short-lived, heavy feeding, farm horse, which works only about three hours per average work day through the year and the heavier dray horse, ought to be radically improved, and who knows how to attack the problem?[53]

Genetics ended up having little immediate impact on horse breeding. It was explanatory, but did not provide the control and guidance that breeders had hoped for. As John Wallace had said, heredity was a "universal law of animal life," but the outcomes "cannot be pre-determined by any rule of arithmetic." In five generations of breeding, sixty-two individual animals play a role as progenitors. "If these . . . are all purely bred in the breed which you are seeking to secure there is a reasonable certainty that your prospective colt will be a good representative of that breed," so long as breeders remembered that "bad qualities are just as certain to be transmitted as good ones."[54]

By 1900 the structure of horse breeding had changed. In contrast to 1850, there was a wide array of specialized horses, varying in size, weight, appearance, utility, and breed. Demand for specialized horses had resulted in the importing and breeding of foreign horses and crossbreeding to improve and modify American horses. American horse breeding was part of national and international markets, where breed designations and market categories advanced the commodification of horses. A network of institutions had developed that included breed associations, veterinary schools, agricultural schools, the USDA, the U.S. Treasury Department (regulating imports), race tracks, and state government agencies.

Americans reveled in their ability to master and reshape nature, yet at the same time they sought evidence of innate, unchanging categories of identity. Consequently, their ideas about horse breeding were complex and contradictory. Americans believed that because horses were highly malleable, a breed was a man-made category; yet they also believed that each breed was a distinct group of ancient origin defined by essential, hereditary traits. Horse breeding raised questions about the mutability of personal and social identity. By implying that biological distinctions might be more constructed than fixed, it subversively questioned the stability of the most fundamental power relations in society, even as purebred horses became a means of bolstering the status quo. As John Wallace observed, arguments about breeding were often arguments about history.[55]

Horse breeding practices developed as part of the energy market of nineteenth-century America. Rising energy consumption was accompanied by demand for horses designed for particular occupations. Americans imported draft horses to add to and vary the traits of the American horse population. At the same time, the way of identifying horses changed from regional labels to breed distinctions. As they created new draft horses, Americans developed an approach of purebred breeding that drew on the traditions of Robert Bakewell and Thoroughbred breeding, but was distinguished by an emphasis on pedigree as a way of creating horses and guaranteeing their quality.

Breeders combined folk beliefs, scientific knowledge, and practical experience in an attempt to formulate universal laws of heredity. They used scientific-sounding language and metaphors of industrial production to frame horse breeding as a contribution to progress and national strength. Growing dependence on horses as prime movers transformed both the size and the makeup of the horse population as industrialization remade the American landscape.

On April 9, 1865, General Robert E. Lee and General Ulysses S. Grant met at Wilmer MacLean's house in Appomattox, Virginia, to arrange the surrender of the Army of Northern Virginia. Lee rode to the meeting on his famous gray horse, Traveller, dressed in immaculate uniform, red sash, and ornate sword. Grant arrived on his favorite horse, Cincinnati, clad in the mud-spattered private's blouse he'd worn since outriding the wagon containing his uniform and sword several days before at Burkeville, as he pursued the Confederate army west from Richmond. Outside the house, Traveller, Cincinnati, and the horses of staff officers, unconcerned with these human matters, cropped the spring grass, their rhythmic chewing audible in the noonday quiet.

Widening the angle of vision on this famous scene brings thousands of horses and men into view. In the Union encampment to the south and west, hundreds of well-shod cavalry horses stand saddled and ready, and harnessed artillery horses are gathered near their parked guns. White-topped supply wagons arrive in trains and are parked in long rows, their teams of horses and mules tethered nearby. Picket lines of horses show the location of the remount depot, where 500 replacement horses arrive each day from the Union Quartermaster Department. Wagons creak through the camp. The intermittent sounds of bellows, ringing blows, static bursts of hammering, commands, shouts, whinnies, and curses announce that the farriers are taking advantage of the lull in the fighting and catching up on the never-ending chore of shoeing the army's horses.

On the other side of the village of Appomattox, the Confederate forces are spread over the ground sloping down into the valley. There are fewer horses with these men. Back in January Lee had had to send many of his cavalry and artillery horses deeper into the South to obtain adequate forage. In February Lee made an urgent request for 3,200 horses and 2,400 mules to replace those killed or unfit for service, but there is no record that he received any from the Confederate quartermaster. By the time he left Richmond and headed southwest toward Danville on April 2, Confederate horses and mules were bony, dull-coated, and listless, many without shoes and harness, all without forage. At one point he reduced his train of 200 guns and 1,000 wagons by a third, choosing the strongest horses and sending the remainder, over 2,000 in number, toward a railroad line in hopes of shipping them south for rest and forage. Cavalry on weak-kneed horses tried to continue scouting duties and to screen the army's movements from the enemy. When he met with Grant, Lee asked him for forage, but Grant had none because he'd been foraging his own horses off the land while pursuing Lee. Until the arrival of the 25,000 soldier rations promised by Grant, Confederate soldiers continued to eat the corn intended for the horses.

The roads leading from Richmond over which Lee had retreated in the last seven days were a tangle of equipment. Broken and deserted supply wagons and field guns were sunk into mudholes and ditches where they had been driven by panicked teamsters or abandoned for lack of teams. Emaciated horses and mules, turned loose when no longer able to pull, wandered in search of food and water, stood head-down with front legs stiffly braced, and lay dead and dying amid dead and wounded human soldiers.[1]

The Civil War was a war of animal power. Thousands of horses accompanied the armies of both sides, pulling artillery and supply wagons, carrying cavalry, cannoneers, and officers. They provided the power for transportation and communication, and made possible the kind of fighting that occurred, and the war's scope and scale. This knowledge alters our understanding of the nature of the Civil War, and reminds us that "troopers" denotes both horses and men, "artillery" both teams and guns, "army" the long trains of horses and wagons as well as the soldiers. The Civil War needed horses for the same reasons that caused the rising use of horses in the antebellum years. Industrialization created both opportunity and means to utilize horse power on an enormous scale. The technological complementarity that characterized the antebellum use of horses meant that the first industrialized war would also have a colossal need for horses.[2]

Wars require energy, and a combatant's energy resources are factors in military decisions and outcomes. After humans, horses were the foremost source of energy needed for the Civil War, and procuring an adequate supply was a critical task for both armies. The war had a distinctive ecology of energy that tied the home front to the battlefield. As prime movers, horses had to be obtained like any other military supply; however, as animals and sentient beings, they resembled human soldiers in their needs. Just as horses on farms, roads, and canals were workers as well as prime movers, Civil War horses were soldiers as well as prime movers. Horses were mobilized for war, purchased, fed, sheltered, outfitted, trained, transported, deployed, maneuvered, doctored, convalesced, and buried. The Civil War provides one of the largest and most focused examples of nineteenth-century dependence on horses.

Just as railroads fueled the growing use of horses before the war, they fueled the need for horses during the war. Railroads changed the nature of warfare just as they changed so much else in American society. They widened the theater of war, extending an army's territorial reach, and thus increased its scale. The capacity of the railroads to move large numbers of soldiers and enormous amounts of war material overland contributed to the unprecedented size and mobility of Civil War armies. These armies, too large to live off the land in most regions, needed enormous quantities of supplies. For field armies to be able to operate away from the immediate vicinity of a railroad track took hundreds of horses pulling supply wagons and field artillery, and protected by cavalry.[3]

Railroads also created a new geography of warfare, rearranging the meaning of terrain, the significance of topography and distance. They constructed a new landscape of roadbeds, embankments, cuts, tunnels, bridges, junctions, switches, and stations. These became strategic sites, important to defend, attack, and control. Whereas a region could be defended without securing every square foot, railroads were vulnerable at every point along their tracks. Union General William T. Sherman, who early on grasped the strategic and tactical implications of the railroads, said, "I am never easy with a railroad, which takes a whole army to guard, each foot of rail being essential to the whole."[4] Railroads constituted a new strategic territory necessitating the use of cavalry and artillery units. In an industrialized war, horses quickly became one of the largest single expenditures in the Union budget.

After Abraham Lincoln's first call for troops in April 1861, the army was deluged with generous and eager offers from many states to raise cavalry regiments—if the federal government supplied the horses. In 1861 everyone, it seemed, wanted to be a cavalier. However romantic the image of cavalry was in popular culture, in practice the United States had a weak cavalry tradition. Neither the Revolution nor the War of 1812 had lent itself to the use of cavalry in battle, and soon after 1815 those regiments were eliminated. In the early decades of the republic, Americans were ambivalent about anything that smacked of a permanent military or aristocratic elite, and even pondered closing down West Point. The militia tradition withered in the North, and there were few mounted companies except for ones like the elite First Troop of Philadelphia. However, in the 1830s Congress reestablished cavalry regiments because of the Indian Wars in Wisconsin and in Florida.

By the 1850s there were five regiments of cavalry thinly scattered across the western territories. However, experience gained fighting the western Indians—who were some of the best light cavalry in the world—was discounted in favor of European ideas about cavalry style, training, and tactics. At the beginning of the war, Union generals did not want to use cavalry, seeing it as both inappropriate and expensive. The heavily wooded terrain of northern Virginia had no battlefields on which traditional cavalry could operate, and most thought the war would be too short to justify the formal three-year program that European experts said was necessary to train cavalrymen for battle.[5]

The Confederate army was quick to use cavalry innovatively and effectively; it took longer for Union leaders to grasp the new tactical and strategic importance of cavalry and to deploy it effectively. Cavalry protected or attacked railroad lines, the telegraph lines strung along the tracks, and the long slow lines of supply wagons. Cavalry were the eyes and ears of the army, reconnoitering, probing the enemy in advance of the force, screening its movements, and protecting its retreat. Armed with improved weapons and using horses for mobility, the cavalry combined concentrated firepower with speed and the capacity for surprise.

Cavalry horses were the best known of the army's equine soldiery, but wagon horses, many of which were mules, or half-horses, were by far most numerous. Huge numbers of wagon horses powered the pipeline of supplies necessary for the gigantic Union armies. An army at rest depended on a continuous line of covered wagons coming up from its rear. An advancing army was accompanied by enormous wagon trains, a team of four horses or six mules pulling each wagon. The standard army wagon was a white-covered wagon with a box twelve feet long, forty-three inches wide, and twenty-two inches deep, providing an interior capacity of approximately ninety-six cubic feet. One army surgeon described a train eight miles long. Since a wagon and team needed fifty feet each of road space, this train would have contained close to 850 wagons and 3,000 to 6,000 horses and mules. During the Tennessee campaign of 1863, two-thirds of the 44,000 horses with General William S. Rosecrans were wagon horses.[6]

As the war continued, the Union army began using more mules to haul wagons, though some generals preferred to have horses in their trains and tried to get a higher percentage of them as wagon animals. Mules were considered less likely to break down in grueling wagon service at the hands of army teamsters. The low status attached to mule riding generally ruled mules out for cavalry use. In 1863 Colonel Abel Streight planned a raid using infantry mounted on mules, thinking that tough, surefooted mules would do better in the rough country of Tennessee and Alabama. Unfortunately, Streight mounted soldiers without riding experience on young, barely broken mules. It was an infelicitous combination. However, the failures of Streight's raid were often blamed on the mules. Because mules were also shorter and lighter than what the army specified for artillery horses, mules rarely pulled field guns; in addition, many people believed that they would panic under fire. So most army mules pulled supply wagons.[7]

The least-known horses were artillery horses. They were like wagon horses, in that their main job was hauling, and like cavalry horses, in that maneuvering and repositioning field guns took them directly into combat. They were the most industrialized of the army's horses, part of the ensemble of the new, light, industrially pro-

Equine and human artillery soldiers training at Camp Randall, Madison, Wisconsin, 1862. Wisconsin Historical Society, image 4225.

duced guns. Field artillery became a salient factor in the many skirmishes that constituted much of the Civil War's fighting. Cavalry units with light guns were known as "horse artillery" and were used for fast-moving raids.

A representative artillery piece was the widely used 12-pounder Napoleon, a field gun that could fire shells, case (shells filled with metal fragments), and shot. It weighed about 1,200 pounds and had a range of 1,100 to 1,600 yards. Mounted on a two-wheeled carriage attached to a four-wheeled carriage called a limber, it was pulled by a six-horse team, with a driver mounted on the left wheel horse. A caisson (a wheeled ammunition chest) pulled by another six-horse team accompanied each gun. An eight-gun battery needed ninety-six horses for the guns, and another five teams of horses or mules for the forge wagon, battery wagon, and three supply wagons. Horse artillery units had extra horses for the cannoneers to ride so that the unit could move fast with cavalry. Industrialized weaponry made the army dependent on horses. The more mechanized the matériel of war, the more essential horses were to move it.

Consequently, with the outbreak of war in April 1861, Union army purchases of horses began escalating rapidly. The complicated logistics of mobilizing an equine army of thousands was the responsibility of the Quartermaster Department within the War Department, headed by General Montgomery C. Meigs. Meigs became quartermaster general in June 1861, over the opposition of two secretaries of war and leapfrogging both high-ranking career officers in the Quartermaster Department and other officers with previous quartermaster experience. He was a military engineer, who after graduating from West Point in 1832 spent twenty years on a variety of construction projects, then came to Washington, D.C., to oversee construction of an aqueduct to bring fresh water from above the Potomac's Great Falls to the swampy capital city. In addition, he took over constructing the half-built Capitol, a project bogged down in cost overruns, graft, and political squabbling. Over the next eight years, Meigs completed both projects and cleaned up the bookkeeping as well, but his financial probity brought him into conflict with congressmen, lobbyists, and his superiors. Secretary of War Floyd relieved him and sent him to the Florida Keys, but military success and political support trumped the animosity of his adversaries, and he returned to Washington.

Meigs took over a department that during the forty-two-year tenure of Quartermaster General Thomas S. Jesup had become a well-established bureaucratic agency. It operated on a transcontinental scale, its main job supplying the army across the vast western territories. Despite the scope of its responsibilities, it was and remained a relatively small office on which Meigs placed his personal stamp. Meigs read as much of the correspondence as possible, writing his answer or instructions on the back in the hieroglyphics that served as his handwriting. The existing structure of the Quartermaster Department and the chaos of state-provided supply in the first months of the war allowed the federal government to take over the task of supply from the states by the end of the 1861. This move centralized authority in the national government, while the Quartermaster Department remained decentralized among the various supply depots. Meigs shaped the logistical conditions of war as well, becoming one of Lincoln's valued advisors because of his formidable organizational skills, unrivaled capacity for detail, talent for military planning, personal integrity, and fierce commitment to the moral righteousness of the Union cause.[8]

As quartermaster general, Meigs was responsible for everything except ordnance, soldiers' rations, and medical operations. In addition to horses, mules, and their forage and supplies, his department had to provide a gamut of supplies, from huge to minuscule: steamboats, wagons, railroad cars, fuel, ambulances, stoves, furniture, tents, hammers, coffins, clothing, blankets, boots, caps, mess gear, sawmills, pontoon bridges, building timbers, pins, buttons, stationery, knapsacks. The Quartermaster Department spent $8 million in the fiscal year ending in July 1861. This figure swelled to $174 million in the next year, to $234 million and $440 million in 1862 and 1863, and to over $400 million in the final year of the war. Horses were one of the largest items in the budget.[9]

The prewar army had perhaps 15,000 animals, most of them used out west. Meigs needed to purchase large numbers of horses and mules quickly, and then to assemble them. Within the Union there were six million horses and mules, but they were scattered on farms and in towns across the states and territories. There were no large breeding operations or centrally organized markets to which the Quartermaster Department could go to purchase large groups of horses. Too many people were authorized to purchase horses for the government—quartermaster officers, regimental staff officers, mustering officers, and state governors among them. People were eager to sell horses to the government. The problem was creating a system for procuring them and getting them to the army, which meant organizing a scattered acquisition process into a process that funneled large quantities of horses into army service as rapidly as possible while providing some kind of quality control.[10]

Required by law to take sealed bids for purchases, Meigs frequently bought from horse dealers to acquire horses quickly. In a market consisting of thousands of small and widely dispersed suppliers, horse dealers were important middlemen. Dealers contracted with the government to deliver a specified number of horses for a prearranged price per head. Contracts ranged in number of horses from a few dozen to thousands. For example, in 1864 Levi Straw of Boston agreed to deliver 1,000 horses, and in Chicago G. M. Gage, C. N. Tomkins, C. T. Watkins, James Mix, and George T. Bergen each had contracts for 2,000 horses, at $120 per head. The largest horse dealers in business with the government came from the region between Pennsylvania and Missouri, the region where the bulk of the horses purchased by the government were located.

Supply officers had been complaining about horse dealers for decades. They argued that horse dealers bidded up prices, worked in combination with one another, and blocked individual sellers out of the horse market. At times supply officers advocated using open-market purchases rather than the contract system, but most horse purchases continued to come through the dealers. For political and economic reasons, the department did try to distribute these contracts widely, although, as happened in the markets for other war goods, the end result was that the large dealers got larger and smaller dealers dropped out of the picture.[11]

Getting enough horses was less of a problem than getting horses that were "serviceable," that is, appropriate for military service. The army wanted to purchase sound horses, free from injury, disease, or any other defect that would reduce their usefulness in military service, whether for cavalry, artillery, or wagon work. Additionally, the army wanted to purchase horses in their prime, between four and nine years of age. Horses had to have the strength and weight to provide sufficient draft, and be uniform enough in size that teams would be balanced and that harness could be of uniform size for interchangeable use. It is not clear if age specifications were met, because there can be difficulties in ascertaining a horse's age; however, complaints from soldiers and civilians about young animals usually referred to mules rather than to horses. Army mules could be used as young as two years, but army horses were usually at least four.

The army specified that horses be male, and preferably geldings because they were considered tractable and easy to use in teams. It is unclear whether the proscription against mares came from concerns about size and strength (though mares can be both large and strong), temperament (a matter of opinion, since some considered mares more even-tempered while others thought them more erratic), mixing horses of different sexes on the battlefield (some generals liked to ride stallions), or from a general notion that the military was no place for a lady, equine or human. In practice, however, mares did get purchased, and Meigs's officers pointed out that if the rule were changed so that they could buy mares, it would be easy to get the number of horses they needed.[12]

A recurring accusation throughout the war was that the government was wasting its money by purchasing unserviceable horses. Army regulations required that all horses be inspected before final purchase, and it was here that the real problems in the procurement process originated. Horse inspection was never a wholly objective process. The ability to assess the quality of a horse could be acquired only through experience, and it always involved a measure of subjectivity. Horse inspection could be only as good as the inspectors. The very nature of inspection offered opportunities for honest error, reasonable differences in judgment, and downright fraud. Because horse dealers wanted to sell as many of their horses as possible, they tried to influence inspectors; some resorted to bribes. The less experienced and confident the inspector, the more vulnerable he was to dealer pressure.

When it came to assessing a horse's serviceability, the only things easy to verify were size and sex. Determining a horse's age depended on being able to "read" the size, hollows, and grooves of its teeth. This was a skill that nineteenth-century books and periodicals often tried to teach, using diagrams and descriptions. In October 1847, for example, *Scientific American* published "To Ascertain the Age of a Horse." As with many of the skills necessary for evaluating horses, there were differences of opinion about how to estimate a horse's age. Judging the soundness of a horse required the ability to "read" the equine body using a working knowledge of how horses should look and move. Horses vary in conformation and in the way they move, and it is not always clear what constitutes unsoundness, or lameness, and what is merely a difference in conformation without much meaning.

Further complicating the process of horse inspection was what it said about the inspector socially. Being known as a good judge of horses was a mark of manhood and honor, and inspectors and sellers alike got touchy if their judgments about horses were challenged. Thus horse inspection was more than a business transaction; it became a matter of personal honor, and sometimes of community or state honor too. As one army officer wrote, "The ability to inspect a horse is a source of great pride. When horses [that men] deem sound are rejected, it's an affront to honor. When 'state' horses are rejected it's worse. It involves both ability to judge horseflesh and human character."[13]

An incident involving Union horse purchases in 1861 suggests the problems of quality control. In central Pennsylvania, supply officer Captain E. C. Wilson needed to inspect 1,700 horses in Harrisburg, 1,000 horses in Huntingdon ninety-eight miles to the west, and another 300 in Chambersburg fifty-six miles to the south. Wilson decided to do the Harrisburg inspections, and hired agents to go to Huntington and Chambersburg. Miller, the Huntingdon inspector, adhered so strictly to government specifications that the horse dealers were in an uproar. Wilson found himself "in a constant quarrel with the sub-contractors on account of so many of their horses being rejected." Though he was convinced that the dealers used "rascally tricks" to get their horses past inspection, neither could he afford to alienate them as a source of needed horses. He sent a trusted friend, General James, to reinspect the Huntingdon horses, and found that the horses that James accepted were "generally sound, though many of them were unfit for cavalry purposes." But James fell ill, so Wilson was forced to hire yet another inspector, a man named Sherbaker, who, he said, came highly recommended by "good and worthy citizens."

If Miller's inspections had left the dealers in an uproar, Sherbaker's outraged the local citizenry. In November 1861 twenty citizens of Huntingdon wrote Meigs claiming that Sherbaker had accepted many horses that were unsound, diseased, or otherwise unserviceable. The citizens said they recognized many of the horses that Sherbaker had approved and knew them to be unsound. They accused Sherbaker of accepting bribes.

> This bold, bald infamy incites universal censure. Corruption so apparent deals a blow as fatal as treason to the life of our country. The citizens almost doubt whether a government so beset by the base and unprincipled and so used by the knavery and cupidity of the vile is worth preserving. Patriotism is sorely tried, because those who coldly support this war have such occasion to talk only of the corruptions which disgrace its conduct. Our country is in a trial,

and surrounded by enormous peril. The honest and faith-
ful citizen . . . must aid in every service where his hands can
help. Duty demands that we expose and strike this mon-
strous evil.[14]

After receiving this letter, Meigs sent Major R. Jones to Huntingdon to investigate. Jones reinspected the Huntingdon horses and
found 100 good workhorses, 30 artillery horses, 150 that he described as "indifferent" but serviceable, and less than 200 fit for the
cavalry, adding up to fewer than 480 out of 1,000 that had passed
inspection. Among the horses that Sherbaker had approved, Jones
found 164 mares, 35 of which were pregnant, 120 horses older than
nine years, 86 younger than three years, 60 that were too small,
8 that were blind, and at least 5 with permanent debilitating conditions. Some horses were already dead of distemper. Jones concluded that the situation in Huntington "furnish[ed] abundant evidence of the determination of the contractors or at least of one of
them to make as much as possible, regardless of the means used."
And Captain Wilson himself, by his own admission, had "no experience in any such business" and "no knowledge whatever of
horses." He too was trying to figure out if a horse was sound or not
while being badgered by dealers, owners, and vigilant citizens.[15]

Meigs continued to receive complaints about faulty inspections
throughout the war. In June 1863 Captain W. Jenkins at the Louisville, Kentucky, depot complained that many of the horses he was
receiving from other depots were of inferior quality, in particular the
horses from Captain G. W. Lee at the Coldwater, Michigan, depot.
Lee's letter defending himself to Meigs reflects the same complicated mix of shock, offended honor, confident judgment, local
pride, and conspiracy as had swirled around the Huntingdon alle-
gations. "I would suggest an immediate investigation as to this inspection," Lee wrote,

for I can get Fifty affidavits from men as good judges as any inspector of cavalry, that those horses were not only *good* but *superior*, and it could not be possible for them to deteriorate so much in the short space of Five days [time in transit]. One of my men said that of 250 Horses sent from Chicago, this board [in Louisville] rejected 130! General, there must be some mistake in this inspection and auction sale . . . I feel myself responsible for the choice of our inspector . . . My inspection has been very rigid in order that reputation should be maintained as I felt a personal pride in the matter. I understand Capt. Jenkins is a very young man and perhaps he has been imposed on in some way.[16]

Meigs had the horses reinspected by Captain Fosser, who rejected 211 of 315 horses from Captain Lee. Of these, 29 were blind, 4 had bad eyes, and 21 had the heaves, or broken wind. Another inspector reported that 174 of 198 horses from Lee were unserviceable. Whether Lee was an incompetent administrator, an incompetent inspector (but convinced otherwise), the dupe of inspectors and dealers, under pressure from local interests wanting to promote Michigan horses, actively engaged in fraud, or all or some of the above is unclear from the record. Meigs established specifications, punished incompetent or dishonest officers and dealers, and tried to get skilled horse inspectors, but the purchase process remained decentralized and hard to supervise. Limiting the number of inspection depots could maximize the number of good inspectors, but it would slow the intake of horses into the army. Field generals complained both when they thought the horses weren't good enough and when they thought that tough inspections kept them from getting enough.[17]

As the war demanded ever more horses, the criteria of serviceability inevitably shifted. Meigs was the purchaser, but not the consumer. The consumers were President Lincoln, his cabinet, and his generals. The assumptions, goals, conflicts, agendas, needs, political calculations, and military decisions of these men, collectively and as individuals, determined how many horses were needed, when, and where. Horse specifications could be trumped by military needs. Meigs's job was to supply the army, and his highest priority always was getting the army what it needed to win the war, even if it meant choosing quantity over quality. If horses were needed for a week's campaign, then Meigs would authorize the purchase of horses that might last for only a week if the choice was between the army having enough horses or not.[18]

Meigs was also purchasing horses in a market with inelastic supply. It was not possible to breed horses to meet the immediate demands of the war market. Horses have an eleven-month gestation period. Once born, they need a minimum of two years before they can be used, and do not really mature until age four. For this reason, the Quartermaster Department required horses to be at least four years old, and in 1863 it raised the minimum age to six years for all categories of army horses. A prescient individual who had begun breeding horses for the war market in 1861, when everyone thought the war would be short, would not have had even two-year-olds to sell to the government until the spring of 1864. Government purchases did stimulate the horse market by causing people to sell horses they might otherwise have kept. The Quartermaster Department, through its depot chiefs, was the visible hand of the war market. As the war went on, the market encouraged people to breed horses to replace those lost in the war. The agricultural press encouraged farmers to breed horses, saying that the war had eliminated surplus horses and made the horse market look promising for years to come. However, as the reaction of citizens to the Huntingdon inspections showed, horses were not just any war commodity, but represented a far more personal and individual connection between the home front and the war effort than hay or oats, and an opportunity for citizens to demand correct behavior from their government.[19]

Thus the Union horse supply for war consisted of the horses on hand in 1861, some of which were young and which would become available for the war market as they matured. Meigs sought to create a system that would elicit as many mature, serviceable horses as possible from the northern economy. In 1863 Lincoln signed an order forbidding the export of horses in order to protect the Union horse supply. The government augmented the Union's horse supply with horses seized by the Union army from southern civilians, captured from the Confederate army, and shipped in from western territories. Horses probably came over the border from Canada as well, though there are no horse imports recorded in the census, agricultural reports, or quartermaster reports for the war years, and some in the Lincoln administration disapproved of buying horses from Canada.[20]

Army horses needed a broad array of supplies and accouterments: hay, grain, horseshoes, nails, harness, saddles, bridles, halters, girths, blankets, salt, medicine, currycombs, horse brushes, buckets, nosebags, blacksmith tools. The most immediate need, always, was for forage; horses' serviceability depended directly upon it. Both tactical decisions and strategic planning rested in part on whether military leaders had enough forage, or thought they could obtain enough forage for their horses in all categories.

The army's daily forage ration was fourteen pounds of hay for horses and mules, and twelve pounds of grain for horses and nine for mules. The hay provided nutrition and the bulk required by the horse's digestive system, while the grain afforded high-energy food for muscle and energy. By modern feeding standards, army horses and mules were probably overfed in camp and underfed while working. On these rations, a single cavalry force of 1,000 horses would be expected to consume seven tons of hay and six tons of grain per

Union army wagons near Brandy Station, Virginia, 1864. The portion of
the wagon park shown contains about 240 teams and wagons. Courtesy of the
Library of Congress.

day. A short supply train of only 150 wagons and 900 horses would
consume between five and seven tons of hay and four to six tons of
grain every day. Advancing armies moved with thousands of wagons. In contrast, the daily food ration for human soldiers weighed
only three pounds, and human soldiers ate a wider variety of food
and could forage for themselves in ways that horses could not. Given
these statistics it is no surprise that forage supply was a never-
ending concern for military leaders, or that requests for and worries
about forage were part of many battle reports and other communi-
cations.[21]

The Quartermaster Department assembled supplies of hay and
grain from individual farmers and from dealers. Purchasing agents
tried to find quality fodder at good prices, but, as with the problems

of horse inspections, they did not always know what they were getting. Under the immediate requirements of war, sometimes any forage would do. Furthermore, demand pushed prices up, especially in areas near supply depots. In addition to the general problem of getting quality forage, opportunities for fraud proliferated in the war market. At one point the government tried to economize on forage by switching from graining the horses with oats to using a mixed feed of oats and the less expensive corn. Detecting the ratio of each in a bushel of mixed feed was difficult, and the government paid mixed-feed prices for mixtures composed mostly of corn until the fraud was uncovered. This and the fact that corn was less nutritious for working horses caused a return to feeding oats as much as possible. Army horses did not always get the hay and grain they needed.[22]

Army horses depended on delivered forage because there were usually too many of them to live off the land. Only the best farming areas, at the right time of year, might have enough hay and grain to support thousands of horses for a short time. Less cultivated areas of the South, such as the wooded, mountainous region of east Tennessee, had very little growth that constituted forage, nor did cultivated areas already ransacked for supplies. When Lee retreated west from Richmond in 1865, he found that Virginia's farmers had already been relieved of forage in the preceding months by Union troops, and again by the Union cavalry directly ahead of him. Horses will eat a number of different things if hungry enough, but they cannot thrive for long nibbling on shrubs and trees.

If a field army ran short of forage, the problem was often delivery rather than supply. In general, the Quartermaster Department was able to procure adequate supplies of forage but not always able to get those supplies to the horses. Forage was a heavy, bulky commodity to ship. Hay was shipped loose because hay baling was still uncommon. Grain was sometimes bagged and sometimes shipped loose. Meigs tried to move forage by rail as much as possible, but loose hay and grain were the kind of freight least favored by the railroads—not only a nuisance to handle, but also less valuable per ton. Away from railheads and supply depots, forage had to move by wagon. This necessity led to an ongoing calculus concerning the numbers of supply wagons traveling with an army. Since wagon horses consumed forage in the process of moving forage, wagons could proliferate to the point of diminishing returns, with horses pulling wagons laden only with forage for themselves. Faced with an unending proliferation of wagons, horses, and forage in 1863, when he tried to impose limits on the number of supply wagons accompanying an army, Meigs asked: "When our army reaches this limit, what is the remedy? Is not every additional horse another subject for starvation? I doubt the wisdom of building up such masses, which crumple under their own weight."[23]

Union horses may have been chronically underfed, as the standard hay and grain rations are on the low side for working horses. At times, however, they underwent true deprivation. Like human soldiers, equine soldiers could be pushed to keep going—both as part of a group of horses and in a working relationship with humans it is in their nature to do so. However, they deteriorated in strength and stamina, becoming what the parlance of the day called "jaded." They then required a commensurate period of rest and good forage in order to return to working condition.[24]

After forage, the most important item of supply was horseshoes. Horses have naturally hard hooves in general, but the hardness and the rate at which they grow varies from horse to horse. Sustained impact and hard surfaces wear hooves down past their natural capacity for regeneration and growth. Horseshoes protect the hoof against this damage. How often a horse needs to be reshod varies according to the hardness or softness of the hooves, how fast the hooves grow, and the nature and difficulty of the usage. The hard usage of army horses required that they not only be shod, since unshod horses could go lame, but shod often.

Consequently, army horses and mules consumed thousands of horseshoes and horseshoe nails, not only in routine shoeing but also in the replacement of shoes lost between shoeings. For example, the 1,000 horses of a cavalry regiment wore 4,000 shoes, and their humans needed to bring along another 4,000, along with the nails and tools to attach them. Grant's 24,000 wagon horses and mules at the Rappahannock wore 96,000 shoes and of course used many more nails.

What made reliable supplies of horseshoes possible was a critical prewar invention. In 1857 Henry Burden, president of the Troy Iron and Nail Works in New York State, patented a machine that made saleable, mass-produced horseshoes. It wasn't the first such machine or patent, but it was the first successful one. By 1860, 11 percent of all horseshoes were mass-produced. In 1861 the shoe produced by the newly established Burden Horseshoe Company became the standard U.S. Army issue. Before, all horseshoes had been made by hand. This process required access to the iron and high-grade coal, skill, and several hours of work in forging. Burden's invention dramatically reduced the time, labor, and expense of shoeing, increasing the number of horses a man could shoe by a factor of seven. It also dramatically changed the geography of horse use: with a portable forge, machine-made horseshoes, nails and simple blacksmith tools, horses could be shod anywhere. It is hard to imagine the massive horse use of the Civil War without the existence of mass-produced horseshoes, and it is not far-fetched to suggest that this invention was a significant factor in increasing the use of horses in an industrialized war.[25]

The Quartermaster Department ordered horseshoes in enormous quantities. It ordered horseshoes and mule shoes (mules have smaller and slightly different hooves than horses), front and hind shoes, and shoes of different sizes. For example, records show one depot officer ordering 100-pound kegs in the following quantities: 300 of #2 size shoes, 300 of #3 shoes, 250 of #4 shoes, and 100 of #5

Shoeing Union army horses near Antietam, Maryland, 1862. Courtesy of the Library of Congress.

shoes, half of them front shoes and half of them back shoes for each size. In addition, he ordered 10,000 pounds of horseshoe nails. In one shipment from Bussing, Crocker and Company of New York City in December 1863, there were 1,190 kegs of horseshoes and 2,000 kegs of mule shoes.[26]

Even though the Burden shoe was standard issue, Meigs purchased shoes from many manufacturers. No single manufacturer of iron products could meet the army's needs, and companies struggled to keep up with orders. Stone, Chisolm and Jones of Cleveland, Ohio, informed Meigs in July 1862 that it could not supply any horse or mule shoes before late August, because "the scarcity of mechanics has seriously delayed us in completing our works for making shoes." Corning Winslow Company of Troy, New York, could fill only one-third of the government's order because "for the remaining 2/3 we shall have to prepare the several patterns, and afterwards make the shoes. This will consume some weeks, and if too great a delay for your wants we suggest that the balance of the order you purchase of other makers . . . your government patterns are different from the forms required for the genl. Market [and] we have not the shoes in stock." Bussing, Crocker promised to deliver, "barring strikes of workers." Yet despite these occasional difficulties there is little indication that, apart from local shortages, the Union lacked for horseshoes or the equally important horseshoe nails (made by a different set of companies).[27]

Forage, horseshoes, and all the other goods needed for both human and equine soldiers generated an enormous amount of business in the form of lucrative government contracts. Companies solicited the Quartermaster Department, submitting samples and testimonials about their products. Meigs and his staff worked hard to keep these contracts as honest as possible in the far-flung and semidecentralized system of army supply, and for the most part they succeeded. Quality control of horseshoes and other items was in the hands of committees of officers, called boards of survey, convened to examine and report on the quality of purchased articles. For example, in February 1863 Lt. Colonel Hollister of the 16th New York Cavalry, Major C. Crowinshield of the 2nd Massachusetts Cavalry, and Major D. Frazar of the 13th New York Cavalry determined that on the evidence of brigade blacksmiths and their own tests, the shoes of two companies in Providence, Rhode Island—Cutler and Perkins, and the Union Horse Shoe Company—were "worthless" and should no longer be purchased or issued.[28]

In addition to procuring, feeding, and outfitting horses, the Quartermaster Department had to assemble them and then move them to where they were needed. Even before horses went into active service, there were substantial issues about keeping them in serviceable condition. Horses were kept at supply depots, located at various points around the country, until needed. In 1863 the depot system was reorganized as part of the larger reorganization of the Quartermaster Department and the establishment of a new agency, the Cavalry Bureau. At that point six major depots were designated at St. Louis, Greenville (Louisiana), Nashville, Harrisburg, Wilmington (Delaware), and Washington, D.C. Each had the capacity to hold thousands of horses. The Giesboro depot, located outside Washington at what is now Bolling Air Force Base, was a 625-acre facility built to accommodate 30,000 horses. Many were kept in fifteen-acre corrals that held 1,000 horses each. With horses continually arriving and departing, and with manure amounting to as much as 700 tons each day, keeping abreast of sanitation was a challenge, as was keeping track of the condition of individual horses. These problems were just extensions of the chronic issues facing horse depots, but on a larger and more dramatic scale.

The first challenge was medical. Just as epidemics swept through the camps of the human army, equine epidemics swept through crowded horse depots as horses from different parts of the country carrying a variety of germs arrived and were put together in the same corrals. Given the way that horses socialize—sniffing, nuzzling, nose rubbing—diseases could spread quickly, especially anything related to the mouth and respiratory system. Horses received little of what would now be defined as veterinary care and were doctored much as humans were. American veterinary science in its infancy at mid-century, and formal veterinary training existed only in Europe and Britain. A person known as a veterinarian might have a degree from a foreign veterinary school, or be a medical doctor who treated animals, or be a self-taught practitioner, or be so designated by the army. In 1863 the army authorized the appointment of "veterinary surgeons" with no proof of training or expertise required.

A "violent and destructive" epidemic of hoof-and-mouth disease put 4,000 of the Army of the Potomac's horses out of commission in the fall of 1862. More serious were the periodic outbreaks of glanders, a highly communicable and incurable equine disease causing ulceration of the lymph nodes and respiratory tract, or pulmonary or bloodstream infections. Glanders spreads through the normal equine behavior of touching and rubbing noses with other horses, and through water troughs, hayracks, and feed bins. It is primarily a horse disease, but can affect donkeys and mules, sometimes goats, cats, and dogs, and is transmissible to humans. Acute glanders was always fatal, death coming a few days after horses showed symptoms. What made the disease especially dangerous was that it had a long incubation period of two weeks, during which afflicted horses were asymptomatic. There was also a chronic form of glanders, in which horses had few or no obvious symptoms and could spread the disease to other horses for years. A glandered horse unwittingly purchased by the army had many opportunities to spread the disease to other horses as it moved through the army's depot system and into active service. There was a severe outbreak of ganders at Giesboro in 1864, during which at least 11,000 horses died in the first seven months. In areas of army operations, farmers and other civilians worried that army horses would spread glanders to their horses, and there was at least one conspiracy theory that the Union was trying deliberately to spread the disease among southern horses.[29]

The dangers of chronic glanders and of the long incubation period of acute glanders were compounded by contemporary beliefs about the nature and causes of disease. Germ theory and other bacteriological discoveries did not emerge until the decade after the Civil War. In the meantime, not everyone agreed that glanders was dangerous or incurable. Filth theories of disease—the idea that disease agents spontaneously generated in or were inherent in various kinds of filth—dominated medical science. In addition, there were theories that some diseases resulted from atmospheric or other environmental changes. Consequently, not all glandered horses, once identified, were isolated and destroyed. Instead, they continued to be kept in large depots and were eventually sent to the army.[30]

In addition to the dangers of disease and injury in the horse depots, transportation exposed army horses to considerable hazards. Railroad travel posed many risks. Early in the war there were no cars constructed to transport horses. Herded into boxcars, many received injuries during the jolting journey, unable to keep their footing, falling, injuring limbs, being kicked, bitten, or stepped on by other horses. Some boxcars were poorly ventilated, and horses suffocated; others were so open that horses died of exposure in cool or cold weather. During the routine long delays and frequent layovers of midcentury railroad travel, horses might be kept confined in the cars without food, water, or care for hours and even days. Few depots were built to allow horses to be unloaded, or had corrals to hold them or the personnel to manage and care for them. Eventually cars were modified to transport horses, and better regulations were drawn up, including a requirement that horses be accompanied by people charged with their care. Even so, railroad travel remained hard on army horses, who routinely needed several days to recover afterward and broke down if pressed too quickly into service.

Moving horses the old-fashioned way carried risks too, as illustrated by an incident in 1863. The Union had to abandon Aquia Creek in Virginia after military reverses in the area, and evacuated men, equipment, and most of the animals by steamboat. However, there were 2,521 horses and mules for which there was no room on the boats. A cavalry company and 200 extra riders began herding the animals northward, heading toward a depot in Alexandria. Near Dumfries the herd stampeded, and 200 of them went into a salt marsh and drowned. Once reassembled and moving, the herd encountered a column of the Union army. Teamsters, artillery soldiers, and cavalry all began appropriating animals from the herd. During the ensuing chaos the horses scattered, turning up in small groups all across northern Virginia. Civilians sighted groups of army horses loose in the fields and woods, and telegraphed the government about the waste of public property and the continuing "great carelessness with respect to the horse." Thereafter Meigs restricted the size of herds on the move to 500 animals accompanied by 150 men. During the war the conditions of transporting horses improved, but its dangers did not disappear.[31]

Overcoming these logistical challenges, Meigs procured and outfitted hundreds of thousands of horses. By gathering horses and supplies at regional depots, he used a hub-and-spoke method of distribution to get horses and associated supplies to field armies as fast as possible. The railroads became cooperative about transporting supplies for the army. The Union's railroads and the Lincoln administration came to an understanding early in the war, after the government persuaded the railroads not to charge high rates in exchange for not being taken over by the government under the authority of the Railroad Act of 1862.

While the precise number of horse purchases made during the war is uncertain, the following figures provide a picture of the unprecedented level of expenditure and acquisition by Meigs's department. During 1861 the Quartermaster Department purchased at least 110,000 horses and 84,000 mules. In 1862 McClellan's army of 112,000 men used 46,000 animals: 34,000 draft horses, 6,850 artillery horses, and 5,000 cavalry horses. Meigs was supplying 1,500 animals per week. In the six months from April to October 1863 the department purchased 35,000 animals, and in early July Meigs had almost 7,000 horses at hand to replace losses after the Battle of Gettysburg. In 1864, when General Grant moved south against General Lee, the 125,000 soldiers of his army crossed the Rapidan River with almost 30,000 horses, 23,000 mules, and 4,000 officers' horses. Later that year General Sherman departed Atlanta to march through Georgia with 64,000 soldiers and 34,000 horses. Between January and August 1864, Meigs remounted the entire cavalry of the Army of the Potomac twice. General Sheridan reported receiving 200 horses a day in the summer of 1864, and by the end of the war Meigs was sending nearly 500 horses per day to replace equine casualties. The Union army used hundreds of thousands of horses. Though there were times when Union commanders found themselves short of horses, the problem one of delivery and not of supply.[32]

Equine soldiers were subject to the same circumstances as human soldiers. They shared the conditions of hard marching, poor food, and exposure to weather; they got wounded, injured, and debilitated; they died. If captured, horses were not imprisoned, but like humans caught in civil wars were pressed into service for the other side. Each kind of army horse encountered the conditions and dangers of military service differently.

Cavalry operations often involved hard riding across rough and thickly wooded countryside. This kind of activity used up horses quickly, increasing their chances of losing shoes, damaging hooves, pulling muscles, and injuring legs and feet. In addition there were insufficient rest, erratic water and forage, and long periods of being saddled, which led to saddle sores and other skin conditions, digestive ills, and general debilitation. One Union cavalry regiment reported traveling 105 miles in twenty-four hours. General D. S. Stanley, pursuing Confederate General Joseph Wheeler in Tennessee in October 1863, marched 247 miles in six days, and on two separate days did 50 miles. "My horses are terribly jaded. I shall return toward Stevenson, but must move slowly, for my horses are so near used up." General Robert B. Mitchell, also pursuing Wheeler, reported, "I think the record of the cavalry service during the entire war cannot show a more severe campaign than the one my command has just closed. There was scarcely an hour during the whole pursuit the horses were unsaddled; for days and nights together the men were in the saddle, almost constantly on the march, and some days making as high as 53 and 57 miles." Mitchell described his horses as "very badly used up." Hard marches, scarcity of shoes, and "miserable worthless saddles that never should have been bought by the Government, or put on a horse's back after they were bought, have ruined many of the horses."³³

Much cavalry fighting involved skirmishing rather than formal charges in open field battle, but in all cases horses were wounded and killed by bullets and fragments. For anyone firing at a mounted soldier, the largest target is the horse's body. Bringing down the horse may injure or kill the soldier; at the very least it leaves him on foot and more vulnerable to being captured, wounded, or killed. Many battle reports mentioned troopers and officers having horses shot out from under them or killed under them.

The conditions affecting wagon horses were first and foremost the conditions of hauling. Road conditions were rarely optimal; if roads were chronically poor in the North, they were dreadful in much of the South. In dry weather, wagon trains jolted over hard-rutted roads, raising choking clouds of dust that encrusted sweaty skin and made the air hard to breathe. In wet weather, the roads turned into unending mires almost impossible for horses to pull wagons through. Every soldier became a specialist in varieties of mud. "We floundered along through the deep red-mud roads," wrote a cavalry officer, "through the worst roads I ever saw, in which our empty wagons could hardly make two miles an hour . . . Horses can scarcely get along alone, they can hardly succeed in drawing the immense supply and ammunition trains necessary for so large an army." Another officer described a stretch in Tennessee as "the most abominable road it was ever our lot to travel, mostly over solid and detached rock, miry lands, miry woods the horses sinking over knee-deep in the mud." As rain fell in the mountains of Tennessee, "the narrow roads . . . had become torrents and sometimes the horses were obliged to swim." This heavy draft left many horses and mules "entirely broken down, and . . . worthless hereafter. Both men and horses had been upon short rations and forage, and it was impossible for . . . trains to follow close upon the troops over such terribly rugged roads."[34]

Wagon horses might be on the periphery of the fighting in large-scale battles, but they were vulnerable to shells and, since wagon trains were the lifeline of armies, a target for raiders. Wagons moved slowly, and under bad conditions lagged behind troops, delaying supplies, and opening dangerous gaps between troops and their trains, even though cavalry and infantry were detailed as escorts.[35]

Bad conditions and susceptibility converged during the siege of Chattanooga in 1863. Defeated at Chickamauga on September 20, Union General William S. Rosecrans and his Army of the Cumberland retreated to Chattanooga, a town on the Tennessee River surrounded by mountains. General Braxton Bragg laid siege to Chattanooga, controlling the river and the railroad and severing Union lines of supply from Bridgeport downriver. The only open route into Chattanooga was through the Cumberland Mountains to the north. Supply wagons had to start southwest of Bridgeport at Stevenson and travel northeast to the Sequatchie River valley and follow it northward to a point called Anderson's Crossroads. From there they picked up a steep, rocky trail up Walden's Ridge, rising nearly a mile in elevation, then down seven miles to the north bank of the Tennessee, crossing into Chattanooga over one of the army engineers' pontoon bridges. From Bridgeport to Chattanooga by rail was twenty-seven miles. The wagon route was sixty miles "over a country destitute of forage, poorly supplied with water, by narrow and difficult wagon roads."[36]

Wagon trains took many days to move supplies over this route at best, but when the autumn rains began to fall in earnest, the roads became impassable. Wagon mules wrestled the wagons through belly-deep mud. Teamsters harnessed sixteen mules to a wagon and assigned two soldiers to each mule—one to pull on the mule, and one to get behind the mule and push. Starving mules died in their traces, were cut loose, and were left at the side of the trail. On October 2, cavalry under General Wheeler attacked the wagon trains on Walden's Ridge. As Wheeler described it,

> We found a large train of wagons, which proved to extend from the top of Walden's Ridge for a distance of ten miles towards Jasper . . . The number of wagons was variously estimated at from 800 to 1,500 . . . The train was guarded by a brigade of cavalry in front, and a brigade of cavalry in rear, and on the flank, where we attacked, were stationed two regiments of infantry. After a warm fight, the guards were defeated and driven off, leaving the entire train in our possession. After selecting such mules and wagons as we needed, we then destroyed the train by burning the wagons and sabering or shooting the mules.

Wheeler destroyed 300 wagons and killed or captured 1,800 mules. Colonel E. M. McCook pursued Wheeler and caught up with him the next day at Anderson's Crossroads, where he was able to recapture 809 mules.[37]

This fragile supply line was not enough to keep Union soldiers and animals in Chattanooga from running out of food. Dead horses and mules lined the streets. To keep the artillery horses alive in case of an attack from Bragg, commanders set guards over the horses' corn to keep the soldiers from eating it. On October 18, nearly a month into the siege, Assistant Secretary of War Charles A. Dana reported:

> The roads are in such a state that wagons are eight days making the journey from Stevenson to Chattanooga, and some which left on the 10th have not yet arrived. Though subsistence stores are so nearly exhausted here, the wagons are compelled to throw overboard portions of their pre-

cious cargo in order to get through at all. The returning
trains have now for some days been stopped on this side of
the Sequatchie, and a civilian who reached here last night
states that he saw fully five hundred teams halted between
the mountain and the river without forage for the animals
and unable to move in any direction.

An offensive mounted by General Grant and General Thomas (who
had replaced Rosecrans) reopened supply lines by the end of October. But the monthlong siege of Chattanooga killed more than
10,000 Union army animals.[38]

Artillery horses were exposed to the same risks as wagon horses
plus the risks of being in battle. Field guns combined firepower with
maneuverability, and they could be positioned and repositioned to
advantage in a battle or skirmish. If a commander called up two
guns, two teams of six horses brought them into position at a gallop,
the guns with their barrels pointing to the rear bouncing over the
ground as they came. The horses would wheel around ("turning
their flanks") to point the guns toward the enemy position. Soldiers detached the guns from the limbers, and the drivers (who were
mounted on the horses) galloped the team and limbers away, to be
held at the ready at a distance from the guns as specified by artillery
regulations.

The accuracy of field guns improved when they were moved
closer to the enemy, but such movements risked bringing the artillery horses into the range of enemy guns. "At this point the enemy
had returned to our front with a battery of two 12-pounder guns . . .
at the first volley from my regiment every horse was killed." Equally
dangerous was bringing the horses out to take guns off the field. "I
immediately gave orders for the battery to limber up," reported an
artillery officer, "but it could not be done as the horses as soon as
they were brought up to the guns were shot down." The life expec-
tancy of artillery horses in service was estimated at seven and a half

Three horse artillery batteries near Fair Oaks, Virginia, 1862. Source:
Henry W. Elson, *The Civil War through the Camera* (Springfield, Mass., 1912).
Rare Book and Manuscript Library, University of Pennsylvania.

months. Killing or disabling artillery horses increased the chances
that guns could be captured or destroyed. Horses would be shot
down or shelled as they were harnessed at the gun. Though regulations specified that the horses must be kept well back from the guns,
artillery soldiers often kept them close at hand for easier access to
their ammunition and so that they could "limber up" and move the
guns quickly if they came under fire from enemy artillery or under
direct attack from enemy infantry. On the third day at Gettysburg
the Confederate barrage went long and did not take out the Union
guns as Lee had planned, but it killed a group of artillery horses.
When the horses were killed or too badly injured the soldiers had to
grab other horses to replace them, pull the gun off the field themselves, or abandon it to the enemy, "spiking" or disabling it if possible.[39]

Lieutenant C. W. Laing, Second Michigan Battery, described artillery action in the Battle of Shiloh in April 1862:

> Meanwhile the Thirteenth Ohio Battery had formed on our right and a little in advance. They had just got unlimbered when one of their caissons was shivered to pieces, and the horses on one of the guns took fright and ran through our lines. All then left the battery without having fired a shot. Two of our sergeants went to the spot and cut a number of the horses loose. Our battery then fell back through an orchard and ceased firing for about twenty minutes. General Hurlbut then told us to advance again and bear to the right . . . Held this position for about an hour and a half, during which time Lieutenant Arndt had his horse shot under him and Lieutenant Bliss' horse wounded; also two team horses on gun shot and two cannoneers wounded.[40]

In another account from Shiloh, Lieutenant Edward Brotzmann of the Missouri Light Artillery wrote:

> After heavy firing of about twenty minutes from both sides the enemy did not respond to our fire any longer and fell back . . . I lost . . . 8 horses. I sent the bugler back to the camp for 6 horses, with drivers, for replacing the loss . . . which were taken from the [team of the] field forge [wagon] . . . [Caught] in a cross-fire, the artillery from the right and the infantry from the front, I sustained a heavy loss of men and horses, and I only returned when our infantry retreated. Two wheel-horses of the second piece were wounded severely, and also the middle driver, which compelled me to leave that piece, a 6-pounder gun, behind; also two caissons, but without ammunition, on which

[some of] the horses were killed and [the remaining] taken to replace the disabled horses on the pieces . . . In overlooking the battery I found that the loss of wounded and killed on this day was 2 lieutenants, 12 men and about 30 horses.[41]

Battle reports, especially artillery reports, form a litany of equine carnage. Artillery horses were shot as they brought the guns onto the field, or while being limbered up to take the guns off. Soldiers tried to cut wounded or dead horses from the traces and stay in action with the remaining horses; infantry soldiers ran over to free horses and help with casualties. If the gun was too damaged to use, soldiers cut horses from the wreckage and harnessed them to other guns. If too many horses were injured, guns were abandoned, in the standard wording of many battle reports, "for want of animals to bring them off."

The behavior of horses under such combat conditions depended on their training and experience, their relationship with other horses and with their drivers or riders, and individual traits such as temperament and age. Horses are not inherently afraid of battle the way humans might be, because for them it does not exist until they experience it. What triggers their fear and flight responses are sights, sounds, and smells, immediate material threats, strange or unexpected events, or encountering something that they remember as dangerous or frightening. Horses can be trained for war so that they are not frightened of the noises and objects they would encounter in combat. Experienced horses, like experienced soldiers, do not panic in combat as a matter of course. There are things that horses do not like to do, such as charge at a solid obstacle (like a line of men) or trample on things, but they can be trained to do so without swerving or shying away. Like most working horses, they listen for and trust the voice of rider or driver.

However, for both horses and men, the environment of a battle created confusing and chaotic conditions. It was difficult if not impossible to be certain that all horses on or near a battlefield had been trained, especially in situations in which horses were scarce or being supplied rapidly to armies during campaigns. Like humans, horses put into service with too little training were unpredictable. Battle could cause experienced horses to behave unpredictably too. "My horses [became] unmanageable when the firing commenced . . . my horses are too green to be serviceable," wrote Colonel Alfred Gibbs. During the battle of Shiloh, "Riderless horses came thundering through the trees with empty saddles, and artillery horse with caisons [sic] attached ran through the squads of men and striking trees caused the percussion shells to explode blowing horses caisons [sic] and everything to atoms." Also at Shiloh, Captain Louis D. Kelley reported: "Horses without riders . . . dashed through our ranks with great speed . . . Our lines were broken several times by horses and mules running away."[42]

As herd animals, horses pick up clues from the horses and humans around them. As wounded humans and horses piled up on the battlefield, horses swerved to avoid them, colliding with other horses and soldiers. As horses became separated from their teams, were cut free from dead and injured horses, lost their familiar riders and drivers, it became more difficult to control them under fire. Artillery horses still harnessed to guns, limbers, and caissons were particularly dangerous. J. R. Purvis described how "shell and bullets were rained on the 12-pounder so fast that the limber was broken and the horses so repeatedly wounded that they could not be held to their places but ran away with both it and the caisson." Artillery drivers were not always skilled and experienced, and not always able to control six horses under battle conditions. Captain Robert C. Stanard explained: "Just as the howitzer entered the road the horses took fright and started off at full speed up the road. The driver of the horses (who was a volunteer and not accustomed to the team) informs me that he attempted to halt just as he got into the road, and that the dashing by of the troop which accompanied us caused his horses to become unmanageable and to run off." Disoriented from wounds, shock, and inexperience, loose and wounded horses careened around battlefields stampeding through the lines of soldiers and inflicting additional injuries on themselves and others. In Civil War combat, horse behaviors were as natural a component of the environment of battle as human behaviors.[43]

Horses became interchangeable in battle. An officer whose horse had been killed or disabled tried to catch a loose one. Horses extricated from the wreckage of one gun or wagon were harnessed to another. Cavalry and wagon horses were commandeered to pull artillery. Under battle conditions, any horse, any mule, was preferable to none.[44]

How many horses did the army actually need? Calculating need was never a simple equation, but a complicated calculus of variables such as horse capacity and condition, terrain, perception, and generals' egos. As the job of procuring, outfitting, supplying, and replacing horses grew ever larger, Meigs challenged what he thought were generals' often inflated notions of how many horses they needed, even as he worked to fill their requests. Field generals demanded enormous numbers of horses, complained that they did not receive enough horses, and sometimes blamed Meigs for military failures related to horses. In the fall of 1862, after Confederate General J. E. B. Stuart had just ridden around the entire Army of the Potomac for the second time in four months and raided and burned Chambersburg, Pennsylvania, along the way, an embarrassed General George B. McClellan complained to General-in-Chief Henry Halleck that Meigs had left him with a "deficiency" of horses that made it "impossible to prevent the rebel cavalry raids." McClellan claimed he had received only 150 horses per week. Meigs, however, supplied documentation that he had sent 1,459 horses a week, and that McClellan had received 10,254 horses in the six weeks preceding Stuart's raid.[45]

Meigs constantly fought with field commanders like Rosecrans who demanded large numbers of cavalry horses. In the early part of the war the cost of horses averaged $110 apiece, about five times the cost of a rifle and ten times the monthly pay of an infantry soldier. Meigs discouraged the use of cavalry because he thought it wasted horses and forage. "Rely more on infantry and less on cavalry which in this whole war has not decided the fate of a single battle rising above a skirmish, which taxes the resources of the country, and of which we now afoot a larger animal strength than any nation on earth," he advised General Rosecrans. Meigs speculated whether officers wanting to be cavaliers were displaying a cavalier attitude about horse care.[46]

The poor performance of Union cavalry for the first two years of the war supported Meigs's economics. Even though General Mc-Clellan had been a cavalry officer, author of a cavalry training manual, and designer of one of the cavalry's standard-issue saddles, he and other Union generals lagged well behind Confederates like General Jeb Stuart, whose innovative tactics exploited the cavalry's potential for reconnaissance and screening and made it into a fast-strike weapon for raids against supply trains, railroad infrastructure, and telegraph lines. Instead of letting its cavalry fight as a unit, the Union army dispersed it among infantry units for picket and escort duties. The cavalry lost only twenty-eight men at Antietam. The infantry began to joke that they had never seen a dead trooper. However, with the creation of the Cavalry Bureau in 1863, the insistence of commanders like General Philip Sheridan that the cavalry fight as its own wing of the army, and a growing understanding of cavalry's uses, Union cavalry improved its record and reputation. By 1863 Union cavalry under General Alfred Pleasanton fought Stuart's cavalry to a draw at Brandy Station, near Culpepper, Virginia. General William Sherman's cavalry was successful in Tennessee during 1863, and General Philip Sheridan's troopers brought the Shenandoah Valley under Union control in the winter of 1864–65.

Meigs tried to reduce the enormous number of wagon horses the army used by setting limits on the number of wagons that accompanied field armies. He wanted the army to adhere to Napoleon's formula of twelve wagons per 1,000 men. However, in a densely populated and cultivated Europe, Napoleon's armies could forage off the land, something not possible in the sparsely populated and cultivated Confederacy. The Union army used between twenty-six and forty wagons per 1,000 men, and averaged thirty-one.

The problem with the proliferation of wagons was forage. Grant's army often had a ratio of one horse for every two or three soldiers, and Sherman's had three horses for every five, which came to 50,000–60,000 horses for an army of 100,000, or approximately 650 tons of forage per day just for the horses, and another 150 tons of food for the soldiers (about three pounds apiece). A team of four horses could pull 2,800 pounds and six mules 4,000 pounds of supplies over a good road; since there were hardly ever any good roads, wagons usually carried 2,000 to 3,000 pounds. Assuming an average wagon capacity of 2,500 pounds, the daily forage ration would take 520 wagons, and the soldiers' rations another 120.

The challenges of horse care complicated the calculus of need. The uncertainties of combat, along with demands that troops be ready and waiting—wagon teams and artillery teams harnessed, cavalry horses saddled—made it difficult to provide good care in the field. Forage was often short, water was time-consuming to locate and provide, and keeping horses clean was an ongoing task. For example, horses need to be cleaned and their skin and hair allowed to dry; if kept saddled for hours or days, sweat and dirt accumulate under saddles and girths and cause sores and other skin conditions. Reported one artillery officer: "Horses wounded, 15; and in consequence of not unharnessing for six days and the hardship they have undergone, I will lose 25 more horses."[47]

Charles Francis Adams Jr. expressed the situation more eloquently and thoughtfully than almost any other observer. He wrote:

"Imagine a horse, with his withers swollen to three times the natural size, and with a volcanic, running sore pouring matter down each side, and you have a case with which every cavalry officer is daily called upon to deal, and you imagine a horse which has still to be ridden until he lays down in sheer suffering under the saddle." It was a question of disciplining oneself and one's troops. A good officer could reduce horse casualties, though Adams noted the limits to what he could do: "An officer of cavalry needs to be more horse-doctor than soldier, and no one who has not tried it can realize the discouragement to Company commanders in these long and continuous marches. You are a slave to your horses, you work like a dog yourself, and you exact the most extreme care from your Sergeants, and you see diseases creeping on you day by day, and your horse breaking down under your eyes." In the final analysis, horses, like human soldiers, were expendable to the larger demands of the war, and people had to put aside their humanitarian feelings. Adams concluded, "I do my best for my horses and am sorry for them; but all war is cruel and it is my business to bring every man I can into the presence of the enemy, and so make war short. So I have but one rule, a horse must go until he can't be spurred any further, and then the rider must get another horse as soon as he can seize one."[48]

Both soldiers and civilians reported poor treatment of horses to the government. J. G. Kennedy of the Census Office wrote to Meigs with suggestions for the care of government horses, especially their tails. "The problem," wrote Colonel W. Halstead of the 1st New Jersey Cavalry to Meigs, "is that supervising the health and well being of horses is seen as an ancillary, not primary duty by many officers." In his own regiment, horse losses outside of battle were only 4 per 1,000 under a commander who understood horse care, but 120 per 1,000 under one who did not. He urged the creation of a board to oversee all the army's horses and make sure that the "noble animals" received proper care. Private A. D. Still wrote Lincoln to complain about the treatment of cavalry horses. Private Peter Lanks wrote to

Edwin Stanton that no attempts were made to rehabilitate disabled animals, and that they were neglected and abandoned, with perfectly good horses and mules wasted. The Quartermaster Department actually did attempt to rehabilitate or "recruit" horses and mules by establishing recruiting depots, and by contracting with farmers to pasture army horses and mules for several months of rest and recuperation.[49]

Meigs lectured field officers and quartermaster personnel about the condition of their horses, investigated complaints, and issued regulations about horse maintenance. He reminded field commanders that "extraordinary care [should be] taken of the horse, on which everything depends." When commanders complained that they did not have enough horses, Meigs asked if they were taking care of the horses they already had, as illustrated by his dispute with General Rosecrans while the latter commanded the Army of the Cumberland in Tennessee.[50]

Early in 1863 Rosecrans began complaining to Secretary of War Stanton that Meigs was refusing to send him enough cavalry horses, and that Meigs's contracting system was restricting the supply. Rosecrans was under pressure from Lincoln and Stanton to move more quickly, but at the end of April Rosecrans claimed, "I have lost control of the country between my infantry and that of the enemy, and all the forage and stock which they have consumed since I arrived here. For want of an adequate mounted force, the fruits of victory have been wrested from me due to that same inexorable necessity." In addition, he complained that the horses he had were not good enough. "Money is being thrown away buying the kind of horses we have bought . . . Cheap horses for service absolutely necessary is the worst possible plan." Soon Rosecrans criticized Meigs for both inspection and purchase policies. "Only 29 horses per day are coming in since the new inspector began to be vigorous . . . We must have delivery as well as quality . . . We can do nothing without horses."[51]

Meigs finally wrote a lengthy response to Rosecrans that was virtually a primer on managing horses and men. Meigs noted that Rosecrans had reported receiving 33,057 horses and mules in the last five months, and having 43,023 horses and mules in March, one for every two men in his army. "Is this not a large supply? . . . You have broken down and sent off as unserviceable, in addition to these, over 9,000 horses, and report that one-fourth or one-third of the horses on hand are worn out. Now, all this it seems to me, shows that the horses are not properly treated. They are either overworked, or underfed, or neglected and abused." Meigs emphasized to Rosecrans that the use of horse technology required considerable management.

> Compel your cavalry officers to see that their horses are groomed; put them in some place where they can get forage, near the railroad, or send them to your rear to graze and eat corn . . . never move off a walk unless they see an enemy before or behind them; to travel only so far in a day as not to fatigue their horses; never to camp in the place in which sunset found them, and to rest in a good pasture during the heat of the day . . . Operate on their communications; strike every detached post; rely more upon infantry and less upon cavalry; which in this whole war has not decided the fate of a single battle rising above a skirmish.[52]

Meigs knew that the care and rest that army horses required did not often fit well with the need for soldiers and horses to be constantly on the move. Furthermore, horse care was a task often relegated to "spare men" and new recruits regardless of their experience or expertise. As this excerpt from the diary of Henry Robinson Berkeley shows, good artillery officers, like good cavalry officers, had to balance the demands of orders with an understanding of how to conserve and maximize the available horsepower.

February 6. We received orders at 8 P.M. to go immediately to Morton's Ford . . . Begged Thomas Jefferson Page, who was in command of our battalion in Col. Nelson's absence, to let us remain in our comfortable quarters until daybreak and get a good night's rest, but he having no practical knowledge, ordered us to be ready to start at ten o'clock that night. We started in wind, rain and utter darkness, and men and horses were floundering in mud, rain and darkness the whole of that night, and when daylight came we had only gotten about a mile or two from camp, while men and horses were worn out and little fit for a hard day's march over a heavy and muddy road.

February 7. Sunday. Continued our hard march toward Morton's Ford. Col Nelson . . . came up with us about sunset, and the first thing he said to Maj. Page was, "Jeff, had you let these poor men and horses remain in their comfortable camp last night, you would be ten miles nearer Morton's ford that you are now." Behold the difference between a practical and theoretical officer![53]

Adding to equine attrition from injuries, wounds, hard usage, poor care, exposure, and underfeeding was outright death in battle. Dead horses were ubiquitous at the scene of every skirmish, siege, and formal battle. At Shiloh, the bodies of dead horses lay so thick upon the ground that in some places one couldn't walk without stepping on them. After the battle of Gettysburg, there were 5,000 dead horses, or 2.5 million tons of horseflesh that needed removal and was burned in huge pyres. Battlefield photographs show the bodies of horses entangled with the wreckage of artillery. Soldiers and reporters frequently mentioned dead horses, perhaps as an evocative but less graphic way of describing battlefields to their civilian readers. "First, in the road, lay a dead horse," wrote Dr. Daniel Holt about coming upon the aftermath of a skirmish. On the battlefield at Antietam, Oliver Wendell Holmes Sr. reported: "At intervals, a dead horse lay by the road side, or in the fields, unburied, not grateful to gods or men . . . at the edge of this cornfield lay a gray horse . . . not far off were two dead artillery horses still in their harness." Charles Francis Adams wrote: "The air of Virginia is literally burdened to-day with the stench of dead horses, federal and confederate. You pass them on every road and find them in every field, while from their carrion you can follow the march of every army that moves." Dead horses became symbols of the tragedy of war, a way to talk about death and suffering by transferring it to the suffering of animals.[54]

Individual horses, usually those belonging to generals, became famous. In addition to Traveller and Cincinnati, these included Little Sorrel (Jackson), Winchester/Rienzi (Sheridan), Virginia (Stuart), Lexington (Sherman), and Old Baldy (Meade). Some lived long after the war and were revered as veterans. Some were stuffed and displayed after death. Old Baldy outlived General Meade by ten years, and when he died in 1882, members of Philadelphia's elite Meade Post (of the veterans' organization the Grand Army of the Republic) had his head mounted on a large plaque (which detailed Old Baldy's fourteen battle wounds) and hung it in its clubhouse. On hearing about Old Baldy's head, members of a GAR post for enlisted men allegedly had the head of an army mule stuffed and mounted in their clubhouse. People drew many meanings from these equine relics that provided a material connection to the war.[55]

The Civil War was more than a litany of great battles. The Union army's horses remind us how much of this war occurred away from the battlefields. Tracing the experience of horses as they were purchased, transported, outfitted, encamped, put into action, wounded, doctored, and killed exposes the fabric of northern Civil war society. It links the home front to the battle front and provides a focus

Dead artillery horses and smashed guns from shelling during the battle of Fredericksburg, 1863. Source: Henry W. Elson, *The Civil War through the Camera* (Springfield, Mass., 1912). Rare Book and Manuscript Library, University of Pennsylvania.

for understanding the relationship between the war's political economy and military management. The Civil War was not the last war in which animal power would be a critical factor, but it was the first war of industrialized animal power, and additional evidence that horses were not marginalized by technological change. The enormous amount of animal energy required to wage the Civil War was available because of the ways in which prewar industrialization had swelled the horse population. In the postbellum years, horses would remain integral to the emerging system of industrial capitalism, but no one organization used or managed horses on the scale achieved by the Union army during the Civil War.

On April 3, 1860, in St. Joseph, Missouri, a growing crowd awaited the inaugural run of the Pony Express to San Francisco, scheduled to depart once the express train arrived from the East at five o'clock. In the afternoon light, people milled around the bay mare of the express rider. They pulled so many hairs from her mane and tail as souvenirs that her rider took her back to the livery stable, where, saddled and ready, she would be safe from further depredations. Finally the train pulled in. The mail was tossed to the express agent, who quickly stuffed letters, newspapers, and parcels into a *mochila*, a poncho with pockets for mail, spread it across the bay mare's saddle, and made it fast. The rider mounted, and the crowd parted as he galloped down to the ferry dock. As soon as the mare's hooves clattered onto the deck, the ferry *Denver* cast off, swung into the current, and steamed to the village of Elwood on the western bank. Another clatter of hooves, then horse and rider galloped away from the ferry landing, followed by the cheers of the crowd as they rode into the sunset on the first leg of the long journey to California. Twenty-three horses and nine days later, a rider arrived at the Pony Express office in Sacramento to deliver the *mochila,* while back in St. Joseph the first rider from California was delivering his.[1]

The horse and its cowboy rider provide one of the most popular and compelling images of horses in nineteenth-century America. As it traverses the expanses of the American West, the Pony Express horse seems the quintessential opposite of Gilded Age industrialization. Reinforced by more than a century of dime novels, Wild West shows, comic books, movies, television shows, cigarette advertisements, car commercials, and presidential rhetoric, the western horses of the late nineteenth century evoke a natural, authentic world in contrast to the human-built world of urban industrial capitalism that was emerging east of the Mississippi.

Yet the horses of the West were integral to nineteenth-century industrialization. Western historians have long recognized the close relationship between the development of the West and the political economy of industrial capitalism. The great cattle ranges came into being because of the extension of the railroads to the West, the development of the meatpacking industry, and the growth of the urban market. Cattle ranches were bankrolled by eastern capital, pastured on the unfenced public domain, and protected by the U.S. military. The western ranch bore similarities to the southern plantation, and the Indian reservation to development of Jim Crow. The farms and ranches of the West were the geographical fringe of urban industrial capitalism. The horses of the West and their human coworkers were industrial workers as much as the horses and their human coworkers of northeastern and midwestern farms and cities. Even the wild horses of the West are industrial creations. These horses are not truly wild, horses having gone extinct in North America over 10,000 years ago, but feral. Living on public lands and protected by the federal government, they symbolize wild and original nature, a concept that gained traction among urban middle and upper classes in the late nineteenth century.[2]

Pony Express riders and horses were some of the first industrial workers of the West. Rather than sending riders across trackless wilderness, the Express built a network of way stations, stables, corrals, wells, roads, and bridges and used a supply system of ox- and mule-drawn wagon trains to provision the way stations with grain, hay, horseshoes, harness, horses, and food supplies, some of which were shipped in from the East. These stations had to be staffed, and horses cared for. At its peak, the Pony Express employed over 400 horses and over 500 people, including 125 riders, who had to sign time sheets so that supervisors could monitor their work. It took industrial management to coordinate operations over thousands of miles in order to carry the mail, just as it took industrial technology to link western ranches with eastern beef markets.

During the Gilded Age the use of horses grew as technological change expanded the opportunities to use horse power. There were startling gains in the number of horses: the national population rose from approximately seven million in 1860 to nearly twenty-five million in 1900. Most of these resided east of the Mississippi River. They were integral in two of the great transformations of the Gilded Age—the growth of the industrial city and the mechanization of agriculture.

Urban horses made up a relatively small percentage of the overall horse population—around 11 or 12 percent—but their role in urban growth gives them an importance beyond their numbers. Horses powered almost every aspect of urban life. Urban herds grew over 350 percent as horses urbanized 50 percent faster than humans. At any time between 1860 and 1920, a Boston banker was likely to encounter more horses than would a cowboy or rancher in Colorado or Texas. Horse populations grew 371 percent during the Gilded

Age. When the Great Epizootic struck eastern cities in the fall of 1872 it underscored the extent to which they relied on these living machines.[3] Philadelphia's center was normally congested with drays, carts, huge brewery wagons, small delivery wagons, city vehicles, omnibuses, carriages, and streetcars that filled the thoroughfares alongside pedestrians, shoppers, street vendors, shopkeepers, city employees and workers of all sorts. However, Monday, November 4, 1872, was no usual day. The streets were virtually empty of traffic. A few delivery boys trundled handcarts, an ox-drawn cart plodded along, its bells swaying in a slow rhythm, and a furniture wagon appeared, two men pulling and two men pushing it down the street. A reporter walking around the city saw only a few horses and one mule between one and eight P.M. The front page of the *Philadelphia Inquirer* reported "The City Well Nigh Horseless." Philadelphia's horses had succumbed to a virulent strain of equine influenza known as "the Great Epizootic" that afflicted the nation's horses in 1872 and 1873.

As horses remained in their stalls, shivering, coughing, runny-nosed, streaming-eyed, and weak, city life came to a standstill, because horses provided the motive power for urban transportation, hauling, and construction. Streetcar companies suspended service, undelivered freight accumulated at wharves and railroad depots, consumers lacked milk, ice, and groceries, saloons lacked beer, work halted at construction sites, brickyards, and factories, and city governments curtailed fire protection and garbage collection. Only a general strike by every teamster, worker, and municipal employee could have produced the same effect. The *Philadelphia Inquirer* noted, "our business houses have been made to feel the important part played by the horse in the daily routine of business life."

The Great Epizootic of 1872 and 1873 was a dramatic demonstration of the extent to which cities relied on horse power. The disease first erupted in Toronto at the end of September, spread northeast to Montreal and Quebec, south to Detroit, Buffalo, and Rochester, and then along the Erie Canal, shutting down traffic. It traveled down the Hudson River and the along the railroad lines, infecting horses in city after city. The epizootic reached Brooklyn, New York City, and Boston by October 22 and spread along the coast and through the interior of New York and New England from the Catskills to Maine. At the end of October it appeared in Philadelphia and New Jersey and progressed to western Pennsylvania, the Upper Midwest, and the Upper South. By December the epizootic was in Atlanta, Memphis, and Milwaukee, then traveled across the West, sickening horses at army outposts early in 1873 and in Sacramento by April. The scale of the Great Epizootic as an animal epidemic was unprecedented—it sickened horses in thirty-three states.

Its worst impact was in urban areas, where the disease spread "with unexampled rapidity . . . attacking its victims with startling violence."[4] A few horses would begin to cough and sniffle, and then the disease would erupt in stable after stable. Horses with influenza suffered symptoms familiar to any human victim of "the flu"—rapid onset of extreme fatigue, muscular weakness, fever, aches, and a general lack of interest in eating or moving. Horses stood or lay miserably in their stalls. Few actually died; the fatality rate from the influenza itself averaged only 1 or 2 percent. Most horses improved within a few days, but full recovery took ten to fifteen days, and working horses not given enough time to recuperate suffered relapses and developed debilitating or fatal secondary complications.

The epizootic was most severe in the cities of the Northeast. In Boston, where it was estimated that more than 50,000 horses shared the city with 250,000 human residents, the disease appeared on Tuesday, October 22, and within forty-eight hours an estimated seven-eighths of the horses were ill. The disease raced through the city's stables, especially the large stables of street railways, stage and omnibus lines, express and trucking companies, and the city government. As one paper put it, "Business requiring the assistance of the equine tribe has received a severe shock." Farmers feared to bring their horses into the city. Funerals and weddings were disrupted by lack of horses for hearses and carriages. The Fire Department suspended the use of horses, and attached drag ropes to steam engines so that humans could pull them to fires. People talked of using small steam engines or "steam dummies" on streetcar lines.[5]

Just as the epizootic abated, events in Boston took another catastrophic turn: on the evening of Saturday, November 9, a fire broke out in downtown Boston that burned sixty-five acres of the business district, destroying 766 buildings and one schooner at the wharves before it was finally contained three days later. One of many factors delaying containment of the conflagration was a lack of fire engines, because many of the fire horses were still too weak to work.

The Great Epizootic brings to light a little-recognized aspect of American history: the dense horse populations that resided in Gilded Age cities. So powerful is the association of horses with nature that to many, horses seem inherently incompatible with urban life. Yet into the twentieth century large populations of horses (and other animals) lived and worked in cities alongside humans.

One source of this misconception is the relative absence of horses from many urban photographs before the 1880s. Photographic wet plates needed subjects to remain utterly still for ten to fifteen seconds—an impossible requirement for horses. Photographers often took pictures on Sundays, when there was little vehicle or pedestrian traffic to blur the image. The resulting photographs gave an imposing, classical impression of American cities but excluded evidence of horse-drawn traffic. Occasionally these pictures contained "ghosts" that upon close examination prove to be legged blurs produced by the movement of horses while the plate was being exposed. All this changed in 1879, when John Carbutt introduced the first commercially successful dry plates, with an exposure time of slightly over one second. These plates had the ability to capture motion. This technological advance brought photography closer to being "an art of actuality." From then on, horses appeared in pictures of urban life.[6]

Horses jammed the streets of Gilded Age cities, working in transit, industry, construction, shipping, commerce, and municipal government. They hauled streetcars, omnibuses, drays, delivery wagons, and private vehicles. Horses delivered raw materials to factories and trucked away the finished products. Horses delivered building materials to construction sites, dug foundations, powered cranes, and hauled away the dirt from excavations. They loaded ships, dredged harbors, and hauled in fishing nets. Horses brought produce, dairy products, meat, grain, and hay from surrounding areas into city markets to feed urban consumers and returned stable manure to hinterland farms. Horses conveyed baggage and packages, carried freight to and from railroad depots and shipping piers, distributed coal, milk, ice, bread, and produce, delivered furniture and other consumer goods to homes and beer to saloons. They pulled fire engines, ambulances, street sweepers, and garbage wagons. Horses provided virtually all the power for the internal circulation of city life because no other prime mover could compete with them technologically.

Railroads stimulated urban growth, but they did not fit very well into urban life. Many municipal governments were reluctant to have steam locomotives traveling within city limits. The chief concerns were fires started by sparks scattered from passing engines, and accidents at crossings. Moreover, locomotives were nuisances: they were deafeningly loud even apart from their bells and whistles; they belched thick smoke, shook foundations, and cracked street pavements. Because of the political and economic power of railroad companies there were tracks through some urban neighborhoods, and their presence prompted ongoing battles between railroad and residents. The files of the Philadelphia and Reading Railroad are filled with letters of complaint about fires that occurred at properties adjacent to the tracks, demands to limit the ringing of bells and whistles, and claims for runaway horses and smashed carriages. The company posted flagmen and constructed barriers at grade crossings, investigated accidents, and determined liability for horses, vehicles, and dead or injured pedestrians and passengers. Chronic conflict over the ways in which railroads disrupted urban life and endangered urban residents fueled labor agitation against the railroads in some cities and contributed to the Great Strike of 1877. Danger and inefficiency kept the use of steam limited in urban transportation except on tracks leading out of the city. There simply was no viable mechanical alternative to horses as urban prime movers.[7]

Photographs taken along Philadelphia's Market Street near the turn of the century reveal a city inhabited by horses and humans. At the Delaware ferry pier at the foot of Market Street, wagons, horse-drawn cabs, and carriages crowd the area, discharging passengers, baggage, and packages. In the first half-dozen blocks away from the river, electric streetcars mingle with heavy wagons, light wagons, covered wagons, two-wheeled drays, buggies, and pedestrians. Large wagons line the street backed into the curb at an angle, their two-horse teams eating a midday meal from small portable troughs set in front of them on the street. Men with wheelbarrows and handcarts trundle through the traffic. By the corner of Eighth and Market, the angle-parked wagons have disappeared, but wagons, carts, and carriages fill the street. Pedestrians are everywhere, on the sidewalk and in the street, crossing at every point and intermingling with the streetcars and wagons.[8]

In 1900, when urban horse populations were at their peak, the average density in the cities of the Northeast was 396 horses per square mile, and in midwestern cities 541 per square mile. (Densities were lower in western and southern cities). The average density for the forty-six largest cities in the country was 426 horses per square mile. In that same year, New York and Chicago each averaged just under 500, Boston nearly 700, Cincinnati over 600, and

Horse market in Madison, Wisconsin, ca. 1900. Wisconsin Historical Society, image 4648.

Milwaukee came in highest with 709 horses per square mile. In Philadelphia there were nearly 400 horses per square mile, or over 50,000 horses in the entire city. Given the still rural nature of the northwestern and far northeastern sections, densities in the center city and its adjacent districts were probably higher.[9]

Horses resided everywhere in nineteenth-century cities. Livery stables hired out horses, wagons, and carriages for temporary use and housed workhorses and private carriage horses. Many hotels maintained livery operations that hired out horses and vehicles in addition to providing transportation for their guests and lodging for guests' horses. Blacksmiths and horseshoers sometimes boarded horses in space alongside their shops, as did many small businesses that already kept a horse or two for their own delivery or production work. The residential patterns of horses reflected the income and occupation of their owners and users. Elite carriage and riding horses lived in private stables in the best neighborhoods or in luxury livery stables. Working-class horses lived in large, sometimes multistoried livery, freight, express, or streetcar stables, or in small stables tucked between homes and businesses. Lower-class horses lived in shacks, sheds, and cheap livery stables with poor sanitation.[10]

Fire insurance maps for the city of Philadelphia in 1872 show stables located in every neighborhood. In the section bounded by Front Street and the Delaware River on the east and Eleventh Street on the west, and from Vine Street on the north to South Street, an area of approximately 130 blocks, there were as many as 175 identified stables of varying sizes. Streets such as Cherry, Arch, and Filbert, which ran parallel to Market Street to the north, had a stable on almost every block, and stables were clustered within a few blocks of Market on the north-south streets as well. In the block delimited by Spruce and Pine and Fourth and Fifth Streets, there were five stables and two livery operations, sharing the area with a Baptist church, the Knapp Barrel Organ Factory, a brick pressing shop, steam laundry, blacksmith and carpentry shop, wheelwright and machine shop, tin shop, locksmith, confectionary, Chinese laundry, "segar" factory, school, and meeting room. In the block formed by Chestnut and Walnut between Sixth and Seventh, the stables of the Central News Company and another stable shared the area with the *Central News* office, Holy Trinity Roman Catholic Church and its cemetery, and the First Presbyterian Church.[11]

Urban horses presented a more varied assortment of breeds and types than were seen in the countryside: teams of enormous draft horses, weighing a ton or more each, pulling the largest, heaviest wagons, mid-sized workhorses and leggy carriage horses, elegant thoroughbreds, hackney carriage ponies with high-stepping action, even the occasional mule and donkey. Purebred heavy draft horses were most likely to be found in the cities, because of their useful status appeal there but also because only year-round urban work could justify the expense of their daily grain requirements. Between 1860 and 1880 crossbreeding with large European draft horses increased the average size of the American draft horse from 900–1,100 pounds to 1,800–2,000 pounds. The majority of horses on the streets were geldings, since stallions were considered dangerous and often banned from city streets by ordinance, and mares were sometimes considered less prestigious or useful as work animals.[12]

Horses were ubiquitous in the urban landscape: standing, walking, trotting, sometimes shying, starting, falling, rearing, plunging, or bolting. They were large beings with which to share space, standing from four to six feet at the shoulder, eight or more feet in length, and weighing 800 to 2,000 pounds. Pedestrians moved around horses on the streets and encountered them at eye level, their work clearly visible in their flexing of muscles, straining, and sweating as they pulled heavily loaded wagons and streetcars. The smells of manure, sweat, and horsehair mingled with other urban smells of garbage, human waste, and industrial production. Horses contributed to the symphony of urban noise—hooves clattering and scrapping on the streets, wagons rattling and banging, wheels creaking, harness jingling, horses whinnying, neighing, groaning, and bugling.

Along with human residents, horses contributed to the growing filthiness of American cities with their rudimentary infrastructures. The average horse produced twenty to fifty pounds of manure and a gallon of urine daily, distributed freely between stables and streets. With 131,000 horses in New York City by 1900, the result was 1,300–3,300 tons of horse manure daily in the city as a whole, or 5–12 tons per square mile given a horse density of 486. The carcasses of horses that died in the streets often lay for several days before being removed by street or sanitation departments or by jobbers contracted to the city. New York had 15,000 horse carcasses per year in the 1880s. Adding to manure and carcasses was the enormous amount of garbage, refuse, and waste generated by humans. City governments established street-cleaning departments and invested in street-sweeping equipment (pulled by horses, who of course dropped more manure as they were driven around cleaning up piles of manure), tried to pave streets with materials that would be easier to clean, and passed ordinances regulating manure piles at stables. They passed laws regarding human waste and garbage as well. Many cities sold stable manure, street sweepings, and night soil to farmers in the immediate hinterlands, whose farms produced the hay, grain, vegetables, fruits, and meat consumed by equine and human urbanites.[13]

Horses were also important urban consumers. Necessities like hay and grain were provided at first by a number of small dealers, and purchased directly from farmers in the local markets. However, the demand for hay and grain from many, large urban horse-based establishments, like the railways, express companies, and teaming firms, aided a shift to larger dealers and commodification of hay and grain. Many businesses supplied an ever-widening array of vehicles and all manner of horse furnishings to urban markets. Abbot, Downing & Company produced a wide range of vehicles for commercial, institutional, and private use: stage coaches, fire wagons, patrol wagons, express wagons, New York drays, and dry-goods wagons (styles unique to New York), ice wagons, hotel buses, ambulances, sleighs, streetcar sleighs. Companies produced an astounding range of products for horses. Some businesses made goods for horses as part of a wider array of products. For example, hatmakers also made straw sunhats for horses; these were good for keeping flies and sun off city horses in the summer and amounted to a sizable business. A long list of jobs depended on urban horses: smiths, farriers, cabmen, stable jobs, carters, horse dealers, horse breakers, horse breeders, knackers, livery stable owners and workers, manufacturers of horse-related objects such as harness and wagons, and the many people they employed. Economic historian F. M. L. Thompson classifies the urban horse as "a producer good with a vital economic function."[14]

The majority of urban horses worked hauling freight into and around the city. There was hardly a raw material or finished good that did not travel by horse power at some point between production and consumption. Large companies, such as the railroads, express companies, and department stores, maintained quite large stables, but smaller businesses kept their own horses and wagons as well. Freighting absorbed horses from mass transit; horses that had worked for four or five years pulling streetcars were moved into urban hauling. As markets and outputs expanded, the number of freight horses rose even higher. The number of urban teamsters grew faster than the rest of the urban population. The electrification of the streetcars in the 1890s that eliminated most of the streetcar horses hardly affected the size of the urban horse population, which underwent one of its largest increases during the same decade. The surge in freighting occurred in tandem with growing mechanization in the wagon industry, which increased production and lowered the price of vehicles.[15]

Horses and wagons helped advertise businesses and products by being part of the message being conveyed to consumers. Some businesses made a specific breed or color of horse their trademark or used elaborate turnouts of wagons, horses, and harness. Horses were a symbol that identified the company on sight. In Philadelphia the department store Strawbridge and Clothier had a fleet of elegant delivery wagons pulled by dapple-gray horses, housed in a large company stable in the center of the city. The R. McAllister Coal Company used matched four-pony teams decked out in elaborately studded harness with jaunty cockades between their ears. Four gray horses in fancy harness and bells pulled the sturdy, elegant wagon of the Great Western Meat Market. The Knickerbocker Ice Company identified its product and address prominently on the side of its boxy covered wagons and put bells on its horses. Small proprietors used their wagons for advertising too—a photograph of Mr. P. Castelli, of Castelli Fruit and Produce, 7286 Woodland Avenue, shows him standing proudly with his wagon and two horses.[16] Less visible were the horses that worked in manufacturing, construction, and shipping. Horse treadmills provided power for small enterprises and enabled people with limited capital to enter mechanized production. Philadelphia brickyards and lumberyards used horses to drive brickmaking machines and saws until the end of the century. On construction sites, horses excavated foundations and lifted materials into place. Horse-powered cranes loaded and unloaded ships; horses powered dredging pumps in the harbors and hauled in nets of shad along the Delaware River.[17]

City governments employed growing numbers of horses, especially in the wake of the city consolidation and reorganization that occurred during the second half of the nineteenth century. As municipal governments achieved more social and political control, they established professionalized departments for fire, police, and public health that used many horses as part of their work. As police departments were responsible for larger urban areas, they organized mounted police units to patrol outlying districts and to provide crowd control in case of riots and strikes. With an expanded jurisdiction, they needed paddy wagons to convey prisoners to jail. Municipal fire departments with paid personnel on duty around the clock replaced volunteer, neighborhood-based hose companies. When heavy steam engines replaced hand-pumped machinery, horses were necessary to pull them. Elaborate mechanisms swung the harness onto the horses and rapidly hitched them to the equipment. Changes in fire-fighting equipment and organization shifted human labor to horse labor. Public health departments maintained fleets of horses, wagons, and equipment for street sweeping and waste removal of all kinds—garbage, human waste, manure, dead animals, and so on.[18]

It is unclear whether urban horses were dangerous, whether nineteenth-century urban dwellers perceived them as dangerous, or whether they saw horse behavior and incidents as normative and took them in stride. On the one hand, horses were a familiar technology whose limits and risks were well known, but on the other hand, many urban dwellers did not directly own or use horses, and their knowledge of their handling and behavior may have resembled the average automobile driver's understanding of the physics of driving and the mechanics of engines. City folk were around horses, but they did not always know very much about them.

Few accident statistics predate the earliest twentieth century, and much evidence is anecdotal. Risk and danger are not inherent conditions, but highly relative perceptions. The cited dangers of horse-driven traffic must be understood within the context of nineteenth-century traffic control, of which there was none. Cities did not institute systems of traffic police and mechanical signals until the twentieth century. Traffic controls relied on systems of one-way streets, parking and speed regulations, and rules about right of way. There were few policemen delegated to traffic duty. New York City gave right of way at intersections to north- and southbound vehicles, mandated signaling by drivers, forbade stopping and parking except in designated areas, and limited speeds to five miles per hour for business vehicles and eight miles per hour for passenger ones. Speed limits could not be enforced because there was no way to measure speed anyway. Since the streets were congested, speeding was rarely an issue. It is hard to imagine that horse-drawn vehicles traveling two to five miles per hour were dramatically more dangerous than heavy metal cars and trucks traveling ten to forty miles an hour.[19]

Since nearly all mass transit was horse-drawn until the end of the century, streetcar horses were the single largest group of equine workers within the urban herd and played one of the most significant roles in urban development. Mass transit appeared during the rapid urbanization of the antebellum period, when operators of interurban stagecoaches began using the coaches within cities as well. Called omnibuses, these vehicles followed established routes like stagecoaches, but picked up passengers at any point along the way. They first appeared in 1829 on New York City streets, where they were immediately popular, multiplying to seventy within a year. In 1831 the Boxall Hourly Stage Coach inaugurated regular service along Chestnut Street in Philadelphia. Philadelphia had eighteen lines of omnibuses by 1848, employing 138 omnibuses, 600 horses, and almost 700 drivers and hostlers. By the 1850s there were 700 New York City omnibuses while Philadelphia had over 300; St. Louis had ten different omnibus routes, each running cars every ten minutes.

As omnibuses proliferated, new vehicles were designed that looked like boxier stagecoaches and could hold twenty or more passengers. Some of these had seating on the roof, accessed by a small, steep stairway on the back. However, they were quite heavy and had a high center of gravity that added to overall draft. Ill-maintained cobblestone streets and unpaved muddy streets made them even harder to pull and maneuver. Competition between omnibus lines sent omnibuses careening through the streets, adding to traffic congestion and chaos and sometimes capsizing at corners or colliding with other vehicles.[20]

The 1850s saw the construction of horse or street railways to replace many omnibus lines, though some omnibuses remained in service where the railways did not run. These omnibuses on rails combined the benefits of horse-drawn transportation with low-friction rails. They traveled six to eight miles per hour, about twice as fast as the omnibuses. The first streetcar operated in New York City in 1832, but it was the 1850s before streetcars were widely adopted, once the technical innovation of using a grooved rail set flush with the pavement removed people's objections to raised rails that obstructed other street traffic. Proponents argued that railways would bring more order to traffic and be easier on the horses. With this technical logjam eliminated, horse railways, "a fundamental American innovation in public transit," expanded rapidly, and the 1860 census listed fifty-seven companies with 403 miles of track in seven cities. Street railways operated under franchise agreements with state or city governments; in many municipalities they were required to purchase the equipment of omnibus companies in order to overcome the strenuous opposition of the latter, which rightly foresaw their own displacement.[21]

Even smaller horse railways employed hundreds of horses, and the largest ones employed thousands, housing them in huge, multistoried city stables. In 1859 the Metropolitan Railway Company in Boston owned 528 horses to operate forty-four cars over twelve miles of track, and the Third Avenue Railroad of New York City owned 570 horses to operate twelve omnibuses and seventy-one cars over six miles of track. In 1890 the eleventh census enumerated 488 companies with 4,062 miles of track employing 84,000 horses in 331 municipalities, and there may have been as many as 100,000. A sixth of these were small railways of less than 10 horses in small towns, newer western towns, or smaller cities with several small lines, while Chicago, Baltimore, Louisville, Detroit, Minneapolis, Brooklyn, New York, Buffalo, Cincinnati, Philadelphia, and Providence had multiple railways, some of them employing more than 1,000 horses. The nine Philadelphia railways that answered census inquiries averaged 527 horses apiece; the largest of the group owned 1,460. The West Chicago Street Rail Road Company listed 4,200 horses and the Brooklyn City Rail Road Company a whopping 5,300. The West End Company of Boston claimed 7,600 horses, and the city was said to contain 10,000 in all, while the City of New York (exclusive of Brooklyn) had 12,000. Railway horses were generally indeed horses, as there was little or no use of mules in northern cities, though southern lines used them. A Minneapolis street railway used mules for a few years but abandoned the experiment.[22]

Streetcar work, with its constant stopping and starting, was fatiguing, and horses could work effectively for only three to six hours a day. Companies quickly learned that it was cheaper to keep more horses working fewer hours than the reverse. Streetcars ran frequently, some lines as often as every five or seven minutes. Companies maintained anywhere from four to twelve horses per car, depending on whether it was a one- or two-horse car, and on length of route, and tried to keep reserve horses to replace those sick or injured, and to augment teams on steep hills or in bad weather.

Street railways were particularly lucrative enterprises, and they attracted the interest of people with capital and power. There was stiff competition for franchises to operate a business for private profit on public streets. Horse railways demonstrated the growing availability of capital and the development of business vehicles that could pool capital and invest in new technology. In keeping with the business trends of the times, horse railways tried to control markets and reduce costs by consolidating into larger systems.[23]

Philadelphia had one of the largest horse railway networks. The state chartered three railways in 1857, and a year later the first one, the Frankford and Southwark, began service. By 1860 franchises had been awarded to sixteen more companies, and the city had 148 miles of track, or 37 percent of the national mileage. By the time crowds poured into the city for the Centennial of 1876, Philadelphia had seventeen companies and 289 miles of track under the cooperative control of the Board of Railway Presidents. That year the city's horse railways carried 117 million passengers. By the mid-1880s there were 429 miles of track over which 222 million passengers rode.

The Union Passenger Railway Company leased the Continental Passenger Railway Company and the Seventeenth and Nineteenth Streets Passenger Railway Company in 1880 to bring its holdings to seventy miles of track, while the People's Passenger Railway Company leased the Germantown Passenger Railway Company and the

Green and Coates Streets Passenger Railway Company to unite forty-four miles of track. Together the Union and the People's served 41 percent of the city's railway passengers. In 1883 two of the wealthiest men in Philadelphia, P. A. B. Widener and W. L. Elkins, merged six companies to form the Philadelphia Traction Company, which soon controlled a third of Philadelphia's 320 miles of track and served 117 million passengers as part of a national syndicate that controlled horse railways in Chicago, New York, and Pittsburgh. Electrification further hastened the process of consolidation, and by 1896 there was only one street railway company in Philadelphia.[24]

Most of the expenses of horse railway companies were horse-related. The companies were large consumers of hay, grain, shoes, harness, horses, horse tools, medicines, and the services of farriers and hostlers on a scale that would have been familiar to any Civil War quartermaster. They also purchased streetcars, rails, paving materials, and other equipment. Railways tried to rationalize their operations as much as possible. Even the smaller horse railways needed considerable management to coordinate diverse inputs of capital, labor, and commodities in order to achieve the complex goal of providing a schedule of streetcar service. Streetcars did not run twenty-four hours a day, but the companies did because of the need to care for the horses.

Railway management wanted to maximize profits by establishing schedules that kept cars fully loaded and by keeping overhead costs down, but they also wanted to provide regular service, maintain the condition of the horses that provided their motive power, and calculate what level of horse care was good enough. Managers read the nutritional analyses from the new agricultural colleges and end-lessly discussed the optimal amount to feed horses, the nutrition and energy content of different horse foods, different types of food preparation—chopped, cooked, steamed, or dry—and the most economical feeding schedule. As they dealt with horse ailments, they considered whether to employ people trained in veterinary medicine. They debated different methods of shoeing and different brands of shoes. They evaluated different paving materials in terms of direct cost and in terms of the traction it provided, perhaps offering savings in horse fatigue and reducing the number of leg injuries, and calculated the maximum gradients for hills. They established operating rules to minimize accidents and liability. Knowing that the work life of a car horse was only three to five years, they calculated the best age at which to buy and sell horses. They might reduce a horse's shift in exchange for getting maximum effort during each hour the horse worked. They looked for lighter, stronger streetcars from manufacturers, and other improvements in horse-drawn rail. They had to meld work schedules, duties, and rules oriented to equine needs with quite different work schedules for humans.

Managers used horse behavior to rationalize operations. They encouraged strong bonds between horses and drivers by assigning horses to the same drivers. They permitted drivers to name the horses and encouraged them to groom them, an activity that copied horse grooming behaviors and encouraged horse-human bonding. In heavy urban traffic, with its lack of traffic controls, horses had to rely on their drivers for direction and reassurance. Horses learned to recognize their own names and their drivers' voices. A skilled driver could steer through traffic, avoid accidents, and limit unwelcome horse behaviors by using his voice as well as reins and brakes in the cacophonous streets. Companies also tried to use new standards of public behaviors, collectively defined as "respectability," as a form of labor control. Owners of railways joined humane organizations, which by raising awareness about animal welfare provided an audience to monitor and enforce driver behaviors and treatment of their horses. But drivers of streetcars (and also drivers of freight wagons) could be caught between the needs of their horses and the needs of their bosses, finding that their job was in public view even as they were squeezed by demands for speed and efficiency from management that a middle-class public did not see or chose to ignore.[25]

Horse railways altered the physical area and spatial organization of the city as a whole. The preindustrial "walking city" had remained geographically compact because the distance a person could commute on foot was approximately two miles. Neighborhoods, though distinguished by social, commercial, and manufacturing differences, still lay in close physical proximity to each other and made the city socially and economically heterogeneous through this physical and visual contact. But the widening use of streetcars—which coincided with many city consolidation efforts—expanded the average commuting distance from two to three miles, and more than doubled the potential residential area of cities from 12.6 to 28.3 square miles. For example, in West Philadelphia real estate developers obtained charters for streetcar lines to connect the central business district with suburban areas and to facilitate the sale of lots and homes. In Boston the number of commuters had already tripled by 1860. Though not alone a sufficient explanation for suburbanization, horse-driven mass transit nonetheless provided the technological component creating the "streetcar suburb."[26]

The horse railways inserted travel space between work and residential areas, and between the neighborhoods of different classes and ethnicities. In doing so they broke the city into components organized around economic function and class, and then rearranged them into a new pattern of concentric rings fanning out from the center. Horse railways eased some of the congestion of the cities but also segmented urban life. Affluent residents began to withdraw from urban life. They moved to the periphery of the city and or the suburbs, fled environments and populations they found distasteful, pursued the pastoral ideal of a country or suburban home, and dealt only with select aspects of city life.

At the same time, the expansion of mass transit began to change the meaning of the streets as urban public space. Urban residents often mounted strenuous opposition to railways, opposing not only the use of steam engines on the streets but also the construction of horse-drawn railways, because *any* railway changed the purpose, meaning, and control of the streets. As a letter from residents of Fifth and Sixth Streets in Philadelphia to the state legislature stated, "But while this company only asks you this year for passenger travel by horse locomotion, what reason have you to believe that next year they will not be knocking at your doors for FREIGHT trains and *steam?*"[27]

Streets had traditionally been multipurpose spaces used for commerce, socializing, recreation, parades, speeches, demonstrations, and transportation, and clogged with vehicles, vendors, pedestrians, playing children, and foraging animals. Owners of street frontage, known as abutters or fronters, considered themselves the owners of the street space between their properties, in part because they traditionally footed the cost of street repairs. Any kind of railway, with its fixed rails, encouraged through traffic and faster-moving vehicles, redefined the street's primary purpose as a transportation artery—a space to go through rather than a place to go to—and lessened the neighborhood's power to enforce invisible social boundaries. Nor were horse railways the only special interest to claim the use of public space. Urban elites persuaded city governments to construct parkways and carriage roads at public expense, which much of the public was prohibited from using.[28]

Urban residents claimed that streetcars would increase traffic congestion, ruin property values, endanger pedestrians, disrupt other traffic, create noise, cause accidents, and make neighborhoods accessible to unwelcome populations. They also objected to city and state governments' asserting authority over the streets through railway franchises and giving public space to private railways to use for private gain. The railways asserted their authority by reconstructing and paving the streets. Horse-powered railways were instruments by which legal principles of reasonable use, powerful private interests, and a broadly defined public interest altered the meanings of common space and neighborhood space. One example was the issue of snow removal. Horse railways needed to clear their rails in order to keep functioning, but residents objected because cleared streets made it hard to use sleighs and other vehicles with runners during snowy weather. Through these and countless other issues, horse-drawn mass transit reshaped the physical, social, and political landscape of cities.[29]

People experimented with alternatives to both horse power and steam power for mass transit and urban hauling. In the innovative spirit of the times, they explored the use of compressed air, ammonia gas, giant batteries, internal combustion, mammoth springs, and mechanical draft animals. While there were some successful prototypes using these power sources, most were less economical, efficient, and reliable than horses. Some cities built cable railways, in which the cars attached to cables that were pulled through underground conduits and driven by steam engines located in central power stations. This arrangement applied steam to mass transit without using steam locomotives. Advocates of cable promised enormous savings, unlimited passenger capacity, and clean, noiseless, effortless operation.[30]

Cable railways proved useful in cities with steep hills where using horse-drawn cars was extremely difficult. San Francisco built the first (and only remaining) cable system in 1873. Newer cities that were just beginning to build transportation infrastructure were interested in cable technology too. Chicago, Los Angeles, and twenty-five other cities constructed cable lines. But cable railways proved to be inefficient, expensive, and cumbersome. Conduits and powerhouses required elaborate and expensive construction. A mile of single cable could cost more than $65,000 dollars, and a double cable $100,000, six to ten times more than an equivalent mile of horsecar line. Ninety-five percent of the energy went into moving the cable, and because the whole cable always had to move, no energy savings were possible during off-peak hours. There were miles of complicated underground mechanisms that frequently broke down. Engine problems, frayed cables, broken mechanisms, and driver error could bring the entire system to a halt because it was so highly centralized. Some cable railways gave up and began using horses. In 1897 a fire in the main powerhouse for the Washington, D.C., cable system shut down the entire system, stranding cars everywhere along the line and leaving managers scrambling to find horses and harness so they could rescue the cars and resume some kind of service. The company converted to electricity shortly thereafter.[31]

Horse railways are often described as deficient and inefficient because horses could get sick or injured. Yet one incapacitated horse did not stop the whole system, while one broken cable or engine brought an entire cable railway to a halt. Horse railways remained sufficiently decentralized in terms of power to prevent systemwide collapse. In 1872 there were those who announced that the Great Epizootic demonstrated the limits of horse power and who called for alternatives. But although the epizootic had shut down entire streetcar systems, such widespread horse epidemics were rare, and despite persistent fears, the Great Epizootic did not repeat itself. Horses continued to be superior prime movers compared to proposed alternatives, and as a result the railways had considerable technological momentum. And as we have seen, horse railways were profitable. Any new technology had to beat the horse on economy, efficiency, reliability, flexibility, and costs.[32]

The only power source that competed successfully with horses was electricity, and its advent trumped cable and, to a lesser extent, steam power. Electric motors had been around for several decades, but it was not until 1888 that Frank Sprague, a former naval officer and employee of Thomas Edison, devised a workable solution to the problems of electric traction and of conveying current to moving streetcars. Sprague demonstrated the success of his innovation by successfully electrifying an entire railway in Richmond, Virginia. Electricity, like cable, was not just a substitute for horse power; it required an entirely different way of organizing the generation, transmission, and application of power and the distance over which it could operate. The initial cost of electrification was high, but the operating costs per mile were quite a bit lower than for horse power. The Panic of 1893 and the resulting depression forced many smaller railways out of business. The result was the consolidation of streetcar railways into more centrally owned and managed systems. Electricity succeeded as motive power because it replicated the decentralization of the horse-based system while employing a powerful, centralized power source. In 1890, 70–90 percent of street railway miles used animal power alone or in combination with steam and cable. By 1902, 97 percent were electrically powered, and the miles operated by horses dropped from over 4,000 to less than 200.[33]

Even after making the transition to electricity, railways did not get rid of horses entirely, but maintained numbers of them for construction work, repair crews, and providing extra traction at hills and crossings. As one writer stated in 1892, "There is room, place and convenience for every system of transportation ever yet devised . . . so, too, horses have still a niche in the methods of transportation." Horses still powered feeder lines and omnibuses connecting with streetcar lines. The West Chicago Railway kept 250 horses for its wrecking or emergency-assistance service. The Chicago City Railway divided its system into seven wreck-wagon districts, kept two shifts of horses harnessed and ready each day, and claimed that the wreck wagon had a response time of eight minutes to any wreck within a radius of two miles. As with steam railroads, electricity could be applied only to vehicles that operated over prescribed routes and remained connected to a central power source. And it powered only mass transit; attempts to include freight transport with streetcar service were not successful, because horses were still needed at each end of the streetcar line. For self-propelled traction, horses had no serious technical competition as the century ended.[34]

The development of the industrial city was inseparable from the industrialization of agriculture in the Gilded Age. Urban growth accompanied the rising productivity of commercial agriculture. Even as urban life became increasingly differentiated from rural life, cities and hinterlands became ever more economically interdependent. Both depended on horse power. For example, the Great Epizootic was not only an urban story. Its impact on the hinterland was less visibly dramatic, but no less serious. *The Nation* described horses as "wheels in our great social machine, the stoppage of which means widespread injury to all classes and conditions of persons, injury to commerce, to agriculture, to trade, to social life."[35]

Mechanization had brought horses into agricultural production during the 1830s and 1840s. It is commonly assumed that horses were always used in agriculture, but before the invention and availability of mechanical agricultural implements in the middle decades of the nineteenth century, most farm work was performed by humans using hand labor and few horses. After midcentury, the widening use of agricultural machines that applied horse power to more aspects of farm work increased the number of horses used. This agricultural revolution followed the transportation revolution that increased farmers' access to new factory-produced machines and new markets. Each stage of agricultural production can become a bottleneck for lack of labor or energy, but mechanization relieved one bottleneck after another in northern agriculture by applying horse power to agriculture. Both the transportation revolution and the agricultural revolution increased reliance on horses as prime movers.

Though often described as "labor-saving," mechanization does not so much reduce labor as relocate it. As the superintendent of the 1860 census noted, "It is now established, as general principle, that machines facilitating labor increase the amount of labor required."[36] Mechanization—replicating the motion of the human hand with a mechanical device that can be driven with a source of power other than human muscle—transfers labor from one worker to another, relocates labor within the process of production, or replaces one kind of job with another.

In northern agriculture, mechanization shifted labor from humans to horses, developing machines that horses could push, pull, or drive with their legs and feet by using the motion of walking or trotting. When humans perform agricultural tasks or any other physical work, they apply muscle power to tools through prehensile hands attached to arms that are not needed for support and locomotion. Since horses don't have prehensile hooves and haven't a leg to spare, the only way to transfer labor to them is to convert their linear motion into the kind of power needed for the machine.

Plowing was one of the most energy-intensive tasks in farming, accounting for over half of the power used to raise a crop. It often took several people as well as draft animals, and was so brutal that people often used oxen instead of horses. For plowing, mechanization involved solving the problem of draft in mass-produced plows. What farmers needed were light, rugged plows that would cut through the soil with as little friction as possible. In 1814 Jethro Wood patented the first successful cast-iron plow, and by the 1860s steel plows and chilled-iron plows that scoured, or shed, soil easily and held an edge had reduced the amount of power needed to pull the plow and made possible other plowing innovations including the sulky plow, with a seat for the farmer, and gang plows, with multiple blades.[37]

Easing the bottleneck of plowing encouraged the invention and production of other agricultural implements. The most important and famous of these was the reaper for harvesting wheat and other small grains. These crops were easy to grow and found ready markets, and were often the first crop of market-oriented farmers in newly settled areas. But few tasks required as much labor as harvesting. If farmers could plant only as much as they could plow, it was equally true that they could plant only as much as they could harvest, and harvesting was tied to the amount of labor they could count on when it was time to bring in the crop. To harvest ten acres of small grain took approximately fifteen laborers—five to scythe the grain and ten to rake, gather, and bind it. As with plowing, the window of opportunity was narrow: when the crop was ready, it had to be brought in quickly to avoid rot and other damage. The president of the Pennsylvania Agricultural Society said, "Nothing is more wanted than the application of animal power in the cutting of grain. It is the business on the farm which requires the most expenditure, and it is always the most expensive labor." The reaper was "the Holy Grail of farm technology."[38]

Obed Hussey in 1833 and Cyrus McCormick in 1834 developed the first workable reapers. The first challenge was to replicate the action of the scythe. Hussey and McCormick circumvented this by using a sawing device to cut the grain. Another problem was draft. Reapers operated on power from the wheels, which was transmitted to the gears of the machine. This entire mechanism had draft. The exterior frame of the reaper was a wheeled vehicle, subject to all the draft problems of any horse-drawn vehicle. The manufacturers of reapers and other farm equipment would address these problems of draft continually as they designed and marketed their equipment.

Since horses provided nearly all the power used for agricultural production, farmers wanted low-draft machines, and they called implements with excessive draft "horse-killers." Manufacturers used draft as a way to compare their machines with those of their competitors. In an 1852 circular the McCormick company promoted "McCormick's Patent Reaping and Mowing Machine!" as having "a rate at which a pair of horses might work for a whole day . . . and with little distress, for this machine appears not only to be lighter in itself, but to work with more ease to the horse than the

Threshing with horse sweep power, ca. 1900. Wisconsin Historical Society, image 31821.

other, being so balanced as to throw a very slight pressure on the horses' backs."[39] Hallenback's "improved" mowing machine was configured to make "the line of draft counteract the resistance of the grass to the sickle," producing steadier motion and "no side draught." In 1866 Joseph A. Saxton took over a patent on a grass harvester, modified "to diminish its pressure on the ground and obviate side draft and friction." The Patent Office reissued Samuel S. Allen's patent for the cutting gear on harvesters in 1870, which established better "center draft" and thus prevented the tendency, "found in other harvesters," to swing around against the horse's shoulder.[40]

Testimonials from farmers about how machines eased the labor for horses were a popular advertising device. A McCormick circular from 1859 quoted farmer John H. Talcott: "I find no difficulty in using the McCormick machines with one span of horses." Solomon and Jacob Call attested that they cut sixteen to twenty acres a day with four horses, and William W. Williams said he had cut seventy acres of grain and grass with a two-horse machine with no change of horses required. Manufacturers also listened to feedback from farmers. As the users of reaper technology, farmers often made their own adjustments to the machines, and they wrote to McCormick and other companies to describe their improvements and offer suggestions. B. F. Northcott wrote the McCormick Company that he had invented a sickle adjuster to "save time, horseflesh and wear and tear . . . [and to] reduce the draft fully one third." Nor were innovations limited to the machines, but included ways of harnessing large teams of horses that would maximize their power and reduce draft and fatigue. Luther Traline informed the McCormick Company that he had applied for a patent on a "three horse draft equalizer especially adapted to binders and wide cut mowers."[41]

McCormick's patent applications showed that he recognized that horses were living machines and that good design was not just a matter of reduced draft. McCormick experimented with different designs, in one patent putting the horses behind the reaper so they

"McCormick Day" in Owosso, Michigan, ca. 1900. These events were sponsored by the company so that farmers could display newly purchased McCormick machines. Wisconsin Historical Society, image 24791.

could push the machine and claiming that the "method of attaching the tongue, when behind, to the breast of the horse, enables him to guide the machine with accuracy."[42]

Horses produced stationary power for threshing, corn shelling, grinding, baling, binding, and winnowing by means of the sweeps and treadmills similar to those used to power horse ferries. These devices went by a variety of names: horse whims, horse engines, horse gins, horse wheels, horse walks, and, most commonly, horse powers. A sweep or capstan device was an ancient method of processing farm and forest products in areas without water power. The sweep had a vertical gear mechanism in the center, with horizontal wooden poles extending to a twelve- to twenty-foot radius. The diameter of a sweep device had to be at least twenty-five feet so that the horses could work effectively. Horses were hitched singly or in pairs to the ends of the poles. As the horses walked, they drove the gears of a differential, spinning a vertical rod that ran down to a universal joint and bearing box on the ground. This transmitted power to a tumbling rod, which extended horizontally to outside the circumference of the horses' path and turned on its longitudinal axis. This rod transmitted power through another joint and box to another tumbling rod, which connected to a machine. Because the tumbling rod crossed the path of the horses, horses had to step over it as they went around. Horses that stepped on the rod damaged it, and often got seriously hurt as well. Sweep manufacturers began to encase the rods and central gears, and some states even passed laws requiring such housings. A one-horse sweep could deliver almost two-thirds of a unit of horsepower (the output of an engine, defined as 33,000 foot-pounds per minute, 550 foot-pounds per second, or 746 watts). Attached to a thresher, a two-horse sweep could thresh 200 bushels a day and an eight-horse sweep 400 bushels or more. Some of the largest sweeps used fourteen horses hitched in pairs to the poles.[43]

The treadmill was also referred to as a railway horse power. A

Horse-powered device (sweep design) for threshing grain. Patent illustration, 1834. Wisconsin History Society, image 46465.

treadmill was a highly tooled, industrially produced mechanism. It resembled a horse stall with half-walls on the long sides and was elevated at one end. Between the side walls, a continuous belt made of wooden slats joined with metal or leather links and, supported by rails, moved across a row of friction wheels along each side and around a horizontal drum at each end. A horse was led into the treadmill and tethered. When the brake was released, the weight of the horse set the belt in motion, forcing the horse to keep walking and turning the treadmill. Treadmills came in one-, two-, and three-horse models and were mounted on wheels so that they could be moved around as needed and parked out of the way when not in use. Whereas work on a sweep resembled pulling a vehicle and, if it involved a lot of horses, used them more as a group of workers, work on a treadmill reduced a horse to nothing more than a machine used for its power.

As historian Joel Tarr has noted, sweeps and treadmills were "the only fractional horsepower motors available before oil engines in the 1890s and rural electrification half a century later."[44] One of their most important use was the processing of hay. Traditionally hay was transported and sold loose, not in bales. Hay is both heavy and bulky, and these factors limited its market range to the distance a farmer was willing to drive. Farmers drove loads of hay to towns and cities and sold it loose from their wagons. Urban hay markets developed where the farmers gathered, and the quality of hay was identified with individual farmers, groups of farmers, or localities. Until the 1830s the only way of making bales involved laboriously stuffing hay into boxes by hand and stamping it down. Most Union Army hay depots during the Civil War had huge mounds of loose hay (which was one reason the railroads disliked shipping hay for the army).

The advent of hay presses in the 1830s made it easier to compress hay into bales. Baled hay was easier to handle and transport, and more of it could be transported. In the 1850s the price of hay presses began to drop and became affordable by ordinary farmers. Some of these were hand-powered, but an increasing number were horse-powered. In 1857 Nourse, Mason & Company advertised "Dederick's Patent Parallel Lever Hay Press," with a horse-driven capstan that formed a bale in just five turns and promised to bale five to nine tons a day. The number of hay presses on the market proliferated, and included a two-horse hay press that baled eight to twelve tons a day. By the end of the century a sweep-powered hay press was advertised as baling twelve to eighteen tons a day with two horses. Hay baling was a task often done by hay-baling outfits that either moved from farm to farm or located their press in a central location where farmers could bring their hay.

Two implements had already affected the labor-intensive process of hay harvesting. The horse-driven hay rake became common after the 1830s, replacing the hand labor of raking and turning the cut hay. The development of the reaper led to the development of the mower, a similar but slightly different machine. Mechanization transformed hay production to meet rising demand. Field implements made it possible to produce more hay, and processing implements made it possible to market more hay. Horse-driven machinery added sufficient value to hay production to cover the expense of using horse labor. Hay production rose from thirty-five million tons to ninety-seven million tons in the three decades after 1879. In the North, 20 to 25 percent of all cultivated acreage was used for hay. With the number of horses employed in the cities and their hinterlands on the rise, the urban hay demand rose. Hay presses expanded the reach of the urban hay market so that more distant farmers could sell hay in the cities through hay dealers. Hay bales were not standard in size or weight, and as face-to-face transactions between producers and consumers declined, it was hard for consumers to know if they were getting fair weight and quality for their money. To bring order to the marketing of hay, urban authorities organized hay exchanges that regulated bale weights and established a grading system for hay quality, ending the identification of hay quality with specific producers and replacing it with impersonal market standards. The commodification of hay resulted from horse-powered hay mowers, rakes, forks, and presses that increased production, sped up processing, and expanded markets.[45]

Steam power entered agriculture production gradually and, as elsewhere in the economy, as a complement to horse power. Steam engines produced stationary power for the tasks of processing. Steam engines had powered sugar mills and cotton gins since before the Civil War. In wheat-growing areas, steam-powered threshing machines appeared in the 1870s and 1880s, drawn by horses from farm to farm. Threshing outfits were like small factories, involving a steam thresher, several reapers, several wagons, large numbers of horses, and smaller numbers of humans. Horse-drawn combines, or combined machines, which cut, gathered, and threshed, were manufactured in California in the 1850s and pulled by twenty-to-forty-foot teams. They became a staple of West Coast and Great Plains agriculture. Once again, horses and steam engines worked together.

Toward the end of the century, small portable steam engines that could be used like sweeps and treadmills to run threshers, fanners, shellers, and the like became more widely available. What remained problematic was combining steam power with self-propulsion. It was one thing to invent a self-propelled steam engine, and another to invent one that worked under actual farm conditions, operating on soft, uneven ground without sinking in or tipping over. In other words, a self-propelled steam engine had to be like a horse. In agriculture, steam worked best for stationary devices until successful steam traction engines were developed at the end of the century. Horses remained the most reliable source of motive power in agriculture until the 1930s.[46]

The industrialization of horse-powered agriculture made gains in productivity and output. The number of people supported by each farm worker rose from four in 1840 to seven in 1900. In wheat production, the number of manhours per acre dropped from 35 in 1840 to 15 in 1900, and manhours per 100 bushels from 250–300 to less than 50. For corn, it dropped from 75–90 manhours per 100 bushels in 1850 to 40 in 1890. Using horse power, agricultural productivity doubled in the second half of the century as technological changes in agriculture reinforced each other.[47]

Horse-drawn agricultural machines cemented the relationship between the individual farmer and the economy of industrial capitalism. Manufacturing was only one step away from agriculture and depended on the rural and farm market. Farming "acted as a magnet drawing people, capital and natural resources into its productive processes." The self-sufficient, idealized yeoman farmer had long disappeared. In the Northeast and Midwest, farmers were fully integrated into the economies of the urban hinterland, and horse-powered machinery emblematized industrialized agriculture.[48]

Mechanization accelerated the change from oxen to horses that had begun during the antebellum period. Most new implements required the fast-paced horse to provide enough speed to drive the ground wheels that operated the internal mechanism and propelled the machine. Oxen were not fast enough, and they could not be made to go any faster. The changes in oxen demographics map the decline of the subsistence farmer and the expansion of industrialized, mechanized agriculture.

The Gilded Age was the age of steam and steel, big business and heavy industry, urban growth and immigration, a railroad network flung across the continent and bridges across the biggest rivers. However, the horse was far from its way to quaint oblivion. There were more horses employed more widely than ever. The majority of horses resided east of the Mississippi, in the most industrialized, populated portion of the country, the cities and hinterlands of the Northeast and Midwest. Horses supplied a majority of the power consumed in the United States.[49]

Horses powered the expansion of industrial capitalism through urban growth and agricultural development, which in turn expanded the use of horses. Whether in city or hinterland, urban street or farm field, horses were indispensable and irreplaceable as industrial workers. As consumers they provided an enormous market for the products of farms and factories. Horses were not a marginal segment of the industrial economy; horses defined the economy. Dependency on the horse peaked in the closing decades of the nineteenth century.

Englishwoman Anna Sewell published the novel *Black Beauty*, subtitled "The Autobiography of a Horse," in 1877. The narrator of this first-equine account is the title character, Black Beauty, a well-bred pleasure horse raised on a country estate. Beauty's life becomes a descent through the equine class system, from fashionable London carriage horse to livery horse, cab horse, and cart horse. Rescued from the slaughterhouse by a kind farmer, Beauty is returned to the countryside of his youth. Beauty's *Candide*-like journey through the urban, industrial world of the late nineteenth century describes this society and its treatment of horses from the horse's point of view.[1]

Sewell wrote *Black Beauty* as a user's guide aimed at the growing number of people owning and working with horses—it was a technical manual for a horse-powered world. She shaped her novel for working-class readers, using a familiar, satisfying plotline, exciting episodes, accessible language, and short, focused chapters that teach simple lessons about using and taking care of horses, or about horse behavior. Sewell often contrasts people who are ignorant about horses with those who are knowledgeable. For example, the man who hires Beauty as a livery horse assumes that his limp indicates laziness, whereas a passing farmer shows that there is a painful stone lodged in Beauty's shoe. Sewell also teaches about equine psychology and behavior, telling readers that horses' senses and instincts are usually sound, and that they are never willfully "bad" so much as misunderstood. Nor are these lessons just for the working class; Sewell also criticizes upper-class folk who abuse horses with cruel practices like checkreins and tail cropping, destroy horses in the careless pursuit of pleasure, and pressure the working class into overworking their horses.[2]

Sewell likes the world of horses and humans as coworkers and coresidents, and never suggests that progress demands replacing horses with other prime movers. However, she does express considerable concern about how other power technologies affect the way horses are used. A recurring theme in *Black Beauty* is the relationship between the treatment of horses and the widening use of steam engines. One of her equine characters complains that humans "think a horse or pony is like a steam engine or a thrashing machine, and can go on as long and as fast as they please; they never think that a pony can get tired or have any feelings."[3] The worst treatment Beauty suffers is from urban folk with a "steam-engine style of driving."

These drivers were mostly people from towns, who never had a horse of their own, and generally traveled by rail. They always seemed to think that a horse was something like a steam-engine, only smaller . . . they think that if they only pay for it, the horse is bound to go just as far, and just as fast, and with just as heavy a load as they please. And be the roads heavy and muddy, or dry and good; be they stony or smooth, up-hill or down-hill, it is all the same—on, on, on, one must go at the same pace, with no relief and no

consideration . . . This steam-engine style of driving wears
us up faster than any other kind. I would rather go twenty
miles with a good considerate driver, than I would go ten
with some of these; it would take less out of me.[4]

As a young horse, Beauty learned not to be afraid of steam locomotives on the railroad tracks adjacent to his field because they "never came into the field, or did me any harm." However, steam engines had changed expectations about speed, power, and endurance, and fundamentally altered perceptions of horses, creating a growing disjuncture between horses and industrial society. It was as if the railroad had jumped its rails and intruded into the horse's sphere after all.[5]

Black Beauty's fame in the United States grew after 1890, when the American Humane Education Society published and distributed the first American edition at the urging of the society's founder, George Angell. Angell felt that the novel described American society as well as British society. He predicted that *Black Beauty* would have "as widespread and powerful influence in abolishing cruelty to horses as 'Uncle Tom's Cabin' had on the abolition of human slavery . . . I am sure there has never been a book printed in any language the reading of which will be more likely to inspire love and kind care for these dumb servants and friends who toil and die in our service."[6]

If any year could be said to mark the apogee of the horse world, the year 1890 would be an appropriate choice. Angell's argument gained its force from the fact that horses, quite literally, had power and were quite vital, valuable, and visible prime movers. Never had the use of horses been as extensive or as intensive. Horse populations continued to burgeon, and the amount of animal power being used increased despite the addition of electricity and internal combustion to the energy ecology. Horses still supplied a third of all power and attracted considerable scientific, technical, and economic attention. Yet even as horses remained of critical importance, there were also questions raised about their role in an urban industrial society. *Black Beauty* mapped the intellectual, economic, and affective underpinnings of the technological world of the late nineteenth century, and pointed to the transition away from horses that would occur in the twentieth century.

Sewell was adamant in *Black Beauty* that horses were not machines, but sentient beings. Nonetheless, horses clearly were the living machines of the nineteenth century. Humans had debated the relationship between animal bodies and machines since ancient times, and in the context of industrial society the question was even more salient. Was the machine a useful metaphor for the animal body, a heuristic device for studying its mechanics and organic processes, or was the machine an *actual* description of the animal body? Sewell's rejection of the machine heuristic was at odds with attempts to expand knowledge about horses that placed the horse squarely within the machine analogy. By the midnineteenth century, developments in biology, physics, and chemistry had blurred the boundaries between the mechanical and the organic, and no more so than in discussions about the nature of energy, and whether living organisms and inanimate movers were powered by the same natural forces. Many technical manuals analyzed the mechanics of equine locomotion and draft alongside those of inanimate prime movers, and increasingly they pondered the nature of horse power in relation to other kinds of power, to determine just what kind of engine the horse was. The dependence of industrial society on horses, the study of motion and energy, and concerns about horses as animals all made horses the focus of engineers, agricultural experts, veterinarians, urban reformers, and social elites during the late nineteenth and early twentieth centuries.

The evolution of photographic technology played a critical role in expanding knowledge about horses as prime movers. Even after centuries of observation, aspects of horse locomotion remained unknown because horses moved too fast for the human eye to track their movements accurately. One of the oldest questions about horses was whether there were moments at the trot or gallop when all of a horse's feet were off the ground. In the 1870s the development of instrumentation that made it possible to measure what the eye could not see revitalized this issue among artists, engineers, cavalry officers, equestrian experts, and elite horse owners. The new technology of photography resolved questions about the ancient technology of horses. The publication of Eadweard Muybridge's sequential photographs of equine motion advanced a mechanical understanding of the horse.

Eadweard Muybridge was born in 1830, immigrated to the United States from England in the 1850s, and became proficient in the new technology of photography. By the 1860s he had a studio in San Francisco, and his acclaimed scenic photographs of the Yosemite Valley made him known to Leland Stanford. Stanford had come to California from New York in the 1850s, became governor of California in 1861, and was elected to the U.S. Senate in 1885. One of the founders of the Central Pacific Railroad, Stanford oversaw the construction of the transcontinental railroad during the 1860s. Like other newly minted millionaires, Stanford acquired a country estate—in this case a ranch in Palo Alto, now the site of Stanford University—and began breeding and training racehorses. In 1872 Stanford engaged Muybridge to photograph the motion of his horse Occident, a record-breaking trotter noted for his unusually long stride. Occident had a rags-to-riches story—Stanford had seen him pulling a wagon in Sacramento and recognized his potential as a trotter. The horse was an equine Horatio Alger.[7]

The challenge for Muybridge was designing an apparatus that could freeze a moment of the horse's motion as it moved past him at approximately thirty-eight feet per second. At this time, the wet collodium plates used by photographers had an exposure time of ten seconds, so that capturing motion was extremely difficult. Muybridge compensated for the exposure time of the wet plate with a very quick shutter speed produced with a specially constructed device. Though the picture he finally obtained of Occident was a blurry silhouette, nonetheless it froze a moment of motion on film. Muybridge became occupied with photographing the Modoc Indian Wars in northern California, and standing trial (and being acquitted) for shooting and killing his wife's lover.[8] In the meantime Stanford continued to explore the subject of equine locomotion and discovered the work of French physiologist Etienne-Jules Marey. Marey wanted to establish universal laws of mechanics for animal and human bodies. Deeply influenced by the work of Hermann von Helmholtz, a German scientist of animal motion who had formulated the first law of thermodynamics, Marey saw the law of the conservation of energy as a fundamental link between the organic and inorganic and the basis for a unified theory of explanation. In his opinion, "The laws of mechanics are applicable to animated motors as well as to other machines." Marey wanted to isolate motion from the physical body and to describe it as a purely abstract relation between time and space. His goal was to "describe that economy of motion and establish the laws of motion of the body." He based his studies on physiological time, or the reaction time of muscular action. Marey invented a number of instruments to easure bodily functions and convert those measurements into graphic inscription. In 1874 he devised an apparatus for graphically recording the paces of the horse. This work was reported in *Popular Science Monthly,* and a subsequent book, *Animal Mechanisms,* was translated into English and circulated through the horse world.[9]

But Stanford thought Marey was wrong about equine locomotion and resumed his project with Muybridge in 1878. Muybridge contrived an apparatus in a shed on Stanford's ranch. He covered one wall in white canvas marked with evenly spaced vertical lines, and parallel to this wall placed twelve cameras at regular intervals with their shutters attached to strings. Occident would move between cameras and wall, trotting over the strings at a steady pace and tripping the shutters as he went. The black lines on the white background would indicate speed. When the strings distracted Occident and caused him to break stride, Muybridge eliminated the strings by using a device with two crossing shutters attached to strong metal springs released with an electric signal. This shutter arrangement also provided a short exposure time. In addition, Muybridge could use the newly invented dry plates, which had an exposure time of slightly more than one second. Muybridge took a sequence of detailed pictures of Occident trotting and of a galloping horse as well. These photographs were published in the San Francisco papers and featured on the cover of the October 19, 1878, *Scientific American* with the caption "The Science of the Horse's Motions." *Philadelphia Photographer,* the most prestigious photography journal in the country, stated that the photographs enabled the viewer to "imbibe all the energy of the horse."[10]

The publication of Muybridge's horse photographs brought him into contact with Marey. In 1881 Muybridge went to Paris and was received as a celebrity by Marey's circle, which included artists and scientists, among them Helmholtz. Muybridge's photographs convinced Marey to use photography instead of graphic inscription in his work, but their work would develop in different directions. Marey, whose work became the foundation for the industrial-motion studies of Frank Gilbreth and others, wanted to abstract motion and link it to time intervals, whereas Muybridge was focused on breaking the motion of humans and animals into component phases.[11]

In Philadelphia Muybridge's photographs attracted the attention of Fairman Rogers. Born into elite Philadelphia society, Rogers was somewhat of a Renaissance man who studied engineering at the University of Pennsylvania, joined Alexander Bache's surveying

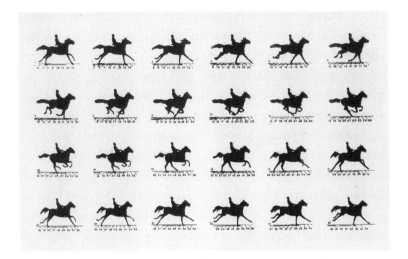

Motion of a galloping horse, based on Muybridge photography. Source:
J. D. B. Stillman, *The Horse in Motion* (Boston, 1882). Fairman Rogers
Collection, University of Pennsylvania.

project in the 1860s, and then taught engineering at Penn for fifteen
years, after which he became a trustee of the university. Rogers was
also a patron of the arts, a trustee of the Academy of Fine Art, and an
avid horseman. Known for the fine carriage horses stabled at his
home on Rittenhouse Square, he was the first man in Philadelphia
to drive a four-in-hand coach, and authored the definitive technical
manual on driving. Rogers also accumulated a large collection of
American and European books on horse care and veterinary medicine, and worked with the veterinarians who founded the Veterinary School at the University of Pennsylvania.

Rogers commissioned the artist Thomas Eakins, who taught at
the Academy of Fine Art, to produce a painting of him driving his
four-in-hand coach that would accurately depict the motion of the
horses. Eakins used the Muybridge photos to understand equine
motion and drew Marey-like representations of the trajectories of
the hooves; he also experimented with motion photography himself. In 1880 he completed the painting *A May Morning in the Park,*

also known as *The Fairman Rogers Four-in-Hand.* It was a pleasing composition of Fairman Rogers, his wife, and others driving along a carriage road in Fairmont Park that employed characteristic Eakins renderings of light, shadow, and color. However, the painting was controversial for challenging centuries-old conventions about how to render equine movement. Before the 1870s, trotting and galloping horses were pictured with legs outstretched front and back, looking, as one writer said, "as if . . . shot from a cross bow and moving at a mark without any agency of their own." Some artists found the new photographic evidence liberating, some doubted it, some were embarrassed to have previous efforts shown wrong, and some raised aesthetic questions about the relationship between photography and painting.[12]

In 1884 the University of Pennsylvania, no doubt influenced by Rogers, now a trustee, and Eakins, a member of the project committee, brought Muybridge to Philadelphia to do an extensive photographic study of human and animal locomotion. Between 1884 and 1897 Muybridge produced hundreds of photographs of humans, clothed and unclothed, male and female, engaging in walking, running, jumping, riding, and various sports. Rush Shippen Huidekoper, the first dean of the Veterinary School, appeared in the photographs, sometimes clothed and sometimes discretely nude, riding and jumping his favorite mare, Pandora.[13] Muybridge photographed horses of all kinds, including workhorses pulling heavy loads and circus horses doing stunts, and he branched out to include farm livestock. He also went to the Philadelphia Zoo to photograph wild and exotic animals such as big cats and camels. He published *Animal Locomotion* in 1887, *The Science of Animal Locomotion* in 1891, *Animals in Motion* in 1899, and *The Human Figure in Motion* in 1901. Muybridge then returned to England, where he died in 1904.

Muybridge's earlier photographs were popularized in 1882 in *The Horse in Motion,* written by one Dr. J. D. B. Stillman and pub-

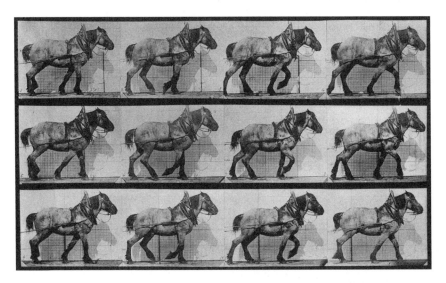

Motion of a draft horse at work. Plate 565 from Eadweard Muybridge, *Animal Locomotion* (1887; reprint, New York: Dover, 1979). Rare Book and Manuscript Library, University of Pennsylvania.

lished by Leland Stanford. However, *The Horse in Motion* contained no acknowledgment of Muybridge, describing the images as made "under the direction of Mr. Stanford" and being "the results of Mr. Stanford's experiments with twelve cameras."[14] What falling-out or misunderstanding occurred between the two men is unclear. After the success of the first photographs in 1878, Muybridge had begun work on a new series in 1879, using twenty-four cameras instead of twelve, and photographing various farm animals and humans in addition to horses. Stanford had underwritten the cost of the apparatus and paid Muybridge's expenses, and the relationship continued until Muybridge departed for Paris. Muybridge sued Stanford but was unable to block publication of the book.

Stillman embedded the purloined photographs in commentary that blended natural history, mechanical science, artistic concerns, and social belief. Stillman argued that the photographs provided scientific evidence for a new theory of animal locomotion. Traditional, commonsense explanations and conventional representations of equine locomotion based on sensory evidence alone were no longer adequate; authoritative knowledge now derived from empirical evidence obtained through instrumentation in laboratory settings that permitted verification through repetition. (Stillman provided descriptions of the methodology.) By isolating the phases of animal locomotion, photographic evidence revealed universal principles of animal locomotion. Reflecting the interests of his patron, Stanford, Stillman focused on the ways in which this knowledge could advance correct artistic representation and improve the breeding and training of racehorses.

In what was becoming almost a ritual in books about horses in the Gilded Age, Stillman framed his discussion by emphasizing the horse's historical, cultural, and religious significance.

> The Horse of all animals, holds the most important relations to the human family . . . the relative importance of the horse as a factor in the progress of civilization has been reduced by the introduction of steam in our century, it cannot be forgotten that he has been the constant of the Caucasian race . . . We have no history that is not interwoven with his; and if by some cataclysm he should be eliminated, we should then be made to realize how indispensable he still is to our business and pleasure. Whatever concerns him will never cease to interest mankind.

The horse revealed the design of an orderly Creator, whom Stillman also referred to as "the Master Mechanic," because the horse was both functional and beautiful. "Beauty of form is never lost sight of in the construction of the horse; and even great sacrifices of mechanical power are made to maintain graceful lines, and that general contour of form that gave to him his matchless beauty,— beauty so great that to the eye of a superficial observer it is difficult to decide whether it is subordinate to strength or conversely." The horse's perfection was evidence for the spiritual origin of the organic world.[15]

Much of the book was an earnest, didactic explanation, using mechanical principles and simple machines, of how the horse was engineered. "A knowledge of the construction of the machine is imperative upon one who would comprehend its action. It is as necessary as for an engineer to understand his engine." Bones were levers, "on which the muscles act, and by means of which their power is made available," analogous to "the piston, connecting-rod and crank of a steam engine." Muscles were pulleys, powered by "will" transmitted through tendons and nerves. Even though muscles were "subject to fatigue, and are unable to respond indefinitely with equal force to the will," yet in the design of muscles and tendons, compared to a "humanly contrived machine . . . nature has done better and contrived a way to avoid friction and wear that human ingenuity cannot hope to rival." Limbs were a system of levers that permitted flexion and extension and got the advantage of length without stiffness. Differences in design and purpose among the horse's limbs and structural elements were subsumed in their functioning according to universal mechanical laws. All the gaits of the horse obeyed these laws. The camera showed each gait to be composed of a never-varying series of positions, shaped by the speed of the horse in relation to the forces of momentum and gravity. Speed, however, came at the expense of power, and vice versa.[16]

Stillman believed that better knowledge of nature gave men power to shape nature with intelligence and skill. A scientific understanding of equine structure and locomotion improved the selection and breeding of horses. Better knowledge of nature gave men power to shape nature with intelligence and skill. "If we have comprehended the movements of a limb and the relative value of the forces that produce them, the levers on which they act and the relation of the limbs to each other, we ought to be able to determine the mechanical elements of the qualities desired in a horse." However, Stillman was less concerned with improving the physical power of workhorses than with artistic patronage and elite horse breeding. Photographs made it possible for artists to represent nature more accurately. "Quadrupeds will be recognized as being possessed of locomotive machinery, self-moving, with all the parts acting in perfect harmony and not passive projectiles" in the conventional way of depicting horses; art based on correct knowledge could present "the true theory of quadrupedal motion."[17]

Much of the work of Muybridge, Stanford, Marey, Rogers, Eakins, and Stillman was linked to aesthetic questions and even elite concerns; this linkage was particularly evident in *The Horse in Motion*. Yet their work also reflected a significant change in the approach to horse technology as a form of knowledge. Traditionally, knowledge about horses had been gained through personal, immediate experience and was often transmitted orally. Learning about horses was a kind of apprenticeship. Muybridge's photographs and Marey's graphic inscriptions and photographs produced a new kind of knowledge. It not only required the mediation of technical apparatus, but it was entirely independent of physical contact with actual horses. This change in the sources and nature of technical knowledge about horses reflected a larger trend toward professionalism that accompanied the rise of industrial capitalism in late-nineteenth-century America.

Professionalism delineates a systematic body of knowledge and skills that are specialized, standardized, goal-oriented, scientific, and acquired through formal education. The emergence of corporate capitalism, the growing importance of technological innovation and industrial specialization as a factor in economic growth, the expansion of a national market, and the development of an urban, cosmopolitan, mobile culture created the conditions for increased professional employment. Many professions asserted the special status of their occupations, legitimized through training in professional schools, credentialing by professional organizations and licensing by the state. By 1900 the majority of the professions had established these institutional structures, setting the stage for a new generation of professionals based in cities and universities. But the success of the professional claim to status rested on the ability to claim their importance to society. Because horses remained an essential source of physical power, professional groups could construct their professional identity and their claim to social and cultural authority around their knowledge about horses.[18]

One of these groups was engineers, who had long been interested in questions of equine locomotion and energy conversion, and for whom the practice of referring to horses (and other animals) as machines was not new. Engineers had both theoretical and applied interests in horses. How were horses like machines? How did they convert energy into power? How did they move? Was it possible to replicate horse motion mechanically? Was it possible to improve equine power, efficiency, and endurance? These questions particularly engaged civil engineers designing and constructing transportation projects, and mechanical engineers working on issues of energy conversion, transmission, efficiency, friction, draft, and work in prime movers. Engineers and doctors studied the photographs of Muybridge and his continuing experiments at Penn with interest. Interest was often rooted in a concern with efficiency, "one of the central concepts of engineering in the late nineteenth century."[19]

Engineering was a profession undergoing a dynamic transition. There were few formal schools in existence before the Civil War. Two of the most important were West Point, whose primary function was producing military engineers such as Montgomery C. Meigs, and Rensselaer Polytechnic Institute, which established an engineering program in 1835. The primary site of engineering education, however, was the construction site of every road, canal, railroad, bridge, tunnel, dam, mill, and steam engine. Consequently, engineering began as a fluid occupation, where the number of men who entered it through apprenticeship on these sites first outnumbered those with formal training, and where the terms "engineer" and "mechanic" were used interchangeably. By the 1880s, however, engineers with formal training were distinguished from mechanics with experience but little formal, scientific education. Furthermore, technological changes fragmented engineering into new specialties. When the American Society for Civil Engineering was founded in 1852, "civil engineering" meant nonmilitary, "civilian" engineering. For example, both Alexander Holley and Robert Thurston graduated from Brown University in the 1850s with degrees in civil engineering. Holley became the first president of the American Institute of Mining Engineers in 1876, while Thurston became the first president of the American Society of Mechanical Engineers in 1880. Other engineers formed the American Institute of Electrical Engineers in 1884. To some extent, engineering divided into those who worked on machinery, those who constructed and supervised public and private works, those who dealt with the mining process, and those who designed large electrical power systems and equipment, though in this time of rapid technological change these distinctions were not always hard and fast. Horses continued to attract attention from all these subspecialties, and the ability to improve horse efficiency and power was related to claims of professional status.[20]

In 1893 Englishman Thomas H. Brigg presented a paper, "Haulage by Horses," at the annual meeting of the American Society of Mechanical Engineers, later published in the society's *Transactions*. Brigg asserted that the conditions of haulage were a critical problem for mechanical engineers, because "a horse is simply a living machine," governed by the same mechanical principles as inanimate machines. "Its power to pull or haul loads is determined by the conditions under which it is placed and the amount of energy it possesses." Mechanical engineers had improved the use of steam and electricity, so why not the use of horses as well? As Brigg put it, "Much attention has been given to the development of breed in horses, and the result has been a vast improvement in their strength, speed and beauty. But while we have been developing horses that are capable of doing better work, we still handicap them by the unscientific methods under which we require them to labor, and there is an absolute loss, in many cases, of 50 percent of their strength."[21]

Brigg focused on the mechanics of harnessing, the means by which power was transmitted from horse to vehicle. "In the simple matter of so hitching a horse to a wagon as to lighten his load we encounter scientific problems based on scientific principles, and yet almost everybody treats the subject as one of common character ... What would the world think of an engineering firm that worked on such a basis?" By observing people and horses doing pulling and lifting, and by using sequential photographs to reveal the mechanics of haulage, Brigg measured the magnitude and direction of draft. Witnessing two horses being beaten for not pulling a load, he asked: "Are the horses attached to the load in a manner which will give then the greatest possible control over it? ... No, they are not because they are relying almost entirely on their own unaided weight for the force they exert, and they are unable, by reason of the direction of their traces, to exert anything like their full natural strength." Correct harnessing enabled horses to deliver more power with less fatigue and longer endurance, just as correct gearing improved the efficiency of inanimate machines.[22]

In order to overcome the resistance of the load, Brigg argued, horses needed traction so that they could engage the strength of their legs (levers, in mechanical terms) to provide pulling power. How much force the horse could exert against the ground—a function of both the horse's weight and the traction or footing—determined how much pulling power the horse had. What horses needed was friction, and the greater the load, the greater the downward force of friction the horse needed. Harnessing mediated the transfer of friction between the horse and the vehicle.

Brigg showed that a horse and vehicle, connected by harness, were each a lever, connected by the front wheels. The angle of the harnessing affected the distribution of weight between the ends of the lever. The vehicle, at one end of the lever, could be loaded and harnessed in such a way as to create an upward or a downward force on the horse. An upward force that lifted the horse literally made it weigh less by counteracting the pull of gravity. In this case "the vehicle supported the horse," an advantage with light loads or on a level or downhill grade. However, if a horse was trying to pull a heavy load or to pull uphill, against gravity, it actually needed to carry more weight to get the friction it needed for traction. Weight could be transferred from the vehicle to the horse through the harness. What was needed was some way of regulating the upward and downward force in accordance with different conditions and loads. "Therefore, to deal justly with our horses, we should not only study cause and effect but should devise some means by which, automatically, every possible advantage could be given to the horse at all times. Otherwise, there must be a constant waste of energy."[23]

Brigg had invented such a device, a spring arrangement for vehicles that would adjust the distribution of weight between horse and vehicle and make horses more efficient. While many people invented devices to ease horse draft during the nineteenth century, Brigg's process of invention differed in that he began with a framework of carefully articulated scientific principles, formulated a series of experiments, and analyzed technical data from photographs and instruments. Brigg's work represented the shift occurring at the end of the nineteenth century to more self-conscious, science-driven invention. He exemplified the growing professionalization of engineering by linking his immediate topic to broader social and economic concerns. For example, unlike Stillman and Stanford, Brigg studied urban workhorses, whose numbers were increasing dramatically at the time. Brigg was concerned with the shift from two-wheeled carts to four-wheeled wagons in city hauling, because wagons put more strain on horses. He linked horse efficiency to social and economic efficiency, and, as shown by the example of the teamster beating the horse, to moral concerns as well, such as the humane treatment of animals.[24]

The audience for Brigg's paper at the ASME annual meeting included Robert Thurston, one of the most eminent engineers of the nineteenth century. Born in Providence, Rhode Island, in 1839, Thurston earned an engineering degree from Brown University in 1859, worked for the family steam-engine works, served in the Navy's Engineering Corps during the Civil War, and afterward taught at the Naval Academy. His growing reputation as an expert on steam engines and industrial production led to an offer to become chair of engineering at Stevens Institute, in Hoboken, New Jersey, in 1871. During his fourteen years at Stevens, he created a curriculum in mechanical engineering, established the first mechanical engineering laboratory in the United States, and in 1880 became the first president of the American Society for Mechanical Engineering. In 1885 Thurston went to Cornell University to head the Sibley College of Engineering, where he remained until his death in 1903.[25]

Thurston was a prolific author of articles, manuals, and textbooks. He wrote extensively on steam boiler design, construction and operation, including *A Manual of Steam-boilers, Steam-boiler Explosions in Theory and Practice, Stationery Steam-engines,* and the two-volume *Manual of the Steam Engine.* One of his most important books was the *Treatise on Friction and Lost Work in Machinery and Mill Work,* a work that paralleled Marey's research in the 1860s and 1870s on the "lost work" between stimulus and response in physiological processes. In addition to these practical works, Thurston was interested in the theoretical aspects of energy and deeply influenced by the formulation of the laws of thermodynamics.

Like Brigg, Thurston believed that improving the use of horse power was important as a matter of science, commerce, and philanthropy. As Brigg said, "We have more to do in the development of horse power in this country than we have yet to accomplish in the development of the steam engine . . . In the application of horse power, the methods of application to useful purposes are comparatively crude, and subject to very great improvement." It was as important to improve horse power as it was to improve steam power, "as a matter of philanthropy, but commercially of great value."[26]

In 1894 Thurston published his own work on animal power, *The Animal as a Machine and a Prime Mover and the Laws of Energetics,* which incorporated the research of Brigg and others on animal mechanics, set within a broad theoretical framework. Though the title referred to "animals," the book focused primarily on horses. Thurston's purpose was "to describe, briefly and exactly, the characteristic of the animals as motors, to describe their methods of action and their sources of gain and loss of energy, and to present the principles of energy-production and transformation illustrated by them." Like Brigg, he was interested in the problems of transmitting power, a topic that had received relatively little attention in the history of power. He believed it was essential that mechanical engineers include horses in their investigations. "The object of the engineer in designing mechanism is to effect this transfer of energy and these transformations at the least cost and with the least 'running expense' and hence with maximum efficiency of apparatus."[27]

In the first section of the book, "Energy and Its Transformations," Thurston offered a primer on energy. He identified six kinds of energy in wide use—fossil fuels, falling water, wind, the tides, electricity, and muscle action—and the six kinds of motors, or prime movers, that transformed this energy into power—animal bodies, heat engines (including steam, gas, and solar), water wheels, tidal machines, windmills, and electrical engines. Prime movers "are those machines which receive energy directly from natural sources, and transmit it to other machines which are fitted for doing the various kinds of useful work." Thurston focused on transmission machinery because it was the greatest cause of inefficiency. While the input of energy always equaled the output of work, this output consisted of both useful work and lost work. According to the law of the conservation of energy, energy was never lost, but according to the law of entropy, some of it could dissipate and become unavailable for use. Friction was "the principal cause, and usually the only cause of energy and waste of work in machinery," and occurred in the process "transmitting energy from that point at which it is received to that at which the work is done, i.e. from the 'driving' to the 'working' point."[28]

Like Brigg and other engineers, Thurston defined horses as machines. "The engineer regards the animal system with peculiar interest, as a machine of singularly complicated structure, a heat-engine or other prime motor—he is not certain as to its classification—of extraordinary efficiency, and as an embodiment of the scientific problems of the greatest interest and greatest obscurity." The problem lay in defining what kind of machine they were. Somehow horses generated thermal, mechanical, electrical, and "vital" energies that resulted in work, both mental and physical, and in waste, which took the forms of heat and of urine and manure, which Thurston referred to elegantly as "the rejected potential energy of incomplete chemical action." Thurston concluded that within itself, the animal machine functioned with high efficiency, but the actual processes by which it converted energy to power remained "a standing riddle and challenge to the man of science and the engineer."[29]

Instead, Thurston concentrated his attention on the effective application of animal power. The primary consideration of work efficiency was the relationship between load and speed. At maximum load, the horse does minimal work (work being defined as the product of weight and the distance moved, measured in foot-pounds), but the same is true at maximum speed when it can carries little or no load. Maximum work occurs at an intermediate load and speed. Thurston reviewed various equations for connecting the time, effort, and power of animals, but noted that they were "approximate, at best, since the conditions of each case are certain to differ." While he estimated the maximum pulling power of a horse to be one-fifth of its weight, the actual work of which it was capable depended "upon its exact accommodation to most favorable conditions for the development of the best work of the individual, and upon its size, natural strength, endurance and spirit." Conditions affecting horse efficiency included breed, health, general condition, training, temperament, food (Thurston analyzed the energy values and nutrition of various foods), road surface, weather, climate, the draft of vehicles and harnessing, and human skill. Animal machines, therefore, were highly specialized; engineers had to select them carefully for both the kind and conditions of work and handle them "in such a manner as to give maximum returns for his expenditures."[30]

Given that animal prime movers were highly specialized and affected by a wide variety of factors, not all of which could be controlled or determined, why was Thurston, who had specialized in steam engines, so interested in them? Because he was interested in all kinds of motive power, and because in the 1890s horses still supplied one-third of all power. Thurston believed that energy was the fundamental, unifying principle of the universe—the "ever-living force," or "the force illustrated in all life and motion." This energy manifested itself in three forms: as physical forces (gravity, electricity, chemical processes, and mechanical forces), as the vital forces of organisms, and as "the forces of the soul and of the intellect—those most wonderful and most mysterious of all known forms of force." Thurston called for a unified understanding of all energies, organic and inorganic, mechanical and vital, physical and metaphysical.

As far as he was concerned, animals had to be included in any consideration of energy. Thurston believed that unlocking the mystery of the vital forces constituted "nature's challenge to the engineer." Studying horses was part of the engineer's professional mission.[31]

As an engineer, Thurston was concerned that the world was going to run out of energy. Steam and electric engines seemed to have reached their maximum efficiency and consumed "rapidly disappearing" fossil fuels. Thurston believed that the foundations of civilization and continued cultural progress depended on increasing the amount of energy by improving efficiency and tapping new sources. "Only the application of the forces of nature without waste and the complete subjugation of all its energies can give maximum result." Thurston thought horses provided a possible model for energy utilization. Even the best engines used only a fraction of their potential power, but "every animate creature is a machine of enormously higher efficiency as a dynamic engine than [man's] most elaborate construction." By implication, the use of animal energies broadened the definition of energy resources to include fields of hay and grain as well as coalfields and oil wells.[32]

The theoretical link that Thurston forged between the energy of animate and inanimate prime movers was part of the project of recasting everything—from city politics to industrial production to domestic practices—in terms of science. It was evident in a well-known and long-used textbook of agricultural education, *A Textbook of the Physics of Agriculture,* first published in 1899 by Professor Franklin H. King, of the University of Wisconsin. King had trained on the Wisconsin Geological Survey in 1873–1876 and had studied at Cornell. After his tenure at Wisconsin he was chief of the U.S. Department of Agriculture's Division of Soil Management from 1901 to 1904. King framed his discussion of soils, drainage, farm architecture, farm mechanics, road building, and weather forecasting as scientific problems, saying, "The great need of agricultural practices at the present time is a keener appreciation and a more thorough comprehension of the principles which underlie them" so that each farmer could "secure his results with the greatest certainty and at the least cost." Physics rather than chemistry or biology provided an underlying unity to agricultural practice. "We might go on enumerating every science and every art to show that there is a physics of each or a necessary treatment of them from the standpoint of mechanical principles of matter and energy."[33]

Like Brigg and Thurston, King saw horses as machines. The horse had the same "essential elements" as other machines "for developing power," such as levers and lubrication; muscles, analogous to "the piston and cylinder of a steam engine"; digestive, excretory, and respiratory organs for fuel supply and waste removal; and a "coordinating and regulating mechanism," or the nervous system, all of these encased within the skin, which protected and insulated the working parts from damage, dirt, and heat dissipation. The horse was one of many motors available to the farmer; unlike Thurston, King expressed little doubt as to what kind of motor the horse was. "The horse, the steam engine and the oil engine each derive its power from the chemical action of the fuel consumed or food eaten and may therefore are called chemical engines ... The chemical engines use the energy derived from the collision of molecules and atoms." However, horses used energy more efficiently and economically than these inanimate motors. "When animals are viewed from the standpoint of machines they are wonderful mechanisms. Not only are they self-feeding, self-controlling, self-maintaining and self-reproducing, but they are far more economical in the energy they are able to develop from a given weight of fuel material, than any other existing form of motor."[34]

King brought scientific precision to the process of using the horse motor, presenting formulas for calculating draft using the variables of horse size, weight, and build, the number of horses being used, the desired speed and distance, road grade, road surface, wheel size, width, and type, harnessing, load weight, load distribution, vehicle rigidity (vertical draft), vehicle friction, and length of time in use. For example, assuming a workday of ten hours and a speed of 2.5 miles per hour, he determined the horse power expected from horses of different weights, required to haul a load over a variety of road surfaces using low, medium, or high wheels, or to plow furrows of different widths and depths. He showed how devices like the two-horse evener and the three-horse equalizer allowed the draft to be most efficiently distributed among the horses of a team, and how horses might be most efficiently used in tread and sweep powers.[35]

As a professor at a major agricultural school and a division chief at the USDA, King was representative of a new breed of professionals that had emerged as a result of the institutionalization of agriculture. During the nineteenth century the informal network of agricultural journals, societies, and fairs that constituted the community of agricultural practice and discourse was replaced by government departments, state universities, and other research institutions, professional organizations, and industry journals.

Congress established the Department of Agriculture in 1862 and raised it to cabinet status in 1889. The Morrill Land Grant Act of 1862 provided for state colleges that included agricultural programs. The Hatch Act of 1887 authorized federal experimental agricultural stations, and state boards of agriculture often had their own stations and programs as well. The Bureau of Animal Industry started in 1884, and the Weather Bureau transferred from the War Department to the USDA in 1891. In order to improve American agriculture, these institutions collected statistics, conducted research, and disseminated information on all aspects of agriculture. There was a growing circle of agricultural professionals, trained in the new universities and agricultural schools, many of whom then taught in those universities or worked for the USDA or state agencies. Like other middle-class professionals of the time, they based their claim to status on trying to restructure American institutions and make them more centralized, scientific, and efficient. Because horses remained virtually the only source of tractive power in agriculture, they were a primary concern for many of the professionals in agricultural institutions, and a way for them to claim authority and status as experts. They addressed horse-machine problems by studying the mechanics of horse draft, researching horse breeding, markets, and nutrition, and supporting the construction of good roads.

For example, the USDA asserted that agricultural chemistry could provide the answer to a common farm problem: How much and what kind of feed did various kinds of farm animals need? Food was fuel for animal machines, so the USDA collected data on the nutritional content of a variety of animal foods—green fodders, grains, hays, root vegetables, beans, and others—to determine their content of protein, carbohydrates, fat, and other nutrients. On the basis of this information, the USDA recommended feeding standards for different animals under a variety of conditions. A table from 1894 mandated different amounts of feed for horses and for oxen at rest, moderately worked and heavily worked, relative to the animal's weight, and noted: "these are the figures which must be consulted in determining the food value of a given material and in selecting feeding stuffs for making up a ration." Basing feeding decisions on this scientific analysis would promote fuel efficiency and farm economy.[36]

The USDA was concerned about the collapse of the horse market during the depression of the 1890s, when plummeting horse prices discouraged many horse breeders. Horses vanished from Chicago market reports, for example, and in agricultural periodicals the usually plentiful advertisements from horse breeders touting their particular breed or prize stallion virtually disappeared. In response the USDA urged farmers to breed for what they said was strong demand for all-purpose carriage horses. The foundation for this horse was the trotting horse, identified as "specially and superiorly adapted to the every-day uses of the people" because it had good action, speed, and endurance. The 1897 annual *Report of the Commissioner of Agriculture* contained a lengthy article on "The National Horse of America," by Leslie E. MacLeod, associate editor of *Wallace's Monthly,* which asserted that racing provided a "turf test" revealing which horses had the qualities "best adapted to the uses of the American farmer and the average American citizen."[37]

The USDA used the new science of horse breeding as a source of authority and status. The rediscovery in 1900 of Gregor Mendel's research on the laws of heredity had created the field of genetics almost overnight. An enormous quantity of unused experimental material that had accrued during the nineteenth century suddenly fitted into the framework provided by Mendel's work and rapidly created a substantial new science with implications for agricultural production. Historian Robert E. Kohler summarizes the situation: "The accumulated genetic traits of domestic plants and animals [were] a windfall for experimental biologists . . . this accumulated resource was put to new uses in the production of experimental knowledge. For the first generation of neo-Mendelians, staking an early claim to a particular organism was a strategy of choice, offering the most likely prospect of payoff." Given the centrality of horses in the agricultural economy, horse breeding immediately linked the scientific authority of the USDA to national prosperity and to the ideological mission of saving farmers at a time when economic depression and declining rural populations seemed to be threatening the very existence of rural life.[38]

The USDA funded several breeding projects to encourage market-oriented breeding. In 1905 it appropriated funds for a project in Colorado for breeding carriage horses. The collapse of the horse market during the 1890s had damaged the breeding of utility horses, but the "coaching craze" that developed during the decade promised a continuing market in lighter horses. The department hoped to study horse breeding, develop breeding stock, and model good

breeding practices. The department also developed a new classification system for carriage horses, which it then presented to farmers at state fairs to encourage small-scale, market-oriented breeding
as a way to increase farm income.[39]

The USDA also cosponsored a breeding project for Morgan
horses with Vermont's state experimental agricultural station. The
purpose of the Morgan breeding project was to "save" the Morgan
from disappearing and make the horse "once more an important
factor in the horse industry." The progressive and scientific aspect
of this breeding project was evident in the assertion of George
Rommel, chief of the Animal Husbandry Division of the Bureau of
Animal Industry, that the purpose was not to replicate the original
Justin Morgan and "the ancient Morgan type." As Rommel said,
Justin Morgan "belonged to his time and he filled his niche," while
contemporary Morgans had to be bred to standard market requirements for "heavy harness" horses used for carriages rather than
road wagons. Since the Morgan project was funded at the urging of
Vermont's Redfield Proctor, who just happened to be the chair of
the Senate Committee on Agriculture, it is possible that part of what
was being saved was a cultural icon, the horse that symbolized the
New England farmer as agriculture in that region declined and rural
areas suffered depopulation.[40]

The USDA continued to think about developing new useful animals for agriculture. In an interesting continuation of the thinking
that had inspired S. F. Baird's 1851 report on domesticating the wild
animals of North America, the USDA sponsored experiments in hybrid breeding. The Bureau of Animal Industry station in Bethesda,
Maryland, produced several zebra-ass hybrids, "beautiful clean-
limbed animals," to study inbreeding, heredity, and similar problems, and with the possibility of designing economic and efficient
animal hybrids.[41]

The USDA also advocated more government involvement in
breeding horses for military use. The experience of the British army

during the Boer War, which sent the British government scrambling to purchase horses abroad—including large numbers of western American horses—and the expansion of the U.S. cavalry from ten to fifteen regiments in 1901 had reinforced the notion that, as one army officer put it, "A nation's strength in war depends not only upon its men, but also upon its horses." The secretary of agriculture recommended that the government establish a national stud to breed horses for the cavalry and artillery use, to maintain the "efficiency of the mounted service" and to provide "experimental possibilities of high value to the horse-breeding industry."[42] These scientific projects asserted the importance of the horse to the nation at a time when its importance as a prime mover in the cities was challenged by the growing viability of automotive technology and by the electrification of mass transit, and when horses were being culturally marginalized as well, thus threatening the status of professionals associated with horses.

The USDA also got deeply involved in the "good roads" movement, along with other urban professionals and interest groups: civil engineers who wanted to plan and build better roads, social reformers concerned about the quality of country life, political reformers interested in centralized administration, urban bicycling enthusiasts seeking weekend recreation, and, increasingly, urban motorists. What defined a good road was its context of use: a road was "good" if it fulfilled its purpose and satisfied its primary users. Though many roads were adequate for the rural populations they served, they were inadequate from the perspective of these urban, cosmopolitan professionals, who adhered to a formal definition of a good road and who considered the nation's roads to be by and large a disgrace. Harvard University geologist and conservationist Nathaniel S. Shaler wrote: "The ancient and more necessary means of transportation afforded by the ordinary wagon roads have remained in a state of shameful neglect."[43]

Throughout the nineteenth century, Americans invested far more capital in iron horses than in roads for real horses. In 1904 only 7 percent, or 154,000 miles, of the two million miles of the nation's roads were classified as improved. "Good roads" became an issue of progress and scientific efficiency. As one enthusiast said, "Roads and civilization go hand in hand . . . it is true now, as it has been for three thousand years, that the degree of civilization to which any people have attained is accurately measured and indicated by the condition of their roads." Another described bad roads as a form of oppression and the good roads movement as a war for independence: "We are annually paying a tribute to our bad roads, more onerous in its nature and more certain in its exaction than the oppression which incited Americans to rise and declare themselves free men. Shall we, who proudly refused to be the minions of government, remain forever the slaves of conditions, fettered with the shackles of our own inaction, and trammeled by the delusion of our hopes?" *Prairie Farmer* stated that "one of the chief factors in creating a dislike to farming is bad roads." Rural reformers saw good roads as a way of retrieving "rural civilization" and relieving the cultural and social oppressions of rural life.[44]

The USDA coordinated some of the good roads movement through its Office of Road Inquiry. Good roads advocates argued that bad roads were costly and inefficient, holding back the rural economy and draining its economic and energy resources. General Roy Stone, director of the Office of Road Inquiry, estimated that $600 million, or a quarter of the value of all farm products, was lost because of bad roads, while another expert estimated the loss per horse per annum due to bad roads at $15, or between $300 million and $360 million.[45] Others noted that bad roads promoted inefficiency, with horses "eating their heads off" when the roads could not be used, and farmers having to haul smaller loads using more horses. A New Jersey farmer explicitly linked good roads to horse energy efficiency when he claimed that "since we have had these

Horse and carriage stuck in a rut on a muddy road in Indiana, 1898. This image was entered in a competition sponsored by the League of American Wheelmen to identify the worst road conditions in the United States. Wisconsin Historical Society, image 1999.

good roads I have disposed of one team and am doing more work with the other one than I did before with both."[46]

Good roads had to be roads that were good for horses in terms of surfaces and grades. Horses had to be able to carry the same load up a grade that it was able to bring over a level road. F. H. King calculated the steepest allowable grade to be 16.5 percent, or a rise of 16.5 feet in 100 feet of road; but he also showed that the better the road was, the less its grade. The reduced draft of a good road increased the amount of weight that horses could pull on the level. However, it was necessary to assure lower grades all along the road to avoid having to use extra horses every time there was a hill. The cost of the extra horses would nullify the energy savings achieved by the improved road.[47] Wide wheels reduced draft, and many states passed laws mandating their use and specifying a width of at least three or three and a half inches for loads in excess of a designated weights or on certain road surfaces.[48] There were experimental proposals for steel-track wagon roads, consisting of two parallel lines of eight-inch-wide steel plates laid a wagon's width apart—a modified railway. Advocates claimed that the steel tracks enabled one horse to pull eleven tons, a weight that required twenty horses on an ordinary dirt road, and that they provided a good surface for bicycles and horseless carriages too. Though the people promoting good roads wanted to improve recreation and rural culture, they had to center their efforts on horses and work. The enthusiastic League of American Wheelmen mounted an effective national campaign for road improvement, but often had to couch their arguments in terms acceptable to rural road users with horses.[49]

Engineers and others defined horses as machines, but veterinarians defined them as patients. Caring for horses was the primary function of veterinarians before World War I. Viewing the horse with clinical detachment as a sentient being served a professional purpose of associating veterinarians with the prestige of science and the medical profession. However, while claiming equality with doctors, veterinarians defined a separate mission by emphasizing the economic and practical value of horses. By defining horses as valuable patients, veterinarians claimed that protecting equine health contributed to the national economy. Yet they implicitly traded on the affective meaning of "valuable" as well, recognizing that people had "complex social, emotional and cultural ties" to their horses and prized them apart from their monetary worth, a fact that also justified veterinary care.[50]

Veterinary medicine developed as an urban profession in the late nineteenth century as a result of the dense and burgeoning equine populations of big cities. Before 1870 there were few professionally trained veterinarians in the United States, and the profession had little status. People identifying themselves as veterinarians, other than a small number trained in Britain and Europe, included farriers, medical doctors willing to treat animals, purveyors of "horse tonics," downright charlatans, and self-taught practitioners relying on knowledge gleaned from classic works by Gervase Markham, Jacques de Sollysel, John Lawrence, and William Youatt and from the many "pocket" horse manuals in circulation. Many of the leading veterinarians in the country were foreign-born and trained abroad, such as the French-born Alexander Liatuard and the British-born James Law. There were only two, short-lived veterinary schools in the United States before 1875. In contrast, nineteen veterinary schools were established between 1879 and 1900, almost all of them in major cities, where large horse populations provided an adequate supply of patients and opportunities for clinical training. In 1886 Harvard located its new veterinary school on Boston's Village Street, near the city stables, railroad depots, and waterfront. James Law was brought to Cornell in the 1860s to found a veterinary school, but was unable to do more than offer some courses until 1897 because of the relatively sparse horse population of the rural Finger Lakes region.[51]

The growth of the veterinary profession was directly related to the growth in horse populations after the Civil War, and was affected by the growing number of animal plagues in the postbellum decades. The increasing mobility of animals in the national and international markets as a result of railroads and steamships led to outbreaks of epidemic disease, such as the Great Epizootic of 1872, which spread along major railroad and canal routes. Glanders, of which there had been a serious epidemic during the Civil War, continued to flare up intermittently, and there were more frequent livestock epidemics such as bovine pleuropneumonia, Texas cattle fever, and hog cholera. These plagues were an opportunity for veterinarians to increase their status and visibility by linking animal health to public health, and laying claim to a role in both. This expanded role could be the basis for more state support for veterinary education and professionalization. The establishment of the Bureau of Animal Industry in 1884 was a response to growing calls for government intervention to control the spread of pleuropneumonia among American cattle and amid concern about declining exports as Europeans rejected uninspected animals and animal products. The first head of the BAI was Daniel Salmon, a veterinarian trained at Cornell by James Law and at the Alfort Veterinary School in Paris, where he was presumably exposed to the science of Pasteur and Koch. Salmon linked new germ theories from bacteriology to veterinary care, emphasizing veterinarians' scientific and medical role and moving away from the position of older veterinarians such as Liatuard who defined veterinarians as sanitarians. The BAI also exerted authority over accreditation of veterinary schools.[52]

Conflict among veterinarians over the place of practical experience versus laboratory experimentation in veterinary medicine and the treatment of individual horses versus the treatment of livestock herds created a division that was to some extent generational but also ideological between older and newer science and older and newer ideas about what it meant to be a veterinarian. Thus veterinarians were besieged by advocates of research science on the one side and by advocates of practical and clinical education on the other. In what has been described as "the golden age" of bacteriology, laboratory science was gaining prestige over field science. Laboratories were thought to be the source of knowledge that was objective and universal, a completely reliable standard of truth. Science was becoming "the paradigmatic knowledge of modern culture and experiment . . . the paradigmatic scientific practice."[53]

Veterinarians resisted the attempts of agricultural schools to bring veterinary education under their aegis, and to include of some animal medicine in vocational training for farmers. At the same time they had to contend with resistance from medical schools, which did not want to be associated with animal doctors. The vets succeeded both in creating medically *defined* schools and in blocking efforts to teach animal medicine beyond the rudimentary level in the agricultural schools. By the 1890s veterinarians were lobbying state legislatures for laws limiting the definition of "veterinarian" and the right to practice animal medicine to graduates of accredited veterinary schools. Veterinarians were adamant and aggressive about distancing themselves from older stereotypes of veterinarians as uncouth, rural animal healers, pejoratively referred to as "horse doctors" or "farriers," and derided for their heroic therapeutics. Veterinarians asserted their scientific training and their similarity to medical doctors even as they established boundaries between animal and human medicine to keep medical doctors from treating horses.[54]

Horses were central in the development of veterinary professionalism. Despite the burgeoning bureaucracy of veterinary science developing around the BAI, which employed a growing number of veterinary graduates, the focus of most veterinarians, and the backbone of their practices, was the urban horse. In no other animal did questions of economic value and affective value intersect so powerfully. Of all the large domesticated American animals, horses were the only ones not slaughtered for human consumption. If engineers viewed horses as prime moves in the urban economy, it might be said that veterinarians viewed horses as urban workers. The economic value of city workhorses provided a financial incentive for railway, express, and haulage companies and livery stables to pay for equine medical care. The epizootic of 1872 had been the functional equivalent of a strike or work stoppage. Owners learned that horses pulled through the influenza because of skilled nursing and adequate recuperation. They also learned that isolating sick horses could stop the spread of disease. Over the next four decades, they increasingly turned to veterinarians to improve stable conditions, contain outbreaks of disease, provide preventive and palliative care, and evaluate horses' ability to work.[55]

Starting in the 1890s, a number of events threatened the livelihoods of urban veterinarians. Severe economic depression reduced horse breeding, electrification of the street railways eliminated the majority of streetcar horses, the bicycle craze threatened to replace pleasure horses, and the horseless carriage raised the possibility of the first technical replacement for the horse. In response, veterinarians emphasized the continuing utility of the horse. "We hear so much of the coming of the 'horseless age,'" proclaimed the *Journal of Comparative Medicine and Surgery* in 1896, but there were "new fields of utility," and went on to describe the use of the horse to produce antitoxin for diphtheria, one of the killer diseases of childhood. Comparing horses and automobiles, veterinarians conceded long-distance travel to cars but noted that for short distances horses were more dependable, economical, relaxing, and better on bad roads.[56]

Veterinarians had cultivated an unsentimental attitude and a detached, clinical approach to horses in order to emphasize the scientific and economic aspects of their profession. However, emphasizing the affective value of horses proved to be a way to promote the utility of veterinary medicine and enhance veterinary status, especially since horses dominated most private practices of urban vets. *American Veterinary Review* suggested that promoting good horse care would keep horses in use. "There is no more danger of the displacement of the horse than there is of the extermination of man," it asserted in 1900; "the horse will ever remain the typical veterinary patient." Veterinarians became involved with the growing humane movement, which promoted an aggressively sentimental image of the horse at odds with the traditional veterinarians' stance. They supported urban workhorse parades, often organized by humane organizations to showcase well-cared-for workhorses and inspire better horse care among the working classes. They argued that horses were not dangerous on the streets. And they noted with confidence the continuing increase in the horse population in the first decade of the twentieth century.[57]

Engineers, veterinarians, and agricultural scientists tried to rationalize the central role of the horse in urban industrial society. But at the same time the horse remained a powerful traditional symbol of social status among members of a new industrial bourgeoisie eager to harness the horse's cultural power to the consolidation of their social and economic power. As the use of the horse became wider and more democratized between the Civil War and World War I, elite groups elaborated the use of horse technology as a social marker to reproduce and maintain social boundaries as old and new elites jostled for power and position. They expressed this effort through horse breeding, display, and appreciation.

Americans revered thoroughbred horses because of their association with the British aristocracy and because the pedigree system secured the purity of the breed. On the one hand, thoroughbreds were celebrated as a human creation, the highest expression of the art of breeding; on the other hand, they were protected from further change or dilution. They had an essential, unchanging quality and thus were a source of good blood to improve other breeds. During the Gilded Age, elites projected their social assumptions and cultural beliefs about American society onto thoroughbreds. Even though the newer moneyed elites favored the breeding of trotters, which did not have to be pedigreed thoroughbreds, they considered thoroughbred blood important for improving the quality of their racehorses through crossbreeding, and the value formerly placed on the "mongrel" trotter declined in favor of pure line breeding methods. J. H. Sanders wrote that there was "scarcely a race of horses . . . but may be improved by a cross with them" and that "civilized" countries regarded the English thoroughbred "as the basis for all substantial improvement" in other breeds. Sanders made the

analogy between horses and humans quite explicit: the laws of heredity were "immutable" and applied equally to humans as to other
animals.

> To know that a man or woman is descended from an old
> family whose record has been honorable, beyond reproach
> and without taint, is the very best evidence, next to this
> own individual record, that he is also worthy of confidence
> and respect; and a taint in the blood of an opposite charac-
> ter should certainly be regarded with as must distrust as a
> similar taint in the blood of any of our domestic animals,
> and for the same reasons. What is "bred in the bone" will
> be transmitted. Beauty of form and feature, strength and
> force of intellect, elegance and grace of motion, integrity
> and honesty of character, susceptibility of culture and re-
> finement or boorish stupidly, as well as all the virtues and
> vices, are as clearly transmissible and inheritable qualities
> in man as hair color and body shape are in horses and
> cattle.

From these beliefs to eugenics would be a very small leap. The relationship between genetics and eugenics in organizations like the
American Breeders' Association would ultimately drive a wedge between elite horse breeding and genetic science.[58]

The style in which horses were used was an important class
marker. People articulated elaborate standards about the keeping of
private stables or the presentations of horses and carriages. The
"coaching craze" of the 1890s contributed to the popularity of private carriages and showy teams. Elite groups lobbied for the construction of carriageways in city parks for promenading and racing.
Etiquette manuals (often British in origin) about horse care, stable management, and coaching techniques communicated the so-

cial grammar of correct horse use and outlined the subtle distinctions necessary for those wanting to signal their arrival and right to belong in the proper social circles. These manuals both promoted access to elite circles and policed the barriers with elaborate rules. They were filled with pronouncements such as "no woman can 'afford' to keep a horse who cannot also afford a capable and presentable servant to attend her."[59]

Distinctions proliferated to a dizzying level of detail, as in this description of correct appointments for the "single brougham" type carriage:

> Harness black; double lined; brass or silver trim according to vehicle, brass being perhaps the smartest, but silver possibly more elegant and less usual; twisted furniture never proper; all buckles square and single, with single billets; bridle, square or D-shaped blinkers; pulley or French bridoon, bearing rein, double-ring drop attached to crownpiece; Buxton bit; single link or square metal brow-band according as D-shaped or square blinkers are used; flowers in headstall rather neat; collar, Kay or rim; hames, anchordraught, jointed terrets, plain tug (no clip nor rivets showing); billet for trace of one piece, but never metal; chain and ring plated like harness; standing martingale from padgirth, through kidney-link ring to nose-band; pad, straight; Tilbury tugs, hook, never post, or bearing rein . . .

and so on. There were separate descriptions for a wide array of carriages, and the number, livery, and even the posture of servants that belonged with each, such as a "park drag," which had "always two servants, groom standing at hinge side of door, robe over left arm, when waiting."[60]

In addition to carriage driving as a form of display, there was new interest in horseback riding among the northern urban classes, especially for young women of the upper classes, advocated "as a means to improved health" but also intended to promote an aristocratic image. Here, too, details abounded, with elaborate prescriptions for behavior and dress competing for space with actual riding instructions. How to mount a horse with male assistance while minimizing physical contact was spelled out in detail. Other chances for public display included horse shows established during the 1890s, such as the prestigious Devon Horse Show in Philadelphia. At the same time British periodicals such as *Spirit of the Times* and *Country Life Illustrated* portrayed the country lifestyle of the English gentry that the new monied classes sought to emulate.[61]

Refined appreciation of the horse as a historical and cultural relic was another class marker. The relationship between horses and civilization was reiterated constantly from early in the century on. William Youatt's much-referenced book *The Horse* stated: "It is natural to imagine that the domestication of the horse was coeval with the establishment of civilization . . . indeed without the aid of the horse, the advancement of colonisation [*sic*] would have been exceedingly slow." W. H. Flower, surgeon, veterinarian, and director of the British Natural History Museum, wrote that the horse "was [man's] domestic companion, friend and servant before the dawn of history. It has accompanied him in his wanderings over almost every surface of the earth." Even divine intention came into play, as when American breeder and publisher J. H. Sanders observed: "It is stated in Holy Writ that 'God made man a little lower than the angels,' and by common consent the horse is voted next highest in the scale of created beings." The horse's connection to civilization was shown in its exemplary character—gentleness, patience, willingness, fidelity, friendship, sagacity, and nobility. The horse was man's friend and servant, "never happier than when employed in our service." Horse etiquette manuals expressed disdain for those servants (usually grooms and stablehands) and classes who they felt had an incorrect and insufficiently refined appreciation for the horse.[62]

During the 1890s the national horse population grew 25 percent. In the cities, horse railways gave way to electrified streetcars, but horse-drawn traffic surged, and wagons grew larger and heavier. In agriculture, horses provided nearly all the power, and the manufacture of horse-drawn agricultural machinery was a leading industry. On the industrial bonanza farms of the Far West, teams of twenty to forty horses pulled combines and other machinery. Federal and state governments promoted good roads designed for horse traction, engineers worked out the physics of draft, a dozen veterinary schools opened their doors, breed associations proliferated, and scientific, upper-class, and middle-class interest in horses had never been higher. As a technology, horses appeared to have considerable momentum in the 1890s.

The term "technological momentum" refers to the extent to which a technology is integral to a society. A technology with momentum is extensively used, engages capital investment, individuals, and institutions, and continues to develop and change.[63] According to this definition, the use of horses had technological momentum in the 1890s. Horses were widely employed and familiar prime movers, valuable to the economy as producers and consumers. Many people were employed working with horses directly or indirectly, and there were businesses, educational institutions, government agencies, professional societies, and other institutions concerned with the use of horses. Knowledge about horse breeding, locomotion, use, and care continued to expand.

Throughout the nineteenth century horse technology had expanded because of the technological complementarity between steam power and horses. The same relationship appeared to exist between horses and electricity. When electrification of the street railways in the 1890s replaced horse-drawn streetcars, it did so in the way that railroads had replaced long-distance hauling during the antebellum period. Electric streetcars replaced the stop-and-start heavy hauling of mass transit, one of the least efficient ways of using horses, but it did not replace the use of horses in freighting, construction, consumer services, or municipal services. Like the steam railroads, electric railways were integrated systems with prescribed routes, very different from the self-propelled autonomous units of horses and wagons. The "energy landscape" of the 1890s was extremely diverse, and, if bicycles and horseless carriages are included, Americans were employing more kinds of power and prime movers than ever before.

Yet there were developments in the 1890s that would undermine the momentum of horse technology. Some of these replaced horses, and some caused people to think differently about them and to suggest a different role for the horse in industrial society from that of prime mover. At the same time, new sources of status for professionals and the upper classes weakened professional and cultural commitments to horses. Contradictions would mount between the different roles of the horse—prime mover, worker, status symbol, and sentient being—and erode the momentum of urban horse technology by the first decade of the twentieth century.

The economic depression of the 1890s, the most serious one in American history up to that time, had a serious impact on the horse industry and eroded some of its momentum as a technology. It depressed horse prices so severely that many horse breeders curtailed breeding by the middle of the decade.[64] Horse production was relatively inelastic to consumer demand; there was a lag between economic recovery and the recovery of horse breeding. Many horse breeders were small, low-capital producers; the large, high-capital horse-breeding operations were the hobby farms of elite breeders like Leland Stanford. As a result of the depression, regular market reports from the Union Stock Yards in Chicago and other sites completely disappeared from agricultural periodicals like *Prairie Farmer* for several years after August 1894, whereas up to that year they had showed sales in a wide range of market categories: roadsters, draft teams, streeters, saddlers, coach horses, plugs, express, general use, drivers, carriage teams. In the cities, the depression pushed smaller horse railways and haulage firms out of business and contributed to the electrification of the railways and the consolidation of railway lines and other firms during the decade. Three critical changes in urban freighting stimulated the humane movement in the 1890s. First, the number of independent teamsters, who owned their own horses and wagons, had declined, and more teamsters were wage employees of large firms. Second, the amount of urban freighting increased dramatically in the 1880s and early 1890s. Third, the trend in freighting was toward bigger wagons. Thus, there were more teamsters, driving horses they did not own, hauling larger, heavier loads on city streets.[65] All these factors made the use of horses and the abuse of horses more prevalent and more public. The American humane movement was already well established. Henry Bergh, a New York City businessman, founded the Society for the Protection Against Cruelty to Animals in 1867 with the primary purpose of protecting urban workhorses. Similar groups appeared in other cities. The Pennsylvania Society for the Prevention of Cruelty to Animals was founded in 1869 in Philadelphia with a mission of reducing cruelty to animals through education, reward, and prosecution. Its first annual report provided a litany of the problems the PSPCA sought to address. "Consider the overloaded horse cars, the cases of fast driving, overdriving, overworking, under feeding, neglect to water, neglect to properly shelter and protect from the weather, tight check-reins, sores worn by harness, twitchings, beatings, kickings, bad shoeing, bad provender, bad stables, bad feeding, bad harness, bad grooming, *bad drivers,* and all other various forms of abuse to which the horse is subjected." Cases cited by the PSPCA included overloading, driving sore or lame horses, beating, bad driving, unsafe street conditions, and bad pavements that injured horses. The PSPCA constructed watering fountains for horses, monitored horses on major streets, tried to pass a law limiting the number of passengers permitted in streetcars, and worked with the presidents of city street railways to improve stabling and horse care. Its reports included tips on feeding, on coping with accidents (such as a six-step process to calm a fallen horse and help it get up again), and on devices that would ease the work of horses. Middle- and upper-class women formed auxiliary groups. Caroline Earle White, barred from leadership of the PSPCA, formed the Philadelphia Women's Branch of the society. It worked for horsecar legislation, employed agents to act as a private police force, and maintained an animal ambulance.[66]

The elite-dominated humane movement emphasized the relationship between humane treatment of animals and social class, and its actions on behalf of animals were often attempts at social discipline. The SPCA seal depicted an angel intervening to stop a teamster from beating his horse, asserting a connection between animal abuse, the working class, and the use of horses for work. Likewise, reform efforts and punitive measures were aimed at individual offenders, not at their employers. Teamsters were stopped and fined, but the owners of the company that set the delivery schedule that resulted in teamsters' beating tired and overloaded horses were not held accountable. Yet members of the PSPCA included the Knickerbocker Ice Company and the Strawbridge and Clothier department store, both of which employed many horses and drivers as part of their delivery operations. By mobilizing middle-class public consciousness about animal cruelty, these companies were able to get the public involved in supervising workers whose jobs took them away from the scrutiny of management.[67]

In the 1890s humane reformers increased their emphasis on prevention rather than prosecution. George Angell distributed *Black Beauty* for a few cents a copy. The Philadelphia Fountain Society, an offshoot of the PSPCA, continued to construct water fountains for men and horses, and also encouraged temperance in order to prevent animal abuse from drunken teamsters. When the Women's Branch ambulance horse got too old to work, it was retired to a country farm, in a reflection of the belief that the country was where horses ultimately belonged. As they drove water wagons and ambulances through the city, provided blankets and straw hats, and sponsored workhorse parades, humane reformers emphasized the individuality of the horse and its special status relative to other species. Humane reformers promoted a sentimental image of the horse as the wise, empathic companion and servant of man. The cultural influence wielded by upper-class humanitarian reformers effected significant changes in the perception of horses, if not always in their actual treatment.[68]

At the end of the century horses' continuing importance as a source of energy had generated a network of social organizations, governmental agencies, and professional societies. Horses were also the center of an intellectual framework of scientific and social thought. Americans pondered the meaning of the horse and how to reconcile its presence with a changing society as they sought to become self-consciously modern.

Black Beauty had contained an unspoken, troubling question: Was there a humane place for horses in an urban industrial world? Sewell's answer was implicit in her narrative solution to ending the novel: she took Beauty from the city and returned him to the presumed stability and order of life in the countryside. In doing so, Sewell seemed to suggest that the contradictions between Beauty's roles as prime mover, worker/servant, status commodity, and fellow being had become too great. In the end, she defined horses outside the world of cities and work and technology, but to do so she resorted to sentimentality—and this would become the way in which Americans defined horses out of the modern world.[69]

7   FROM HORSE POWERED
          TO HORSELESS

A central focus of *The Magnificent Ambersons,* Booth Tarkington's
1918 novel, is the rising use of automotive and electric power, and
their consequences for American society. Tarkington's protagonist
is George Amberson Minafer, the scion of an upper-class family that
epitomizes Gilded Age wealth. One day when George is driving a
horse and sleigh with his prized trotter, Pendennis, going at a good
three-minute mile, he is passed by a horseless carriage, but a few
minutes later finds it stopped along the road as its inventor-owner
does repairs. Shouting "Git a hoss! Git a hoss!" he circles the sleigh
to jeer some more, but the horse breaks into a gallop and swerves
toward a ditch. "George turned too late; the cutter's right runner
went into the ditch and snapped off; the little sleigh upset, and, after
dragging its occupants some fifteen yards, left them lying together
in a bank of snow. Then the vigorous young horse kicked himself
free of all annoyances, and disappeared down the road, galloping

cheerfully." George and his broken sleigh are left lying in a ditch at the side of the road. The automobile, formerly described as a "sewing machine" and a "broken down chafing dish," is easily repaired and comes to his rescue.[1]

Written from the perspective of 1918, Tarkington's scene encapsulates the rapid technological and social changes occurring since the 1890s. *The Magnificent Ambersons* uses the advent of the automobile as a symbol of how changing energy technologies launched widespread changes in American society. George represents the older industrial class of the Gilded Age, an old-style aristocracy, which, horses and all, must adapt to the altered social conditions and political economy of the new century or be left behind.

For many Americans, then and since, the advent of the automobile marked a distinct break with the past and the beginning of the modern world of the twentieth century. Depictions of the automobile recalled those of the steam-powered railroad decades before, as a symbol of inexorable progress sweeping everything else aside. But whereas the "iron horse" of the railroad did not replace real horses, the horseless carriage did, supplanting prime movers that had been in use for five millennia. This complicated technological transition was hastened by other significant long-term cultural conditions prevailing in the years from 1890 to 1920. These included the values of Progressive reformers, the adoption of electricity, and changes in Americans' ideas about nature.

In the 1890s middle-class Americans felt a growing sense of crisis about their cities as immigration, congestion, sanitation, and corruption strained physical infrastructures, political institutions, and social relations. They worried about the fate of democratic government given the concentrated economic power wielded by large corporations. With a growing feeling that in modern society "all that is solid melts into air," they yearned for moral order and stability. Their response was the widespread reform impulse called Progressivism, which found expression in politics, reform, and social thought and would be the driving force in American society for three decades.

During these same years there was an enormous change in Americans' energy use. The expansion of electrical networks brought the electrification of most streetcar lines by 1903. Even more significant, for the first time in history there was a mechanical alternative to animal power that replicated both its scale and its self-propelled versatility. While only around 4,000 horseless carriages were sold in 1900, nearly 900,000 were sold in 1915. During the same years registrations of the vehicles soared from 8,000 to over 2.5 million. Together, electricity and internal combustion represented a revolution in the ways people perceived and consumed energy.[2]

In the transition from animal to automotive power, Progressivism was a catalyst, through its critique of animal power. Its rhetoric about American society emphasized a particular set of values and concerns. The key words of this rhetoric were "sanitation," "efficiency," "order," "safety," and "monopoly." These were the terms in which urban Progressives argued against horses. Starting in the 1890s, Progressives identified urban horses as the cause of a host of social ills and prescribed adoption of the automobile as a solution.

Concern about the stability and moral order of cities intensified after the violence and upheavals of the Great Strike of 1877. The 1880s may have marked the nadir of urban life in terms of stress on the social and material environment. Urban populations swelled as a result of migration from rural areas and immigration from abroad. Industrial production concentrated in urban areas. Sanitary, transportation, and housing infrastructures were strained to the breaking point. Political institutions seemed unable and unwilling to provide solutions. Continued labor and political agitation was highlighted by incidents such as the Haymarket bombing in Chicago. The monied classes, fearful of revolution, built armories and organized private militias. In the 1890s immigration intensified, and the newcomers seemed more alien; there were significant outbreaks of disorder around the Homestead and Pullman strikes and agrarian issues, and the worst depression in national history to date.

Progressive reform emerged out of a widespread belief that American society had become profoundly disordered, but was infused with optimism about the possibilities of change. Progressives fused an older concept of benevolent moral reform with the application of scientific methods and technological solutions to political and social problems. The growing influence of corporate structures and industrial management, and the spread of professional education, with its emphasis on science and technique, led many in the middle and upper classes to believe that creating a more sanitary, efficient, orderly, safe, and democratic society was primarily a technical problem. Once it was solved, moral order would follow. Progressive efforts began in the cities and targeted the growing population of urban horses.

Progressives believed that cleaner, more attractive, and more efficient urban environments would produce the moral order and social control they sought. Since inculcating moral hygiene depended on improving material hygiene, they advocated sanitary measures such as street cleaning, garbage collection, and waste disposal, and they targeted specific sources of urban pollution. Progressive municipal reformers did not analyze pollution as a comprehensive problem. Instead they focused on immediate, visible material dirt. As urban environmental historian Martin Melosi writes, "Pollution problems were most often approached as isolated cases . . . Urban reformers had yet to consider pollution in terms of its root causes—the processes of urbanization and industrialization." Progressives tended to link pollution "to wastefulness and inefficiency, but in such as way as to avoid the conclusion that industrial activity was intrinsically responsible for despoiling the environment."[3]

If the immediate problem was public dirt, then horses were quite visibly a source of copious amounts of it. With an average urban density in 1900 of 446 horses per square mile, horses could generate as much as 5 tons of manure per square mile per day. The city of Philadelphia, with 129 square miles and a horse density of 394 in each, received 500 tons per day. Horse manure littered city streets, and along with other kinds of dirt was churned and pounded into a carpet that turned into muck in damp weather and dust in dry weather. As George Waring proved in New York City, it took an army of white-coated street sweepers working constantly to keep thoroughfares moderately clean. In addition to the scattered manure droppings, large manure piles accumulated in and around stables. Urban sanitarians who subscribed to the older "filth" theory of disease had no trouble identifying the source of at least one kind of obvious filth. Urban stables had already been the targets of cleanup campaigns and legislation during nineteenth-century epidemics of cholera and other diseases. Proponents of the newer "germ" theories also saw manure as a source of disease, although they battled older sanitarians over the scientific issues.

Scientific knowledge about disease underwent enormous changes during the Gilded Age with the growing acceptance of germ theory, based on the bacteriological discoveries of Louis Pasteur, Robert Koch, and Rudolf Virchow. By the 1890s germ theory was widely accepted as part of the growing ascendancy of laboratory science as the source of knowledge. It became the basis for what historian Nancy Tomes calls "the gospel of germs," the belief that hygiene provided the means to eradicate disease agents and control disease, especially traditional killer diseases such as typhoid. By the end of the century there was substantial awareness of the measures required to kill germs and prevent illness, and there had been significant changes in American beliefs and personal behaviors around sanitation.

One of the forms that the battle for urban sanitation took was the antifly campaign, which was an effort to increase awareness of flies as germ-carrying insects and to encourage people to install window screens, cover food, and swat flies. Antifly reformers identified manure and carcasses as sites that incubated germs and attracted flies, which then carried germs on their feet into homes and spread them onto food, dishes, clothing, and skin. Waging war on the fly united reformers whether they believed in a "filth" theory of disease or in germ theory. Even though there was little evidence that manure was longer a specific cause of disease, Progressive reformers attacked it as such.

Dr. L. O. Howard of the USDA Bureau of Entomology estimated in 1895 that 95 percent of all flies were bred in piles of horse manure. In *Popular Science Monthly* W. E. Britton, Connecticut's state entomologist, described the many places where flies could breed— "almost any place where suitable moisture and food conditions exist"—but placed particular emphasis on manure. "The stable manure which is shipped in carloads from the cities to suburban or county districts is an excellent breeding place for flies." Antifly campaigns made invisible germs visible in the form of manure and carcasses, and implied a tight connection between horses, flies, and disease even though there was no scientific evidence for it. The editor of the *Journal of the American Medical Association* complained in 1910 about health crusaders "who assume that they have discovered the origin of a typhoid epidemic if they observe a few piles of horse-manure."[4]

In addition to being seen as a germ-breeding site, horse manure attracted an untidy collection of organic life quite visible to the naked eye, including rats and other rodents, flies and other insects, and nuisance populations of yet other unwanted animals, particularly flocks of English sparrows. These birds, brought to the United States in the 1860s to combat urban insects, had to everyone's dismay proliferated in the cities beyond what was thought to be their usefulness as insect eaters. They thrived on the spillages of feed that were inevitable in and around horse stables, and they flocked around the horse manure in the streets to eat the undigested grain found there. English sparrows also displaced native species of song-birds, a result that alarmed middle-class bird watchers. During the 1890s there was rising awareness among the middle and upper classes about environmental issues, and rising concern with pro-tecting nature, especially animals. One issue that attracted wide support from the expanding network of women's clubs was bird protection. Birds were traditionally seen as exemplary role models for human behavior, displaying patience, ingenuity, bravery, indus-try, dignity, fidelity, and familial devotion; in addition they were seen as adding beauty to the world with their plumage and song. The Audubon Society was founded in 1896 in order to protect native birds from a variety of threats. The animal world, perennially em-ployed as a metaphor for the social world, seemed in the case of the English sparrows to be a metaphor for the social crisis of the city. Doing something about horse manure would reduce vermin in gen-eral, and possibly eliminate an undesirable nonnative bird popula-tion from urban life.[5]

The new emphasis on sanitation accompanied visions of a differ-ent kind of American city. The single best expression of this new urban aesthetic was the "White City" of the Columbian Exposition of 1894, held in Chicago on a massive site specially designed by Frederick Law Olmsted in conjunction with engineers and other ar-chitects. Though the White City has been rather overworked as a metaphor for turn-of-the-century society, it nonetheless represented a distinct urban vision as the centerpiece of a world's fair celebrat-ing American civilization and progress. With its enormous, white, monumental buildings and wide, clean streets devoid of horse ma-nure (because of the use of electric-powered vehicles) and festooned with electric lights, the White City was a rationalized, sanitary envi-ronment. It was devoid of the organic messiness and many animals of traditional urban life. It contained no horses. Its beautifully land-scaped grounds on the shores of Lake Michigan placed nature in carefully planned and bounded areas. Clean, spacious, scientifically planned and managed, brilliantly lit at night, the White City exemplified modernity.

The streets of real cities were less orderly. The economic depression of the 1890s began to alter the urban horse world, and the public nature of horse work became more problematic. The depression pushed many horse railway lines to the brink of bankruptcy and led to the consolidation of many smaller lines into larger companies, some of which monopolized mass transit services. As it became clear that the difficulties of electric traction had been solved, electrification and expansion often accompanied consolidation.

Despite the disappearance of horsecars from public transit, the number of horses on the streets increased as urban freight and delivery haulage expanded. As the depression drove smaller urban hauling enterprises out of business, larger firms often absorbed them. Individual teamsters had already largely disappeared from freight work, but this new round of consolidation further changed the conditions of urban haulage. More of the teamsters plying city streets were wage employees of larger companies. Instead of driving their own horses, they drove company horses. In addition, bigger wagons came into use during the 1890s as an attempt to cut costs by moving larger loads. These vehicles were both longer and heavier than before. Consequently, more teamsters were driving horses they did not own and were paid by the size and weight of the load as well as speed of delivery. These conditions may have led to more overworked and overloaded horses as drivers were pressed by management to push their horses and stay on schedule. Furthermore, the larger freight concerns may have been more ready to cut costs on horse care and to use up and discard horses, especially as the collapsing horse market drove prices down. Conditions were such that more abused horses and more incidents of abuse may have been on the rise even as there were also more teamsters on the streets.[6]

Teamsters had always been a target of animal-welfare efforts—the

Society for the Prevention of Cruelty to Animals seal depicted an angel descending to stop a teamster from beating his horse—but they came under greater scrutiny than ever before as the animal-welfare movement expanded. This multifaceted movement included animal-welfare, humane-education, and wildlife-conservation organizations. One of these was the American Humane Education Society, whose particular focus was teaching children kindness to animals, and who distributed the free copies of *Black Beauty* provided by George Angell. Middle- and upper-class members of these organizations continued to agitate for humane legislation to control the public behaviors of teamsters directly.

These groups, often dominated by increasingly activist middle-class women connected through a network of women's groups, sought support from the owners of haulage and express companies, for whom public opinion about humane treatment functioned as a way of controlling employees who worked away from direct supervision. These groups subscribed both to a stereotype of teamsters as marginal, shiftless, and smelly and to the traditional image of the livery stable as a center of lower-class male socializing.

Animal advocates used several means to help urban horses, one of which was the construction of public water fountains for horses and humans. Finding regular sources of water for horses, especially during hot weather, was a perpetual problem, and groups known as "fountain societies" spun off from advocacy organizations with the specific purpose of providing water. They solicited private monies to build fountains at key intersections on major haulage routes into and around the cities. Some of these fountains were quite elaborate and offered different levels of basins and spouts of water to serve dogs, horses, and humans. These groups provided a link between temperance reformers and animal advocates, since fountain societies hoped that providing water would also encourage teamsters not to stop at saloons and thus reduce drunken abuse of horses. Hu-

City street (probably Black River Falls, Wisconsin) with livery stable, horse-drawn snowplow, blanketed horses, sleighs, and wagons, ca. 1900. Wisconsin Historical Society, image 42207.

mane reformers wanted to improve both the moral and material environment of the urban horse world.

Although humane reformers had a legitimate case regarding the teamsters, they were not always people who knew horses and horse work well enough to distinguish between a working horse and an overworked horse. They were uncomfortable with the yelling and swearing that were part of the style of teamster culture, and interpreted it as abusive anger and in pejorative class terms. By distributing the novel *Black Beauty* and other stories written in the equine first person, humane reformers encouraged a sentimentalized image of horses as individuals of special sensitivity and intelligence. They opened the door to the idea that having horses do any work, apart from pleasure riding and driving, was automatically a form of abuse. Emphasizing teamster behavior linked the physical work of horses to the unsanitary conditions and moral disorder of the streets. Humane and other reformers fused an older concept of moral reform with scientific methods and technological solutions to resolve political and social problems.[7]

The animal-welfare movement was part of the large constellation of reform movements that came to be known as Progressivism. Even more than a desire for cleanliness and order, an emphasis on scientific efficiency was perhaps its defining characteristic. It was a separate value, and yet one that also subsumed those of order, sanitation, and safety. For Progressive reformers who aimed to reengineer institutions, cities, governments, and even bodies, efficiency was the trump card; to argue against efficiency was to argue against American progress itself. Progressive criticism of the horse emphasized the horse's inefficient work hours, its wastefulness of food resources, and its contribution to urban disorder through urban pollution, danger, and traffic congestion.[8]

Building on the ideas of motion first studied in the photographic work of Muybridge and Marey, efficiency experts tried to devise more efficient work methods. For example, efficiency expert Frederick Winslow Taylor disaggregated the work process for different industrial jobs into separate components, then tried to reassemble them into a new work process intended to be more efficient. By eliminating what he deemed as extraneous motion Taylor sought to reduce wasted energy among workers and make them more productive. But when applied in the workplace, Taylorism seemed to mechanize workers by making their motions conform to Taylor's model.

Although the sequence of horse motion could also be studied, the actual work of horses could not be broken down into a chain of tasks and then reorganized differently. However, as prime movers horses could make the humans who worked with them inefficient, at least from an employer perspective. For example, railway horses generally worked four-hour shifts, but their drivers worked longer shifts. The need to take their horses back to the barn and get a new team in midshift gave the drivers time away from their own work. Furthermore, stables were traditional sites of male gathering and sociability, representing the kind of workplace autonomy and "soldiering" (slacking off) that employers wanted to eliminate.

Horses were seen as doing some soldiering of their own. Unlike mechanical engines, which did not consume fuel when they were not running, horses kept eating even when not working. "Eating their heads off" was of course a function of horses' need to eat a large volume of food each day in order to get enough nutrition. Draft horses in cities had to eat for most of the time they weren't working. Those on farms still had to eat during the winter and other slack periods. In the context of a growing conservation movement largely concerned with the efficient use of natural resources, horses were seen to be wasting the nation's farmland. Estimates were that it took three to six acres of farmland to support a single horse for a year. Instead of seeing this farmland as a renewable mine of animal energy, critics of the horse saw it as the source of a waste of more than seventy-five million acres.[9]

The increased size and number of wagons on the streets caused ever more congestion. Meanwhile, traffic regulation and control remained largely nonexistent. (Not surprisingly, this was the time when Philadelphia began building an elevated railway and New York its subways.) Urban traffic was also more diverse than ever before, combining horse-drawn vehicles of all sorts with electric automobiles and trucks, steam automobiles, internal combustion automobiles, and electric streetcars. The different styles, surface requirements, and speeds of these prime movers complicated traffic

Horse-drawn fire wagon sharing the street with automobiles and horse-drawn wagons, Milwaukee, Wisconsin, 1910. Wisconsin Historical Society, image 1950.

flow even more. The very largest vehicles, and the source of clogged traffic when they parked along curbs loading and unloading, were heavy horse-drawn wagons.

Urban Progressive reformers defined the horse as a specific problem and were eager to welcome a technological solution that would replace the horse and remove it from the city. It was a removal they could defend on grounds of sanitation, social and material order, and efficiency. The first technology they found was the bicycle.

The bicycle first appeared in the United States in the 1870s and was manufactured with modest success, but the introduction of the safety bicycle in 1887 set off a ten-year "bicycle craze." The bicycle craze had a significant impact on horse technology. Bicycles offered the opportunity for people of both sexes and a variety of ages to enjoy the popular pastime of going for drives or rides for recreation without having to ride a horse or drive a carriage. Despite the fact that women rode and drove, riding and driving were still remarkably gendered activities in the nineteenth century. Bicycles allowed an efficient translation of human muscle effort into motion, and their popularity alarmed veterinarians and livery stable owners, who were convinced for a time that the bicycle would put them out of business.[10]

Bicycle enthusiasts, or "wheelmen," tended to be affluent urbanites who saw themselves as modern and were eager to embrace new technologies. Their enthusiasm for cycling took them out of the cities and into the countryside. There they encountered the notorious public roads of America, unpaved, uneven, rutted, muddy, or dusty depending on the season. They became ardent advocates for good roads and organized effective lobbying groups through their bicycle clubs and used their magazines, such as *American Wheelman* and *Outing,* to publicize their views, joining their voices with those in other periodicals such as *Good Roads.*

The rhetoric of good roads was utterly reasonable. Horse travel over bad roads was difficult, and when the roads were truly bad, travel in some areas stopped altogether. In conjunction with the growing concern about rural life that would culminate in the "Country Life" movement of the early twentieth century, good roads advocates urged the construction of better roads to reduce physical isolation and improve the social and cultural opportunities in rural areas, as well as to improve rural farm prosperity by connecting them to markets.

In the first volume of *Good Roads,* "The Gospel of Good Roads" by Isaac Potter defined road taxes as an investment that would allow farmers to benefit more from their work, and discussed the cost of bad roads. If the roads were impassable for four weeks in a region with 10,000 horses, the cost of individual upkeep at twenty-five cents per day amounted to a total cost of $2,500 per day, $17,500 per week, and $70,000 for the four weeks. "A bad road, you see, is an expensive thing." It was not only costly but also inefficient. "Granting the necessity for the liberal use of horse-power in the maintenance of agricultural traffic, it is easily certain that the farmers of this country are keeping at least two millions of horses more than would be necessary to do all the hauling between farm and market, if only the principal roads were brought to a good condition."[11]

Following reformers' prevailing view of farmers, Potter extolled farming as a profession but then excoriated American farmers for being backward, suspicious, and reactionary and for eroding the quality of rural life. "His sons desert the farm life for the more profitable and enlightened conditions of city life, and the allurement of profit which is held out in every community of successful farmers is not so conspicuous in the United States today as to entice our farmers' sons from the greater promise of success offered by mercantile occupations." Farmers should stop resisting the use of engineers and scientific management for their roads. After all, all the farms in an area were simply analogous to one big partnership, and all farmers had to work together to devise ways of "curtailing expenses and making the business profitable . . . the first suggestion in order would be that of reducing the number of horses and hired help and of devising some way by which more and quicker trips could be made and large loads hauled between farm and market." Farmers had to rationalize their operations.[12]

Some were more sympathetic to farmers. Walter Preston Brownlow, a congressman from Tennessee, pointed out that farmers had had to carry the entire cost of building and maintaining roads on which others depended as well. "It is not the farmer's fault, but it is his misfortune, that, while there has been a great advance in railway and water transportation to which the National Government has largely contributed, he has not seen improved transportation on his roads . . . he cannot afford to pay for it unaided; he has not, and never will have, the money to pay for good roads."[13]

The bicycle performed a transitional function in manufacturing technology, and the wheelmen performed a transitional function in political culture, by advocating an increased role for the state and national government in what had been the largely local responsibility for road funding and road building. However, even as roads advocates listed the economic benefits that farmers would enjoy from improved roads, they made it an imperative to bring farmers into year-round connection with the market and objected to farmers' autonomy from those demands and standards. They implied a connection between farmers, bad roads, horses, and resistance to progress.[14]

The rhetoric about bicycles and about roads exposed the sharp distinctions that were emerging between rural and urban life by the turn of the century. As cities became less organic, they resembled rural life less. Electricity also drew a line between urban and rural life, with its capacity to reorganize the temporal, spatial, and sensory conditions of life, such as turning night into day with the bright luminosity of city streets. By 1910 only 2 percent of farmers had electricity. There was also a growing distinction between the city as "culture" and outside the city as "nature" or as a space where urban residents went for recreation and refreshment. The new suburban ideal as described in the writings of John Burroughs and others encouraged this view. There was a tendency to feel that farmers did not live up to the expectations of urbanites in terms of country living. If in the 1890s and early twentieth century Progressive reformers increasingly articulated an ideal of urban life in which there was no place for organic nature, they were no less comfortable with the condition of rural life.[15]

Along with bicycles, urban residents turned to automobiles as the technological means to their social and political ends. Like bicycles, automobiles were initially urban vehicles, because that was where the good roads and the consumer dollars were located.

Though at first automobiles seemed very much the playthings of the rich, the advent of the automobile was greeted with technological enthusiasm by magazines and other media catering to urban middle-class audiences. City dwellers who had resisted having steam locomotives on the streets were urged not confuse automobiles and locomotives.

> Editors who regard the motor wagon as a road locomotive can hardly be expected to have correct ideas of the nature and scope of the new invention. With such a fundamental misconception it is not singular that they should believe the motor wagon as impractical except on smooth asphalt pavements, and should picture these ponderous "road locomotives" rushing with the speed of a express train through city streets. The locomotive is a track vehicle, and the motor wagon a trackless vehicle, and if we would understand the latter we must first rid our minds of the locomotive idea.[16]

As the number of automobiles and their enthusiasts increased, the image of the horse began to change from benign to dangerous. The magazine *Horseless Age,* a popular magazine for automobile enthusiasts published between 1895 and 1918, illustrates the shift in how people thought and talked about horses. The magazine, like *Motor World* and others, served the interests of a distinct group of middle-class technological boosters and Progressives. The perspective offered by *Horseless Age* on the transition from animal to automotive power is worth exploring in some depth.

The editorial in the inaugural issue in 1895 was a litany of Progressive values, starting with the notion of progress itself.

> Progress is no respecter of persons or trades . . . Sufficient that they possess the energy, the brains, the capital, and

above all the confidence to fulfill her commands. Without this latter qualification all others are of no avail. Even now the bugle call has sounded. The muster roll is called. Willing and able volunteers are responding. These will go out to do valiant service in the cause of Progress, but the sluggards who will not heed the call . . . will be but stragglers in its rear.

The editors went on to stress the roles of efficiency, economy, sanitation, humane values, alleviation of congestion and stress, and general safety in the use of the automobile:

From the gradual displacement of the horse in business and in pleasure, will come economy of time and practical money saving. In cities and in towns the noise and clatter of the streets will be reduced, priceless boon to the tired nerves of this overwrought generation . . . On sanitary grounds too the banishing of horses from our city streets will be a blessing. Streets will be cleaner, jams and blockages less likely to occur, and accidents less frequent, for the horse is not so manageable as a mechanical vehicle.[17]

At times the magazine did modify its claims, as when it admitted that "there is not the slightest hope that the motor vehicle will relieve the congestion of cities; for the congested districts are inhabited by the very poor, who cannot afford to buy vehicles of any kind." But in general it welcomed the automobiles as a technological solution for a range of problems.[18]

Conventional sentimental language about the horse as an "obedient beast" began to vanish as *Horseless Age* expressed attitudes that became downright hostile. The horses that during the nineteenth century had been lauded as loyal companions and humble servants were now depicted as ungrateful and unruly. Horses repaid human care by with kicking, bucking, and causing accidents. In contrast, the automobile was the perfect servant. "At our will [the automobile] stopped, and at our will it would start again, and barring accidents it would do what we asked." Soon horses were portrayed as wild brutes that endangered pedestrians and passengers alike. "Scarcely a day passes that some one is not killed or maimed by a wild outbreak of this untamable beast . . . These frightful accidents can be prevented. The motor vehicle will do it." The "willful, unreliable brute" caused an intolerable number of accidents. "The everrecurring accidents due to horses which are daily set forth in the papers prove that the horse is a dangerous motor."[19]

Traditional practices, such as hitching horses in the streets or letting the milkwagon horse walk untended from house to house, following the route by memory while the milkman walked back and forth delivering the milk, came under attack as unsafe. That safety is a relative concept and not always a compelling reason for change is clear from the often appalling accident rate of the popular railroads and steamboats of the nineteenth century. However, there were changing ideas about risk, liability, and accident prevention in the Progressive era, when reformers raised safety to an absolute if abstract value. They sought to criminalize traditional practices of people who used animals in their work. "One of our correspondents last week called attention to the number of horses he encountered unattended in the street on a recent motor outing, and suggested that owners of motor carriages and the public in general needed protection from these 'ownerless' beasts. To leave horse unhitched in the streets or to permit them to make their way alone in the streets, as is frequently done, is criminal carelessness and a violation of law."[20]

Horse drivers in general came under attack, much like the horses themselves. They were inconsiderate and selfish nuisances, who made enormous demands about the behavior of automobile drivers but were unwilling to accept responsibility for their role in incidents or for their horses' behavior. "The average driver prides himself on his horsemanship and praises the intelligence and obedience of his horse, but as a matter of fact he begs his way through the world. He is constantly lifting his hand and signaling the motor vehicles to stop until he can get his horse under control; which in reality means until the horse himself decides to go ahead."[21]

As *Horseless Age* railed against horses and their drivers, it also railed against suggestions of regulations, speed limits, or licensing requirements for motorists; it was horses and their drivers who posed danger, not automobiles and their drivers. An editorial attacked the "motophobia" of the city of Chicago for requiring that drivers be licensed and demanded to know why horse drivers were not licensed. Cars "immediately obey a driver's will" whereas horses did not. The editorialist did admit that motorists had displayed "a disposition to exceed the limit of speed which can safely be taken in crowded thoroughfares," but concluded that speed limits would stop the problem. Car drivers should not be licensed "when in strict justice horse drivers are in greater need of restraint." *Horseless Age* expressed the hope that "when the inferiority of the horse as compared with the motor is generally admitted, the horse will be quietly and quickly dropped until the responsibility as between horse and motor will be clearly fixed where it has always belonged—on the owner of an untamable brute which man has cowed and beaten into partial subjection, but which in revenge bursts his bonds occasionally carrying ruin and death through our streets."[22]

If horses did not belong on city streets, where did horses belong? According to *Horseless Age*, "The horse belongs in the country . . . In the city he is a nuisance and an object of pity, a menace to the public health, and a dumb servant compelled to work under conditions not natural to him, and to which he cannot properly adjust himself." The automobile had become "a fact—a necessary concomitant of our advancing civilization"[23]

To show that automobiles were more sanitary, clean, safe, and efficient, *Horseless Age* devoted an entire issue to medical doctors in 1903, collecting their accounts of the benefits of using an automobile in medical practice instead of a horse. Doctors were quick to adopt automobiles in their practices, especially if they served more rural areas, and their professional status made them good advocates to showcase in the magazine. This issue showed that because automobiles were faster, they allowed doctors to respond faster to urgent cases and thus save more lives. Because the vehicles could be left unattended, they allowed a doctor to focus exclusively on the patient without being distracted by concerns about his horse. The doctor who arrived in a car was cleaner and did not bring dangerous stable filth into the sickroom. And finally, in a stressful age, automobiles provided rest and recreation. Automobiles were less tiring, because "of the perfectly even motion compared to the jog of a horse." There was also a pleasure in tinkering with the car, according to several doctors who enjoyed relaxing with their vehicles. Thus automobiles were pronounced to be healthy because they alleviated the stress of the modern age and provided a source of recreation.[24]

Automobiles were considered more efficient than horse-drawn vehicles, though as prime movers horses and automobiles have comparable energy efficiency. However, the process of using an automobile is often more convenient that using a horse. The desire for energy efficiency imposes one set of conditions, but the desire for convenience imposes another, which may or may not be energy-efficient. Progressives conflated the scientific meaning of efficiency as an energy ratio with the cultural meaning of convenience. What was convenient for Americans was control over personal autonomy in terms of time, mobility, and space. Most of what were cited as technical differences between horses and internal-combustion automobiles that made automobiles "better" were actually social and cultural preferences.

A recurrent theme in the automobile and bicycle literature was liberation from using streetcars and railroads. Auto enthusiasts expressed deep antagonism toward railroads and streetcars. They complained constantly about the inconvenience of timetables, about late trains, and about being at the mercy of large corporations. Middle-class commuters fumed over the fares and service of municipal streetcar companies, which often won city contracts in a corrupt political environment. People had always complained about the horse railways, but the faster speeds and service provided by electrification seemed to come with the consolidation and political corruption that made streetcar companies seem more distant and more powerful. Streetcar companies and other monopolies of public services became targets of Progressive political reform in the cities. Concern about railroads and other "trusts" were prominent national political issues. Automobiles seemed to provide a way for individuals to remove themselves from the control of these transportation monopolies.

Automobiles made private transportation more available to urban residents, most of whom did not own horses and carriages, but rented them from livery stables as needed. They relied on trains and streetcars to move between and within cities. However, many urbanites who would not have owned horses did own automobiles. Automobiles permitted first the rich and then the middle classes to withdraw from a public transportation system that they found increasingly distasteful. Automobiles gave them an alternative to crowded railroad cars and close contact with people whom they found unsettling or alien. Automobiles also provided an increasingly protected, private space, an extension of the private home, which surrounded people even as they traveled farther and faster than ever before.

Automobiles changed the meaning and use of public space. They turned city streets into arteries of through traffic, filled with the fast-moving cubicles of automobiles. Urban streets were traditional public social spaces, but in the wake of the disorders of the Gilded Age the urban middle and upper classes saw them as dangerous sites of urban disorder and public displays of resistance to authority. In the name of safety and efficiency, urban Progressives moved children into supervised urban playgrounds, installed new traffic regulation devices, placed policemen on the streets, and encouraged changes that turned streets from spaces in a neighborhood to spaces through a neighborhood.[25]

Automobile use did clean up public space by eliminating much of the horse manure and horse carcasses from the streets. The electrification of the streetcars had accomplished some of this, but between 1910 and 1920 the number of urban horses dropped by nearly 50 percent. However, the elimination of horses did not make the cities substantially cleaner, though it may have made them look cleaner. Instead it replaced a visible, solid, stationary form of pollution (piles of manure) with an invisible, mobile, gaseous form, namely the exhaust of internal-combustion vehicles.

By the 1920s urban air pollution was a public issue. However, political solutions were difficult to achieve. Because air pollution ignored political boundaries, it required political cooperation between local governments or between states. As an issue, air pollution involved the same problems of centralization and rivalry that had made the politics of internal improvement so contentious a century before. At that time, Americans had turned to private enterprise, in the form of railroad companies, to construct public infrastructure. The automobile privatized the problems of transportation, and one consequence was that air pollution was more difficult to deal with as well.

A significant factor in the replacement of horse power was the increasing electrification of American society and the way electricity changed how Americans thought about energy. Electricity was an extraordinarily different kind of power. It was invisible, yet extremely and dangerously powerful, its current contained in wires that only those with technical skills could handle. Using electricity required a system designed by engineers, the secular heroes of the Progressive era. Most significant, however, electricity's revolutionary capacity for transmission over distance, and thus its capacity to separate the production of power from the consumption of power. This gave it a magical quality—Thomas Edison was referred to as a wizard for his electrical creations. Henry Adams expressed the same sense of wonder when he described a dynamo: "The planet itself seemed less impressive in its old-fashioned, deliberate, annual or daily revolution, than this huge wheel, revolving within arm's-length at some vertiginous speed, and barely murmuring . . . Before the end one began to pray to it; inherited instinct taught the natural expression of man before silent and infinite force." Electricity also addressed another great concern, based on the implication of the third law of thermodynamics, that the fixed supply of energy would eventually be used up and become inaccessible through entropy. Electricity provided material benefits while delaying this possible end. It promised a modern kind of energy, with bountiful consumption, complete commodification, and invisible production. In contrast, the horse seemed cumbersome, inefficient, and old-fashioned. Its visibly working and straining muscles were an uncomfortable reminder of the costs of harnessing and consuming power.[26]

Another factor in automobile adoption was a strengthening cultural dichotomy between nature as a wild, separate realm and culture, or the human-built world that had developed as a response to industrialization during the nineteenth century. The closing of the frontier in 1893 contributed to a growing belief that the supply of wild nature was limited and needed protection. A burgeoning preservation movement sought to change the idea of nature as a source of exploitable energy to nature as a source of spiritual renewal and respite from the stresses of urban industrial society. When access to nature was limited by reliance on railroads, the idea of protecting nature for recreation instead of as a productive source of common wealth was still contested. But when the automobile began to make nature more accessible to more people, the idea of keeping it removed and separate gained cultural strength. To the idea that horses were making the cities unclean, disorderly, unsafe, and inefficient was added the idea that as bits of nature they should not be in the city at all.

The view that automobiles easily replaced horses obscures the fact that each was part of a very different kind of technological system. Horse-drawn transportation was a decentralized system. Because it was expensive to own private carriages in urban areas, it limited individualized mobility but encouraged the use of public transportation and public space. As automotive transportation became more affordable for urbanites, it provided unlimited individualized mobility and discouraged public transportation and public space. Yet it was a much more centralized system because of the large automobile makers and oil companies that provided the vehicles and the fuel. The demands of automobile users for increased government spending for infrastructure and for increased regulation of ownership and use promoted the centralization of power in state and federal governments.

However, the material environment that had been created by and for horses made it possible for automobile adoption to occur rapidly. Automobiles did not need new infrastructure in order to be used. Unlike railroads, which had had to construct rails for the steam-powered locomotives, automobiles could take advantage of the existing infrastructure of streets and roads that had been constructed for horse-drawn vehicles. Automobiles did not require massive public or private capital investment in new infrastructure. Automobiles could also be housed and parked in many of the same spaces as horses. With no immediate investments of capital or radical changes in use of space required, it became exceptionally easy for American society to adopt automobiles.

Automobiles were the "weeds" of the turn-of-the-century technological world. In biology, a weed is defined as "any plant that spreads rapidly and outcompetes others on disturbed soil."[27] Weeds are successful and ubiquitous because they are opportunistic. They exploit opportunities and quickly make themselves at home in a new environment. For automobiles, the "disturbed soil" was found in the loss of momentum suffered by horse technology in the decades straddling the turn of the century, and in the culture of the urban middle and upper classes that embraced automobiles as a technological solution to a variety of issues and saw them as a symbol of progress.

Apart from their similarity as self-propelled, mobile prime movers, automobiles and horses occupied different niches. These surface similarities would mask differences between horse energy and automotive energy in the sources, production, and consumption of power that over time would have considerable consequences for American society, one of which was the enduring belief that the transition was a matter of simple substitution.

Nonetheless, the cultural transition was faster than the material transition. The decline in the horse population and the disappearance of horses from most of American life was far slower than most people came to believe, and took nearly half a century to accomplish. Urban horse populations declined rapidly but did not disappear completely. Horses continued in construction work. Much urban hauling continued to use horses; hauling firms experimented with electrical trucks, internal combustion trucks, and horse-drawn wagons for many years until the internal-combustion truck won out. There were draft horses on the streets of American cities through the 1920s, and in some urban occupations until the 1950s. For example, the city of Philadelphia continued to use horses in its sanitation department and retired the last ones only in the 1950s.

Equine populations remained steady through the 1920s, in part because the number of mules continued to increase, and then dropped, hitting their lowest point around midcentury. In geo-

Horses being used in house construction, Milwaukee, Wisconsin, 1926.
Wisconsin Historical Society, image 47934.

graphical terms, horse populations dropped off from east to west. After 1910 the states with the largest horse populations were all west of the Mississippi.

The transition was much slower in agriculture, where the use of horses remained a good technological choice. Not only did it take a long time to develop tractors that were reliable, but also tractors could not entirely substitute for horses on many farms. Horses did more than pull machinery; they were workers as well as prime movers. There were many tasks on the farm that needed a horse's knowledge of routine or response to command. For example, in clearing stones from a field, the farmer walked beside a horse and wagon, starting and stopping the horse by voice command. Using a tractor for the same work required either using another worker to drive it or getting on and off the tractor repeatedly and consuming fuel by starting, stopping, and idling. Additionally, much horse-drawn equipment, such as harrows, drills, cultivators, tenders, and mowers, was not geared for the power and speed of tractors and would need replacing or retooling. Since horses were used for transportation as well as work, tractors replaced only one of their jobs. A lively and often acrimonious debate in agricultural circles about tractors versus horses lasted through the 1930s as the Horse and Mule Association of America, led by Wayne Dinsmore, argued about the consequences of the motorization of agriculture.

Motorization affected the agricultural sector in profound ways. As prime movers, horses did not operate in a vacuum, but were part of an economic and cultural network. The decline in urban horse use diminished an important market for horses, grain crops, and equipment. Motorization at first affected the horse market by increasing the number of unemployed horses. The military absorbed some during World War I, a conflict that relied extensively on ani-

Horses and trucks at the McCormick Works (International Harvester) in Chicago, Illinois, 1928. Wisconsin Historical Society, image 25707.

mal power. Some horses were sent to the slaughterhouse, and many were retired. Declines in horse breeding resulted in a smaller horse supply that eventually encouraged tractorization. As reductions in the horse population accelerated, the intensifying trend affected a network of producers and consumers in all horse-related markets even as the effects of motorization burgeoned and rippled through the economy. One result was that many veterinary schools closed their doors, and the number of veterinarians declined so precipitously that many believed that the profession was in mortal danger.

More immediately affected were manufacturers of horse-drawn vehicles. Less than a handful of these firms, including Studebaker, were able to shift into automobile production. Automobile production was an entirely different industry from the production of horse-drawn vehicles, which involved producing a frame, usually with wheels, to be used by prime movers supplied by the purchasers. Automobile manufacturers produced both frames and motors.

Also affected was the grain market. As the decline in the horse population accelerated during the 1920s, acreage was shifted from pasture and hay into grain production. The immediate impact of this increase in supply on the grain market was muted by the demand for grain during World War I. However, high grain prices during the war encouraged American farmers to increase production. When European nations resumed grain production after the war and international trade picked up, these two factors caused American grain production to rise as world grain prices were dropping.

The effects of a declining farm horse population were substantial. The agricultural sector was depressed throughout the 1920s, remaining a chronically weak sector in an economy that otherwise appeared prosperous. In 1933, during the nadir of the Great Depression, the Bureau of the Census suggested that the transition from animal to automotive power was "one of the main contributing factors of the present economic situation." A report titled "The Farm Horse" argued:

> At least 18,000,000 acres of crop land, formerly required to produce horse feed, have been put in other crops in the last decade. This added acreage augmented by the release of that part of 3,000,000 acres of plowable pasture formerly devoted to horses, has resulted in surpluses of various crops and livestock; in many crops the surpluses have resulted in decreased prices for these farm products, greatly lowering farm purchasing power; and the reduction in the latter has affected the entire country.[28]

Surpluses had not only depressed crop prices but also caused rural unemployment and depressed urban industries dependent on processing agricultural products. Furthermore, horse breeding, which had always been a source of extra income for farmers, was declining, and the farm horse population was aging. These factors raised the possibility of an animal-power shortage just as 1.5 million people were returning to the farms because the conditions of the Great Depression were forcing them out of the cities. The causes of the Great Depression were complex and remain contested. However, the use of horses was so integral to American society that the effects of their replacement affected a number of other enterprises and rippled through the economy, possibly contributing to the economic conditions of the 1920s and the subsequent depression.

At the turn of the century, the culture of Progressivism facilitated the technological transition between animal and automotive power, and made it appear simple and swift, with only benefits and no costs. Reformers and technological enthusiasts emphasized themes of efficiency, order, sanitation, safety, and democracy that resonated with the urban middle and upper classes, which valued scientific management and rationalization. The automobile was the symbol of a modernity they were ready to embrace.

The transition from animal to automotive power would prove to be gradual, complicated, and troubling. Assertions of its inevitability are misleading and irrelevant. The central issue is that the replacement of animal power took a particular form that was the result of cultural choices made about energy consumption at the turn of the century. Many economic, political, and technical factors contributed to the near-demise of horse power. Of all these contingencies, however, the most important was a growing objection to using horses as prime movers. Though motivated in part by humane concerns, the overriding objection came from the discomfort of the visible, physical work of power production. Americans wanted bountiful energy and abundant consumer products without having to deal with the moral, social, political, or environmental implications of their choices. As they consumed electricity from distant power plants, fossil fuels from still more distant foreign countries, and food from industrialized farms and processing plants and placed workers inside rationalized factories, they rendered the connections between production and consumption invisible. Tarkington's scene in *The Magnificent Ambersons* in which George receives his comeuppance in a snow-filled ditch would prove to be a metaphor for how Americans viewed the fall of horse power. The scene concludes with the horse shaking off its traces and disappearing from sight. The politics of energy, which had taken form during the conflicts over internal improvements in the antebellum period, would construct a new energy landscape in the twentieth century on the foundations of the world created by horses in nineteenth-century America.

On Saturday, May 20, 2006, a magnificent spring day, a record crowd of over 118,000 gathered at Maryland's Pimlico Race Course for the 131st running of the Preakness Stakes. What drew them to the track and millions to their television sets was Barbaro, the dark bay three-year-old colt that had won the Kentucky Derby. Barbaro's victory in the Derby by the largest margin in history raised the possibility that he might be the first horse in twenty-six years who could go the distance and win the Triple Crown.

The race began with a false start as Barbaro burst early out of the gate. After being inspected by the track veterinarian for injuries, he was loaded back into the starting gate. The bell rang, the gates opened, and horses surged forward, Barbaro in the middle of the pack as it headed for the first turn. Suddenly he dropped back, then veered sideways, awkwardly hopping and trying to hold his left rear leg off the ground. Jockey Edward Prado leapt off his back and tried to hold the agitated horse steady. People converged on the injured horse, and screens were erected around him. One woman screamed repeatedly from the rail, "Don't you put that horse down!" The race, unnoticed, continued around the far side of the oval as a silent crowd watched Barbaro loaded into an ambulance. Soon, under police escort, Barbaro was en route to the New Bolton Center of the University of Pennsylvania School of Veterinary Medicine. The next day, in a five-hour operation, Dr. Dean Richardson, one of the leading equine surgeons in the country, and his team pieced the leg together with more than twenty-four titanium implants. It was one of the worst injuries Richardson had ever seen, with multiple broken bones; the operating team had gasped when they saw the extent of the damage. The pastern bones alone were in more than twenty pieces. The operation was an immediate success in that Barbaro was able to put weight on the splinted and bandaged leg. This was significant because horses must keep standing and moving for reasons of health. But Richardson warned that the horse remained in critical though stable condition, in danger of laminitis (hoof inflammation), infection, respiratory problems, and digestive disorders.

Meanwhile, at the modest entrance to the center, located on an old, sunken country road in Chester County, it was a mob scene. Not only had the media converged on New Bolton, but also well-wishers traveled there to hold prayer vigils and to leave offerings of carrots, apples, flowers, and get-well cards. One man drove two hours so that his young daughter could bring carrots to Barbaro. By Wednesday the Veterinary School had created a special website so that well-wishers could send e-mail messages to the racehorse. The Barbaro story dominated national news for days. Like the racehorses Ruffian and Secretariat before him, Barbaro had become, in the words of one columnist, "a national pet." In the days leading up to the Preakness, Barbaro had been described as a "big, long-striding high-cruising dude" and as "a monster . . . the real article." After his injury, the word "fragile" appeared frequently. "This is what can happen when a 1,000-pound racehorse balanced on the legs of a ballerina takes a bad step on the track," wrote Bob Ford in the *Philadelphia Inquirer*.[1] All over the country there was an emotional outpouring as Barbaro's plight captured people's sentiments. Many were inspired by what they described as the horse's nobility, courage, and sweet temper in the face of having the greatest prize in American racing snatched from him. People in all conditions and classes spoke of the importance of his example to them in their lives.

Barbaro's injury raised questions about the injuries sustained in horse racing. Many noted that injuries were simply part of the sport. One pedigree specialist said, "These horses are bred to compete, they want to do what they are doing. They really want to do this." Some criticized the extravagant attention paid to Barbaro in contrast to other horses. Four days after the Preakness, a four-year-old filly named Lauren's Charm died of a heart attack in a race at Belmont Park in New York. "One horse breaks an ankle in a Triple Crown race and sets off a national outpouring of emotion," wrote William Rhoden in the *New York Times*. "[Another] collapses and dies in full view on a sunny afternoon and not many seem to notice."[2]

For months Barbaro's recovery remained uncertain. He underwent several more operations. At one point he improved so much that he was able to go outside every day. But the severity of the injuries to leg and foot made him susceptible to laminitis, a hoof disease that was a constant topic of discussion in veterinary literature through the nineteenth century. In February 2007 Gretchen and Roy Jackson, Barbaro's owners, and Richardson made the difficult decision to put the horse down to spare him further suffering from the incurable condition.

The story of Barbaro reveals much about the fate of the horse in the twentieth century. The use of horses for farm work and haulage dropped away, but the use of horses for sport, recreation, and companionship continued. During the nineteenth century the horse was the center of a masculine world of work, associated with status and manly virtue. In the twentieth century the horse became the center of a feminine world of play, associated with young girls. Even race jockeys, with their diminutive size, were childlike in appearance. People felt increasingly uncomfortable when seeing horses working, often criticizing the horse-drawn tourist carriages found in historical districts, and complaining to humane societies about seeing farm horses at work.

The decline of the horse as a source of power was accompanied by an increase in its traditional power as a symbol of natural and mystical forces, wealth, and prestige, while sentimentality about horses rivaled that of the Victorians. The thoroughbred remained at the top of the equine class system. Horse status reflected owner status, and in most cases considerable income. Thus horses returned to their traditional roles as elite animals and potent symbols. They continued to serve as blank slates onto which humans projected their values and concerns.

Horse populations remained steady through the 1920s, then dropped steadily until midcentury, declining in a pattern from east to west. The majority of the horse population was west of the Mississippi, joined by a substantial mule population in the South. By the late 1940s the last of the farm horses were disappearing from use except among the Amish and a few others, and in cities the remnants of delivery and vending by horse-drawn vehicles were vanishing as well. In 1950 the horse population was six million; by 1960 it had dropped to three million.

During the 1970s an upsurge of interest in riding and racing, combined with expanding affluence, led to new increases. Traditional horse work such as pulling and driving became boutique hobbies attracting people who had not grown up on farms or previously used horses. The energy crisis of the 1970s renewed some interest in using horses in farming. Specialized farmers found horses to be efficient prime movers in small operations or in small fields. Vineyards found that using horses instead of tractors avoided compressing the soil and damaging valuable rootstock. Environmental concerns and forest management brought them back into logging to avoid the damage caused by large, heavy machinery. By the end of the century, however, most of the estimated seven million horses in the United States were used for recreation and sport rather than work.

The changing roles of veterinarians followed the fortunes of horses. The decline of the urban horse created a professional crisis for veterinarians. Many veterinary schools closed, and for years the greatest employment opportunity was with the USDA in public health work with livestock. Care of small pets now constitutes the majority of veterinary practice in the United States. As the example of Barbaro shows, horses are at the center of continuing innovations and advances in large-animal veterinary medicine. Much as in human health care, the benefits are not equally distributed and are largely a function of (owner) wealth.

Human interest in horses has remained constant over the centuries, though its focus and the uses of horses have changed. Despite the intensity of popular attraction to horses, Americans have lost sight of the history of horses as a source of power and the role they played in the development of industrial society. Now, at the beginning of the twenty-first century, rising energy prices, complicated geopolitics, and grave environmental concerns suggest that energy may not continue to be indefinitely plentiful and cheap for Americans, and that the energy landscape that evolved in the twentieth century may have to undergo changes. The energy history of the nineteenth century reveals the possibilities of using different kinds of power sources in ways that complement one another. One such possibility might be to use horses as an appropriate technology in certain settings. Certainly, though, Americans will never recapture what they had in the nineteenth century, a society of horses and humans living and working together.

Appendix:

Horse Population and Power

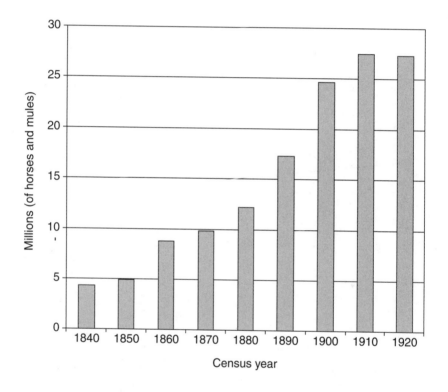

United States horse and mule population, 1840–1920. *Sources:* U.S. Bureau of the Census, decadal censuses, 1840–1940; Clay McShane and Joel Tarr, *The Horse in the City: Living Machines in the Nineteenth Century* (Baltimore: Johns Hopkins University Press, 2007); Philip Teigen, National Library of Medicine, National Institutes of Health, Bethesda, Md., 2002.

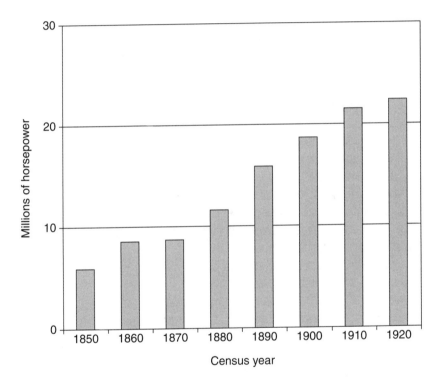

Horse power from animal power, 1850–1920. *Source:* U.S. Bureau of the Census, *Historical Statistics of the United States,* Part 2 (Washington, D.C.: Government Printing Office, 1975).

Horses per square mile

City	Horses per square mile
Chicago	463
Detroit	537
Cincinnati	615
Milwaukee	709
Kansas City	440
Boston	680
Albany	392
Buffalo	395
New York	486
Philadelphia	394
Baltimore	645
Washington	214
Atlanta	326
New Orleans	308
Nashville	471
Richmond	615
Denver	561
Los Angeles	298
Portland, Ore.	633

Population density of horses in selected cities, 1900. *Source:* Philip M. Teigen, National Library of Medicine, National Institutes of Health, Bethesda, Md., 2002.

INTRODUCTION

1. "The Position of the Horse in Modern Society," *The Nation* 15 (31 October 1872): 277.
2. Ibid.
3. Ibid., pp. 277–278.
4. Ibid., p. 278.
5. Erik Schatzberg, "Technik Comes to America: Changing Meanings of Technology before 1930," *Technology and Culture* 47 (2006): 486–487, 492–493, 511–512.
6. William Cronon, *Nature's Metropolis: Chicago and the Great West* (New York: W. W. Norton, 1991), p. 98; Edmund Russell, "Evolutionary History: Prospectus for a New Field," *Environmental History* 8 (2003): 215–216.
7. Juliet Clutton-Brock, *Horse Power* (Cambridge, Mass.: Harvard University Press, 1992), pp. 179–180; Harriet Ritvo, *The Animal Estate: The English and Other Creatures in the Victorian Age* (Cambridge, Mass.: Harvard University Press, 1987), pp. 18–20.
8. Charles Elton, *Animal Ecology* (1927; reprint, London: Sidgwick and Jackson, 1951), p. 63; Philip Scranton, *Endless Novelty: Specialty Production and American Industrialization, 1865–1925* (Princeton: Princeton University Press, 1997), p. 8.

9. John Lauritz Larson, *Internal Improvement: National Public Works and the Promise of Popular Government in the Early United States* (Chapel Hill: University of North Carolina Press, 2001).

10. Cronon, *Nature's Metropolis*, p. 268; Daniel Siegel, "The Energy Concept: A Historical Overview," *Materials and Society* 7 (1983): 411–424.

11. Susan D. Jones, *Valuing Animals: Veterinarians and Their Patients in Modern America* (Baltimore: Johns Hopkins University Press, 2003); Bruno Latour, *Aramis, or the Love of Technology,* trans. Catherine Porter (Cambridge, Mass.: Harvard University Press, 1996).

12. David Edgerton, *The Shock of the Old: Technology and Global History since 1900* (New York: Oxford University Press, 2007), p. ix; Thomas P. Hughes, *Networks of Power* (Baltimore: Johns Hopkins University Press, 1983), pp. 2, 5–6.

13. Carolyn Marvin, *When Old Technologies Were New* (New York: Oxford University Press, 1988), p. 235.

14. John Kasson, *Civilizing the Machine: Technology and Republican Values in America, 1776–1900* (New York: Grossman, 1976).

1. WHY HORSES

1. *American Farmer* 1 (1819): 17.

2. Ibid., p. 35.

3. Ibid., pp. 43, 178.

4. Tamara Platkins Thornton, *Cultivating Gentlemen: The Meaning of Country Life among the Boston Elite, 1785–1860* (New Haven: Yale University Press, 1989); Adele E. Clark and Joan H. Fujimura, "What Tools? Which Jobs? Why Right?" in *The Right Tools for the Job: At Work in Twentieth-Century Life Sciences,* ed. Adele E. Clark and Joan H. Fujimura (Princeton: Princeton University Press, 1992).

5. John Lauritz Larson, *Internal Improvement: National Public Works and the Promise of Popular Government in the Early United States* (Chapel Hill: University of North Carolina Press, 2001), pp. 9–10.

6. Jared Diamond, *Guns, Germs, and Steel: The Fates of Human Societies* (New York: W. W. Norton, 1997), chap. 9.

7. Edward Everett, quoted in Edwin T. Layton Jr., ed., *Technology and Social Change in America* (New York: Harper and Row, 1973), p. 91; Judith A. McGaw, *"Most Wondrous Machine": Mechanization and Social Change*

in Berkshire Paper Making, 1801–1885 (Princeton: Princeton University Press, 1987), p. 1; *Horsepower Applied to Railways* (London: John Ollivier, 1844).

8. J. H. Reeves, *The Orange County Stud Book* (New York: Jason H. Tuttle, 1880), p. 69.

9. Robert H. Thurston, *The Animal as a Machine and a Prime Mover, and the Laws of Energetics* (New York: John Wiley and Sons, 1894), pp. 32–33; Vaclav Smil, *Energies* (Cambridge, Mass.: MIT Press, 1999), p. 39.

10. Stephen Budiansky, *The Nature of Horses: Exploring Equine Evolution, Intelligence, Behavior* (New York: Free Press, 1997), p. 186; Smil, *Energies*, pp. xvi–xvii.

11. Daniel S. Mills and Sue M. McDonnell, *The Domestic Horse: The Evolution, Development and Management of Its Behaviour* (Cambridge: Cambridge University Press, 2005).

12. Donald R. Griffin, *Animal Minds: Beyond Cognition to Consciousness* (Chicago: University of Chicago Press, 2001); Budiansky, *The Nature of Horses.*

13. Brian Cottrell and Johan Kamminga, *Mechanics of Pre-Industrial Technology* (Cambridge: Cambridge University Press, 1990); Drew Conroy, *Oxen: A Teamster's Guide* (Gainesboro, Tenn.: Rural Heritage, 1999); Michael R. Goe and Robert E. McDowell, *Animal Traction: Guidelines for Utilization,* Cornell International Agriculture Memo (Ithaca: Cornell University, 1980).

14. *Rural New Yorker* 6 (1855) and 69 (1910).

15. *American Agriculturist* 23 (1864): 171.

16. George B. Ellenberg, "Mule South to Tractor South: Mules, Machines, Agriculture, and Culture in the Cotton South, 1850–1950" (Ph.D. diss., University of Kentucky, 1994), pp. 15–16.

17. Harvey Riley, *The Mule: A Treatise on the Breeding, Training and Uses to Which He May Be Put* (New York: Dick and Fitzgerald, 1867); Kyle Dean Kauffman, "Why Was the Mule Used in Southern Agriculture? Empirical Evidence of Principal-Agent Solutions," *Explorations in Economic History* 30 (1993): 336–351.

18. *American Agriculturist* 21 (1862): 360; *Rural New Yorker* 6 (1855): 21.

19. *Rural New Yorker* 6 (1855): 134; ibid., 7 (1856): 174; ibid., 8 (1857): 294.

20. U.S. Census Office, *Agriculture in the United States in 1860* (Washington, D.C.: Government Printing Office, 1864), pp. cxi–cxii.

21. Harriet Ritvo, *The Platypus and the Mermaid, and Other Figments of the Classifying Imagination* (Cambridge, Mass.: Harvard University Press, 1997), pp. 94–95.

22. *Ohio Cultivator* 12 (1865): 262.

23. S. F. Baird, "American Ruminants: On the Ruminating Animals of North America and Their Susceptibility of Domestication," in *Report of the Commissioner of Patents: Agricultural Report, 1851* (Washington, D.C.: Wendell and Benthuysen, 1852), pp. 104, 108.

24. Arthur H. Cole, "Agricultural Crazes," *American Economic Review* 16 (1926); James B. Davis, "Introduction of the Asiatic Buffalo, the Brahmin Ox, and the Cashmere, Scinde and Mata Goats into South Carolina," in *Report of the Commissioner of Patents: Agricultural Report, 1853* (Washington, D.C.: A. O. P. Nicholson, 1854); D. J. Browne, "Proposed Introduction of the Yak-Ox from Tartary to the Great Plains of the West," in *Report of the Commissioner of Agriculture, 1858* (Washington, D.C.: William A. Harris, 1859); "The Alpaca—No. 2," *American Agriculturist* 5 (1846).

25. Odie B. Faulk, *The U.S. Camel Corps: An Army Experiment* (New York: Oxford University Press, 1976).

26. Peter Benes, "To the Curious: Bird and Animal Exhibitions in New England, 1716–1825," in *New England's Creatures: 1400–1900,* ed. Peter Benes, Annual Proceedings of the Dublin Seminar for New England Folklife, 1993 (Boston: Trustees of Boston University, 1995); Rev. John M. Wilson, ed., *Rural Cyclopedia* (Edinburgh: A. Fullerton, 1852), pp. 658–659; D. J. Browne, "Importation of Camels," in *Report of the Commissioner of Patents: Agricultural Report, 1853*, p. 61.

27. U.S. Senate, *Report of the Secretary of War . . . in Compliance with a Resolution of the Senate of February 2, 1857 Respecting the Purchase of Camels,* 34th Cong., 3d sess., 1857, Exec. Doc. No. 62; "Stated Meeting, 6 November," *Proceedings of the American Philosophical Society* 6 (July–December 1857): 275–276.

28. Smil, *Energies,* p. 63; R. T. Wilson, *The Camel* (London: Longman, 1984); *American Agriculturist* 25 (March 1866): 99–100.

29. U.S. House of Representatives, *Report of Edward Fitzgerald Beale to the Secretary of War . . . April 26, 1858,* 35th Cong., 1st sess., Exec. Doc. No. 124, in Lesley Lewis Burt, ed., *Uncle Sam's Camels: The Journal of May Humphreys Stacey Supplemented by the Report of Edward Fitzgerald Beale (1857–1858)* (Cambridge, Mass.: Harvard University Press, 1929), pp. 147, 156, 233; *Scientific American* 13 (1858): 155.

30. George Perkins Marsh, *The Camel: His Organization, Habits and Uses, Considered with Reference to His Introduction into the United States* (Boston: Gould and Lincoln, 1856).

31. May Humphreys Stacey, in Burt, *Uncle Sam's Camels*, p. 43.

32. William Stanton, *The Leopard's Spots: Scientific Attitudes toward Race in America, 1815–1859* (Chicago: University of Chicago Press, 1960).

33. U.S. Census Office, *Synopsis of the Sixth Census* (Philadelphia: S. Augustus Mitchell, 1843), p. 192; U.S. Census Office, *Compendium of the Seventh Census* (Washington, D.C.: Beverly Tucker, 1851), p. 164; U.S. Census Office, *Twelfth Census*, vol. 5 (Washington, D.C., 1902), p. clxxxix; U.S. Bureau of the Census, *Thirteenth Census*, vol. 5 (Washington, D.C.: Government Printing Office, 1913), pp. 331, 437.

34. U.S. Census Office, *Preliminary Report of the Eighth Census* (Washington, D.C.: Government Printing Office, 1862), pp. 198, 210.

2. A Landscape for Horses

1. Thomas Weber, *The Northern Railroads in the Civil War, 1861–1865* (New York: King's Crown Press of Columbia University, 1952), pp. 107–108.

2. George Rogers Taylor, *The Transportation Revolution, 1815–1860* (New York: Rinehart, 1951), p. 3.

3. Fairman Rogers, *A Manual of Coaching* (Philadelphia: J. B. Lippincott, 1900), pp. 186–187; W. Kingsford, *History, Structure and Statistics of Plank Roads in the United States and Canada* (Philadelphia: A. Hart, 1851), p. 26; Robert F. Hunter, "Turnpike Construction in Antebellum Virginia," *Technology and Culture* 4 (1963): 189; John R. Stilgoe, *Common Landscape of America, 1580–1845* (New Haven: Yale University Press, 1985), p. 112.

4. Albert C. Koch, *Journey through a Part of the United States of North America in the Years 1844 to 1846*, trans. Ernst A. Stadler (Carbondale: Southern Illinois University Press, 1972), p. 132.

5. William Cobbett, *A Year's Residence in the United States of America* (1819; reprint, New York: Augustus M. Kelley, 1969), pp. 476–477; Horace Greeley, *An Overland Journey from New York to San Francisco in the Summer of 1859* (New York: C. M. Saxton, Barker, 1860), p. 46.

6. *Journal of the Franklin Institute* 65 (1858): 294; Jacob Bigelow, *Elements of Technology*, 2d ed. (Boston, 1831), pp. 204–205; John McAdam, "Ad-

dress to the President of the Board of Agriculture of England," *American Railway Journal* 1 (1832): 499.

7. "Plank Roads.—No. 1," *DeBow's Review* 7 (1848): 463.

8. William Gregg, "Plank Roads," ibid., p. 378.

9. W. M. Gillespie, *A Manual of the Principles and Practice of Road-making: Comprising the Location, Construction and Improvement of Roads (Common, Macadam, Paved, Plank, etc.) and Rail-Roads* (New York: A. S. Barnes, 1847), p. 15.

10. Taylor, *The Transportation Revolution*, pp. 16–17; Hunter, "Turnpike Construction in Antebellum Virginia," pp. 177, 186–187.

11. Ausable River Plank Road Company, *Proposed Association for Constructing a Plank Road from Ausable Forks in Clinton Co. to Some Point on Lake Champlain near Port Kent or Port Douglas . . .*, Adirondack Museum Library, Blue Mountain Lake, N.Y.

12. William Owen, *Diary of William Owen*, ed. Joel W. Hiatt (1906; reprint, Clifton, N.J.: Augustus M. Kelley, 1973), p. 29.

13. Richard John, *Spreading the News: The American Postal System from Franklin to Morse* (Cambridge, Mass.: Harvard University Press, 1995), pp. 108–109.

14. Ibid., p. 91.

15. Waybills, Abbot-Downing Collection, box 19, folder 5, New Hampshire Historical Society, Concord.

16. Taylor, *The Transportation Revolution*, p. 140; Edward C. Kirkland, *Men, Cities, and Transportation: A Study in New England History, 1820–1900* (Cambridge, Mass.: Harvard University Press, 1948), p. 55.

17. John, *Spreading the News*, pp. 63–64, 91–96.

18. J. L. Ringwalt, *Development of Transportation Systems in the United States* (1888; reprint, New York: Johnson Reprint, 1966), p. 29; Owen, *Diary*, p. 27; Charles Dickens, *American Notes* (1842; reprint, New York: Penguin, 2000), p. 213; Frances Trollope, *Domestic Manners of the Americans* (1839; reprint, Oxford: Oxford University Press, 1984), pp. 159, 334.

19. Julius F. Sachse, *The Wayside Inns on the Lancaster Roadside between Philadelphia and Lancaster* (Lancaster, Pa.: New Era Printing, 1912), p. 114.

20. Dickens, *American Notes*, p. 105.

21. Twain quoted in Harry N. Scheiber, *Abbot-Downing and the Concord Coach* (1965; reprint, Concord: New Hampshire Historical Society, 1989), pp. 5–6; Thomas A. Kinney, *The Carriage Trade: Making Horse-Drawn*

Vehicles in America (Baltimore: Johns Hopkins University Press, 2004), pp. 15–16.

22. Bigelow, *Elements of Technology*, p. 252.

23. Franz Anton Ritter von Gerstner, *Early American Railroads: Franz Anton Ritter von Gerstner's Die Innein Communicationen,* ed. Frederick C. Gamst, trans. David J. Diepenhouse and John C. Decker (Stanford: Stanford University Press, 1997), pp. 2, 91.

24. Peter Way, *Common Labour* (Cambridge: Cambridge University Press, 1993), pp. 134, 137.

25. Jenny M. Parker, *Rochester: A Story Historical* (Rochester, N.Y., 1884), quoted in Ronald E. Shaw, *Erie Water West* (Lexington: University of Kentucky Press, 1966), p. 197.

26. *Scientific American* 13 (1858): 251; Gerstner, *Early American Railroads,* p. 102.

27. *Off-Hand Sketches: Companion for the Tourist and Traveler over the Philadelphia, Pottsville and Reading Railroad* (Philadelphia: J. W. Moore, 1854), p. 80.

28. *Scientific American,* n.s. 13 (1858): 405; ibid., n.s. 27 (1872): 15.

29. Koch, *Journey through Part of United States,* p. 115; Dionysius Lardner, *Railway Economy: A Treatise on the New Art of Transport* (New York: Harper Brothers, 1850), p. 331; Peregrine Prolix [Philip Nicklin], *A Pleasant Peregrination through the Prettiest Parts of Pennsylvania* (1836; reprint, York, Pa.: American Canal and Transportation Center, 1975), pp. 37, 120–123.

30. Alvin F. Harlow, *When Horses Pulled Boats* (York, Pa.: American Canal and Transportation Center, 1987), p. 66; *Scientific American,* n.s. 27 (1872): 246 and 181.

31. Koch, *Journey through Part of United States,* p. 114; Kevin J. Crisman and Arthur B. Cohen, *When Horses Walked on Water: Horse-powered Ferries in Nineteenth-Century America* (Washington, D.C.: Smithsonian Institution Press, 1998), pp. 61–62, 74–75.

32. *Niles' Weekly Register,* quoted in Crisman and Cohen, *When Horses Walked on Water,* p. 33; Harriet Martineau, *Retrospect of Western Travel,* vol. 1 (New York, 1838), p. 73; Owen, *Diary,* p. 29; Richard Champion Rawlins, *An American Journal, 1839–1840,* ed. John L. Tearle (Cranbury, N.J.: Associated University Press, 2002).

33. U.S. Census Office, *Agriculture in the United States in 1860* (Washington, D.C.: Government Printing Office, 1864), pp. clxiv–clxv.

34. U.S. Bureau of the Census, *Historical Statistics of the United States*, Part 2 (Washington, D.C.: Government Printing Office, 1975), p. 73.

35. *American Railway Journal* 1 (1832): 36; *New York Times*, 9 August 1864, p. 4.

36. Comparison to a dragon: Frances Kemble, quoted in Charles Francis Adams, *Railroads: Their Origins and Problems* (New York: G. P. Putnam's Sons, 1878), p. 13; the verse comes from *Locomotive Sketches . . . from Philadelphia to Pittsburg* (Philadelphia: J. W. Moore, 1854), p. 13.

37. Dickens, *American Notes*, pp. 74–75; D. W. Walker, "Rail Road Song," *Lancaster Gazette*, 13 July 1854, quoted in David H. Mould, *Dividing Lines: Canals, Railroads, and Urban Rivalries in Ohio's Hocking Valley, 1825–1875* (Dayton, Ohio: Wright State University Press, 1994), p. 204; "Statistics and Speculations concerning the Pacific Railroad," *Putnam's Magazine* 2 (September 1853): 271; Henry D. Thoreau, *Walden* (New York: Perennial Classics/Harper and Row, 1965), pp. 87–88.

38. Bigelow, *Elements of Technology*, p. 212; Gerstner, *Early American Railroads*, pp. 144–145; Ringwalt, *Development of Transportation Systems*, p. 103.

39. Carl Russell Fish, "The Northern Railroads, April 1861," *American Historical Review* 22 (July 1917): 785; Robert C. Black, *The Railroads of the Confederacy* (Chapel Hill: University of North Carolina Press, 1952), pp. 9–10; Weber, *Northern Railroads in the Civil War*, pp. 7–10; Edward L. Ayers, *Southern Crossing: A History of the American South, 1877–1906* (New York: Oxford University Press, 1995), p. 9.

40. "Improvements in Machinery," *North American Review* 14 (1822): 414; *Journal of the Franklin Institute* 9 (1830): 352.

41. W. J. M. Rankine, *A Manual of the Steam Engine and Other Prime Movers* (London: Griffin, Bohn, 1861), p. 81.

42. Dickens, *American Notes*, p. 173; Bruce Sinclair, *Early Research at the Franklin Institute: The Investigation into the Causes of Steam Boiler Explosions, 1830–1837* (Philadelphia: Franklin Institute, 1966); Louis C. Hunter, *A History of Industrial Power in the United States, 1780–1930*, vol. 2 (Charlottesville: University of Virginia Press, 1979), pp. 355, 371, 382; *Journal of the Franklin Institute* 54 (1852): 267.

43. "Ode to the Iron Horse," *United States Democratic Review* 34 (September 1854): 207–209.

44. *Journal of the Franklin Institute* 2 (1826): 148; Dolores Greenberg, "En-

ergy, Power and Perceptions of Social Change in the Early Nineteenth Century," *American Historical Review* 95 (1990): 695.

3. REMAKING HORSES

1. J. H. Reeves, *The Orange County Stud Book* (New York: Jason H. Tuttle, 1880), p. 34.

2. John Strohm, "The Conestoga Horse," in *Report of the Commissioner of Patents: Agricultural Report, 1853* (Washington, D.C.: A. O. P. Nicolson, 1854), pp. 176, 178–179; Albert I. Drachman, "Summary of the Development of the Conestoga Horse," in George Shumway, Edward Durell, and Howard C. Frey, *Conestoga Wagons, 1750–1850* (York, Pa.: George Shumway Publisher, 1966), p. 135; Stonehenge [John Henry Walsh], *The Horse in the Stable and the Field* (New York: George Routledge and Sons, 1869), p. 43.

3. William H. H. Murray, *The Perfect Horse* (Boston: James R. Osgood, 1873), p. 369; D. C. Linsley, *Morgan Horses* (New York: C. M. Saxton, 1857), pp. 9–10, 24–25; *Ohio Cultivator* 12 (1856): 230.

4. Elias Smith to Simon Cameron, 9 April 1861, Record Group 92, box 839, National Archives; *American Agriculturist* 42 (1883): 556.

5. "What Are We Coming To?" *Atlantic Monthly* 8 (October 1861): 490; E. H. Denby, "Resources of the South," ibid., 9 (October 1862): 506; *Spirit of the Times,* quoted in Michael C. C. Adams, *Our Masters the Rebels* (Cambridge, Mass.: Harvard University Press, 1978), p. 76.

6. Emory M. Thomas, *Bold Dragoon: The Life of J. E. B. Stuart* (New York: Harper and Row, 1986).

7. Frederick Law Olmsted, *A Journey in the Back Country, 1853–54* (1860; reprint, New York: Schocken, 1970); Gavin Wright, *The Political Economy of the Cotton South* (New York: W. W. Norton, 1978).

8. *American Agriculturist* 1 (1842): 250; ibid., 23 (1864).

9. Margaret E. Derry, *Bred for Perfection: Shorthorn Cattle, Collies, and Arabian Horses since 1800* (Baltimore: Johns Hopkins University Press, 2003), pp. 3–5.

10. Nicholas Russell, *Like Engend'ring Like: Heredity and Animal Breeding in Early Modern England* (Cambridge: Cambridge University Press, 1986), p. 58.

11. Edward Constant, "The Social Locus of Technological Practice: Com-

munity, System, or Organization?" in *The Social Construction of Technological Systems: New Directions in the Sociology and History of Technology*, ed. Wiebe E. Bijker, Thomas P. Hughes, and Trevor Pinch (Cambridge, Mass.: MIT Press, 1989), p. 232.

12. F. R. Marshall, *Breeding Farm Animals* (Chicago: Breeders' Gazette, 1911), p. 189.

13. Reeves, *Orange County Stud Book*, p. 93.

14. J. H. Sanders, *Horse Breeding* (Chicago: J. H. Sanders, 1885), pp. 9–10.

15. George B. Ellenberg, "Mule South to Tractor South: Mules, Machines, Agriculture, and Culture in the Cotton South, 1850–1950" (Ph.D. diss., University of Kentucky, 1994).

16. Harriet Ritvo, *The Platypus and the Mermaid, and Other Figments of the Classifying Imagination* (Cambridge, Mass.: Harvard University Press, 1997), p. 130.

17. Murray, *The Perfect Horse*, p. 387.

18. Charles Darwin, *The Variation of Plants and Animals under Domestication*, vol. 2 (1883; reprint, Baltimore: Johns Hopkins University Press, 1998), pp. 397–399.

19. Richard S. Reynolds, *An Essay on the Breeding and Management of Draught Horses* (London: Balliere, Tindall and Cox, 1882), p. 14; D. J. Browne, "Domestic Animals," in *Report of the Commissioner of Patents: Agricultural Report, 1854* (Washington, D.C.: Beverly Tucker, 1855), p. 2.

20. John H. Wallace, *The Horse of America, in His Derivation, History and Development* (New York: Privately published, 1897), p. 465.

21. *American Agriculturist* 1 (1843): 339–340; Browne, "Domestic Animals," pp. 2–4.

22. Herman Biddell et al., *Heavy Horses: Breeds and Management* (London: Vinton, 1894), p. 23.

23. Sanders, *Horse Breeding*, p. 64; Sperry [pseud.], *Hints and Helps to Horsemen* (New York: Albert Cogswell, 1877), p. 9.

24. Marshall, *Breeding Farm Animals*, p. 115.

25. Agassiz quoted in Sanders, *Horse Breeding*, p. 61; McGillivray quoted in Stephen Lincoln Goodale, *The Principles of Breeding* (Boston: Crosby, Nichols, Lee, 1861), pp. 52–53. On Law, see Manly Miles, *Stock-Breeding* (New York: D. Appleton, 1879), pp. 265–267.

26. Eugene Davenport, *Principles of Breeding: A Treatise on Thremmatology* (Boston: Ginn, 1907), pp. 186, 188–189; *Southern Planter* 38 (1877):

716–720; Linda Schiebinger, *Nature's Body: Gender in the Making of Modern Science* (Boston: Beacon, 1993), pp. 138, 140.

27. Goodale, *Principles of Breeding*, p. 25; Wallace, *The Horse of America*, pp. 478–479; Davenport, *Principles of Breeding*, pp. 232–233.

28. Miles, *Stock-Breeding*, p. 255.

29. *Spirit of the Times* 87 (1874): 28.

30. R. J. Moore-Colyer, "Aspects of the Trade in British Pedigree Draught Horses with the United States and Canada, c. 1850–1920," *Agricultural History Review* 48 (2000): 48.

31. Margaret E. Derry, *Horses in Society: A Story of Animal Breeding and Marketing, 1800–1920* (Toronto: University of Toronto Press, 2006), p. 70; *Southern Planter* 38 (1877): 268.

32. *American Agriculturist* 45 (1886): 197, 366.

33. Derry, *Horses in Society*, p. 74.

34. Ibid., p. 77; Sperry, *Hints and Helps to Horsemen*, p. 22.

35. *American Agriculturist* 48 (June 1889): 287.

36. Biddell et al., *Heavy Horses*, p. 6.

37. Marshall, *Breeding Farm Animals*, p. 210.

38. Department of Agriculture, *Yearbook of the United States Department of Agriculture, 1900* (Washington, D.C.: Government Printing Office, 1901), pp. 647–648.

39. Sanders, *Horse Breeding*, pp. 31–32.

40. Biddell et al., *Heavy Horses*, pp. 36, 8.

41. Derry, *Horses in Society*, p. 79.

42. Clay McShane and Joel A. Tarr, *The Horse in the City: Living Machines in the Nineteenth Century* (Baltimore: Johns Hopkins University Press, 2007), p. 12.

43. *American Agriculturist* 50 (1891): 198.

44. *American Agriculturist* 52 (1883); *National Livestock Journal* 11 (1880): 249; *American Agriculturist* 50 (1891): 682; ibid., 42 (1883): 277; ibid., 52 (1893): 328.

45. Philip Scranton, *Endless Novelty: Specialty Production and American Industrialization, 1865–1925* (Princeton: Princeton University Press, 1997), p. 10.

46. *American Agriculturist* 42 (1883): 328.

47. Sanders, *Horse Breeding*, pp. 137–138; *American Agriculturist* 42 (1883): 14; ibid., 45 (1886): 97; ibid., 48 (1889): 229; ibid., 53 (1894): 6; Derry, *Horses in Society*, pp. 86, 91.

48. Phillip Thurtle, "Harnessing Heredity in Gilded Age America: Middle-Class Mores and Industrial Breeding in a Cultural Context," *Journal of the History of Biology* 35 (2002): 44–46.
49. Holmes quoted in ibid., p. 50; Wallace, *The Horse of America,* pp. 519–521.
50. Sanders, *Horse Breeding,* pp. 80–81.
51. *American Agriculturist* 50 (1891): 607.
52. *American Agriculturist* 53 (1894): 1–5; Tamara Plakins Thornton, *Cultivating Gentlemen* (New Haven: Yale University Press, 1989), p. 207.
53. American Breeders' Association, *Proceedings,* vol. 1 (1905), pp. 10, 12–13.
54. Wallace, *The Horse of America,* pp. 461–462.
55. Ibid., p. 459.

4. CIVIL WAR HORSES

1. Charles W. Ramsdell, "General Robert E. Lee's Horse Supply, 1862–1865," *American Historical Review* 35 (1930).
2. Russell F. Weigley, *History of the United States Army* (New York: Macmillan, 1967), p. 220; James M. McPherson, *Battle Cry of Freedom* (New York: Ballantine, 1988), p. 306 n. 41 and p. 325; *Official Records of the War of the Rebellion,* Series III, 5 vols., 4: 1212 (hereafter *OR*). The *OR* as a whole was published from 1880 to 1901 in 70 volumes: Series I, 1880–1898 (53 vols.); Series II, 1894–1899 (8 vols.); Series III, 1899–1900 (5 vols.); and Series IV, 1900–1901 (4 vols.).
3. John G. Moore, "Mobility and Strategy in the Civil War," *Military Affairs* 24 (1960); Edward Hagerman, "Field Transportation and Strategic Mobility in the Union Armies," *Civil War History* 34 (1988).
4. *OR,* Ser. I, 4: 353; 31, pt. 1: 737.
5. Edward W. Coffman, *The Old Army* (New York: Oxford University Press, 1986), pp. 76–78; Stephen Z. Starr, *The Union Cavalry in the Civil War,* vol. 1 (Baton Rouge: Louisiana State University Press, 1979), pp. 52–53.
6. Daniel M. Holt, letter, 27 September 1864, in *A Surgeon's Civil War: The Letters and Diary of Daniel M. Holt, M.D.,* ed. James M. Greiner, Janet L. Coryell, and James R. Smithen (Kent, Ohio: Kent State University Press, 1994), p. 260; Russell F. Weigley, *Quartermaster General of the Union Army* (New York: Columbia University Press, 1959), p. 264.
7. Moore, "Mobility and Strategy in the Civil War," pp. 75–76; Weigley, *Quartermaster General,* p. 269; *OR,* Ser. I, 3, pt. 5: 243; Myers to Meigs,

28 September 1863, box 297, Record Group 92, National Archives (cited hereafter as RG).

8. Mark R. Wilson, *The Business of Civil War: Military Mobilization and the State, 1861–1865* (Baltimore: Johns Hopkins University Press, 2006), pp. 36–37; Weigley, *Quartermaster General;* Sherrod E. East, "Montgomery Meigs and the Quartermaster Department," *Military Affairs* 25 (Winter 1961–62).

9. Wilson, *The Business of Civil War,* pp. 138, 140.

10. The figure of 15,000 animals is the author's estimate based on the size of the army in 1860; McPherson, *Battle Cry of Freedom,* p. 313.

11. Potter to Ekim, 21 March 1864; McKim to Ekim, 22 February and 5 March 1864, Consolidated Correspondence File (hereafter CCF), box 1267, RG 92; Johnson to Thompson, 22 August 1863, CCF, box 839, RG 92.

12. "Horse Specifications," 2 July 1863, CCF, box 840, RG 92; Jenkins to Meigs, 22 May 1863, CCF, box 839, RG 92.

13. Lee to Meigs, 14 August 1863, CCF, "Horses 1863," box 839, RG 92.

14. Citizens of Huntingdon to Meigs, 2 November 1861, CCF, ibid.

15. Wilson to Jones, 9 December 1861; Jones to Thomas, 18 December 1861, ibid.

16. Jenkins to Meigs, 10 June 1863; Lee to Meigs, 23 June 1863, ibid.

17. Fosser to Meigs, 25 June 1863, ibid.; Kealey [*sic*] to Ekim, 8 April 1864, box 1267, file 418, RG 92.

18. *OR,* Ser. I, 23, pt. 2: 303; "Rules and Regulations," CCF, box 838, RG 92.

19. *American Agriculturist* 22 (1863): 231; ibid., 23 (1864): 70, 102.

20. *OR,* Ser. III, 1: 432–433.

21. Nash to Meigs, 21 November 1861, CCF, box 839, RG 92; *OR,* Ser. I, 25, pt. 2: 547.

22. East, "Meigs and the Quartermaster Department," p. 192.

23. *OR,* Ser. I, 23, pt. 2: 301.

24. Hagerman, "Field Transportation and Strategic Mobility," pp. 149, 157; *OR,* Ser. I, 29, pt. 2: 420; 31, pt. 3: 70, 130, 179; 33: 853–854, 920–921.

25. *Scientific American* 13 (1858); Richard Morris, "Horseshoe Economics: To Shoe or Not to Shoe, That Is the Issue," *Nevada Historical Society Quarterly* 30 (1987): 304–315.

26. Rucker to Meigs, 28 July 1862, CCF, box 839, RG 92.

27. Stone, Chisholm, and Jones to Sibley, 21 July 1862; Corning Winslow Co. to Sibley, 5 August 1862; Bussing and Co. to Gully, 15 December 1863, ibid.

28. Proceedings of a Board of Survey, 18 February 1863, CCF, box 840, RG 92.

29. G. Terry Sharrer, "The Great Glanders Epizootic, 1861–1866: A Civil War Legacy," *Agricultural History* 69 (Winter 1995): 79–97; *American Agriculturist* 24 (1865): 269.

30. Dr. Asche-Berg, "Veterinary Matters in America: Mainly from the Civil War in 1861 and 1862," National Institute of Health Library Translation, trans. Ted Crump, *Magazine für die gesamte Theirheilkunde* 29 (1863): 1, 10.

31. Anonymous to Eckert, 18 June 1863; Peirce to Sawtelle [*sic*], 26 June 1863; Stanton to Meigs, 18 June 1863; Sawtelle [*sic*] to Ingalls, 29 June 1863, CCF, box 839, RG 92.

32. *OR*, Ser. I, 27, pt. 2: 543, 590; Journal of William Bolton, 51st Pennsylvania, Civil War Library and Museum, Philadelphia; *OR*, Ser. I, 33: 853–854; 52, pt. 1: 702; 36, pt. 1: 797–798; *American Annual Cyclopedia* (New York: D. Appleton, 1864), p. 37.

33. *OR*, Ser. I, 30, pt. 2: 648, 668–673.

34. Charles F. Adams Jr., 30 November 1862, in *A Cycle of Adams Letters*, ed. Worthington Chauncey Ford, 2 vols. (Boston: Houghton Mifflin, 1920), 1: 202–203; *OR*, Ser. I, 10, pt. 1: 46–49, 57, 64.

35. Adams, 30 November 1862, in *A Cycle of Adams Letters*, 1: 201.

36. *OR*, Ser. I, 30, pt. 1: 49; 30, pt. 3: 929.

37. Baker to Meigs, 6 October 1863; Dudley to Meigs, 26 October 1863; Doolittle to Reynolds, 29 October 1863; Asmussen to Fisher, 30 October 1863, "Letters and Telegrams," box 297, RG 92; *OR*, Ser. I, 30, pt. 2: 723, 30, pt. 4: 62; 31, pt. 1: 70.

38. *OR*, Ser. I, 30, pt. 1: 221; *OR*, Ser. III, 4: 879.

39. *OR*, Ser. I, 10, pt. 1: 209; 30, pt. 1: 195, 309, 354.

40. *OR*, Ser. I, 10, pt. 1: 245.

41. Ibid., p. 246.

42. *The Civil War Diary of Cyrus F. Boyd, Fifteenth Iowa Infantry, 1861–1863,* ed. Mildred Throne (Baton Rouge: Louisiana State University Press, 1998), pp. 32–33; *OR*, Ser. I, 29, pt. 2: 221; 10, 29, pt. 1: 46–49, 226–227; 30, pt. 1: 597.

43. *OR*, Ser. I, 3: 234; 2: 189–190; John Keegan, *The Face of Battle* (New York: Penguin, 1976), pp. 95–96, 158–159.

44. *OR*, Ser. I, 10, pt. 1: 146.

45. George B. McClellan, *Report on the Organization and Campaigns of the*

Army of the Potomac (New York: Sheldon, 1864), p. 418; *OR,* Ser. I, 19, pt. 2: 422–424.

46. *OR,* Ser. I, 23, pt. 2: 303.

47. *OR,* Ser. I, 30, pt. 1: 324.

48. Adams, 12 May 1863, in *A Cycle of Adams Letters,* 2: 3–5.

49. Kennedy to Meigs, 31 January 1862; Halstead to Meigs, 2 February 1862; Still to Lincoln, 2 November 1863; Lanks to Stanton, 14 April 1863, CCF, box 839, RG 92.

50. *OR,* Ser. I, 29, pt. 2: 419; 10, pt. 2: 270.

51. *OR,* Ser. I, 23, pt. 2: 271, 288–289; Halleck to Meigs, 14 January 1863; Meigs to Stanton, 14 January 1863; Stanton to Rosecrans, 18 January 1863; Rosecrans to Meigs, 24 April 1863, CCF, box 839, RG 92.

52. *OR,* Ser. I, 19, pt. 2: 423; 23, pt. 2: 301–303.

53. Henry Robinson Berkeley, *Four Years in the Confederate Artillery: The Diary of Private Henry Robinson Berkeley,* ed. William H. Runge (Chapel Hill: University of North Carolina Press, 1961), p. 67; John D. Billings, *Hardtack and Coffee; or, The Unwritten Story of Army Life* (Boston: G. M. Smith, 1887), p. 207.

54. Constance Sullivan, ed., *Landscapes of the Civil War* (New York: Alfred A. Knopf, 1995); Holt, diary entry, 16 September 1862, in *A Surgeon's Civil War;* Oliver Wendell Holmes Sr., "My Hunt after 'The Captain,'" *Atlantic Monthly* 9 (December 1862): 745–748; Adams, 8 March 1863, in *A Cycle of Adams Letters,* 1: 294; ibid., 12 May 1863, 2: 5.

55. Drew Gilpin Faust, "Equine Relics of the Civil War," *Southern Cultures* 6 (Spring 2000): 22–49.

5. Horses as Industrial Workers

1. Details drawn from Waddell F. Smith, *The Story of the Pony Express* (San Francisco: Hesperian House, 1960); Alvin Harlow, *Old Post Bags* (New York: D. Appleton, 1928).

2. Donald Worster, "Cowboy Ecology," in *Under Western Skies: Nature and History in the American West* (New York: Oxford University Press, 1992), pp. 35–36.

3. Joel A. Tarr and Clay McShane, "The Centrality of the Horse in the Nineteenth Century American City," in *The Making of Urban America,* ed. Raymond A. Mohl (Wilmington, Del.: SR Books, 1997), p. 107.

4. *Philadelphia Inquirer,* 24 October 1872, p. 2.

5. *Boston Daily Advertiser,* 24 October 1872, p. 1.

6. Elizabeth Atwood Lawrence, *Hoofbeats and Society: Studies of Human-Horse Interactions* (Bloomington: Indiana University Press, 1985); Ted Steinberg, *Down to Earth: Nature's Role in American History* (New York: Oxford University Press, 2002), pp. 157–159; Alan Trachtenberg, *Reading American Photographs* (New York: Hill and Wang, 1989), p. 288.

7. John H. White Jr., "Steam in the Streets: The Grice and Long Dummy," *Technology and Culture* 27 (1986): 106–109.

8. "Broad Street, Looking East," ca. 1907, Print Collection, Library Company of Philadelphia.

9. Phil M. Teigen, "Counting Urban Horses in the United States," *Argos* (Utrecht) 26 (2002): 273.

10. Clay McShane, "Gelded Age Boston," *New England Quarterly* 74 (2001): 295–297.

11. Ernest Hexamer, *Barnes' Map of the Whole Incorporated City of Philadelphia* (Philadelphia: R. L. Barnes, 1864).

12. McShane, "Gelded Age Boston," pp. 283–285.

13. Clay McShane, *Down the Asphalt Path: The Automobile and the American City* (New York: Columbia University Press, 1994), pp. 48–52; George Waring Jr., *Report on the Social Statistics of Cities,* Part 1 (1880; reprint, New York: Arno, 1970).

14. Abbot, Downing & Company, "Chart A: Catalogue and Price List," (ca. 1871; reprint, Lexington: Carriage Association of America, 1984), Abbot-Downing Collection, New Hampshire Historical Society, Concord; F. M. L. Thompson, "Nineteenth Century Horse Sense," *Economic History Review* 29 (1976): 78.

15. Tarr and McShane, "Centrality of the Horse," pp. 107, 119.

16. Strawbridge Wagon, ca. 1900; Knickerbocker Ice, ca. 1900; Castelli wagon, ca. 1910, Print Collection, Library Company of Philadelphia; McAllister pony team, ca. 1895, Davis Collection, ibid.

17. As described in Louis C. Hunter, *A History of Industrial Power in the United States, 1780–1930,* vol. 3 (Charlottesville: University of Virginia Press, 1991); Joel A. Tarr, "A Note on the Horse as an Urban Power Source," *Journal of Urban History* 25 (1999): 434–448; Donna Rilling, *Making Houses, Crafting Capitalism* (Philadelphia: University of Pennsylvania Press, 2001), pp. 92, 105, and 168; Susan D. Jones, *Valuing Animals: Veterinarians and Their Patients in Modern America* (Baltimore:

Johns Hopkins University Press, 2003), pp. 18, 23; *Street Railway Review* 10 (1900): 724.

18. For example, *Annual Report of the Board of Health, 1890* (Philadelphia, 1891); ibid., *1893* (Philadelphia, 1894); Waring, *Report on Social Statistics of Cities.*

19. Brian J. Cudahy, *Cash, Tokens, and Transfers: A History of Urban Mass Transit in North America* (New York: Fordham University Press, 1990); Clay McShane and Joel A. Tarr, *The Horse in the City: Living Machines in the Nineteenth Century* (Baltimore: Johns Hopkins University Press, 2007), p. 54.

20. John H. White Jr., *Horsecars, Cable Cars, and Omnibuses* (New York: Dover, 1974).

21. Alexander Easton, *A Practical Treatise on Street or Horsepower Railways* . . . (Philadelphia: Crissy and Markley, 1859), pp. 5, 8–12; *Street Railway Review* 1 (1891): 587; Frederic W. Speirs, *The Street Railway System of Philadelphia: Its History and Present Condition* (Baltimore: Johns Hopkins Press, 1897), p. 11; Louis P. Hager, ed., *History of the West End Street Railway* (Boston: n.p., 1892), pp. 59–60.

22. U.S. Census Office, *Eleventh Census,* vol. 5 (Washington, D.C.: Government Printing Office, 1895), pp. 704–720, 728–729; John H. White Jr., "Horse Power," *American Heritage of Invention and Technology* 8 (1992): 41–51; Hager, *History of West End Street Railway,* pp. 59, 119; Waring, *Report on Social Statistics of Cities,* p. 564.

23. Easton, *Practical Treatise on Street Railways,* p. 96.

24. Speirs, *Street Railway System of Philadelphia,* pp. 30–32.

25. *Street Railway Review* 1 (1891): 33, 560; ibid., 2 (1892): 615; ibid., 7 (1897); McShane, "Gelded Age Boston," pp. 293–294.

26. Tarr and McShane, "Centrality of the Horse," p. 111; Sam Bass Warner, *Streetcar Suburbs* (Cambridge, Mass.: Harvard University Press, 1978); Peter Schmidt, *Back to Nature: The Arcadian Myth in Urban America* (New York: Oxford University Press, 1969).

27. *Addresses and Remonstrances against Fifth and Sixth Street Railways* (Philadelphia, 1857), p. 3.

28. Easton, *Practical Treatise on Street Railways,* p. 5; *Street Railway Review* 5 (1895): 418; *Munsey's Magazine* 20 (1898–99).

29. Citizens' Municipal Reform Association, *Passenger Railways* (Philadelphia, 1874), p. 1.

30. *Street Railway Review* 2 (1892): 407; National Cable Car Company, *System of Traction Railways for Cities and Towns* (New York, 1883), pp. 6, 12, 15.

31. *Street Railway Review* 1 (1891): 33.

32. *Spirit of the Times* 87 (1874): 35.

33. U.S. Census Office, *Eleventh Census,* pp. 704–720, 728–729; U.S. Census Office, *Twelfth Census,* vol. 5 (Washington, D.C., 1902), pp. 387–395.

34. *Street Railway Review* 2 (1892): 561; ibid., 4 (1894): 339; ibid., 10 (1900): 199–200.

35. "The Position of the Horse in Modern Society," *The Nation* 15 (31 October 1872): 278.

36. U.S. Census Office, *Agriculture of the United States in 1860* (Washington, D.C.: Government Printing Office, 1864), pp. xii, clxiv.

37. *Country Gentleman* 1 (1853): 21, 117; Leo Rogin, *The Introduction of Farm Machinery in Its Relationship to the Productivity of Labor in the Agriculture of the United States during the Nineteenth Century* (Berkeley: University of California Press, 1931); *American Agriculturist* 30 (1871): 166.

38. *American Farmer,* quoted in Clarence Danhof, *Change in Agriculture: The Northern United States, 1820–1870* (Cambridge, Mass.: Harvard University Press, 1990), pp. 218, 228.

39. "McCormick's Patent Reaping and Mowing Machine!," circular, January 1853, folder 5X-1, McCormick Collection, State Historical Society of Wisconsin, Madison (hereafter McCormick Collection).

40. *Country Gentleman* 2 (1853): 117; Patent Reissues, 1861–1870, folder 5X-1, McCormick Collection.

41. Northcott to McCormick Co., 16 April 1888; Traline to McCormick Co, 7 March 1888, folder 2x, McCormick Collection.

42. Application for reissue of original McCormick patent of 21 June 1864, United States Patent Office no. 1270, 27 October 1870, folder 5X-1, McCormick Collection.

43. J. Sanford Rikoon, *Threshing in the Midwest, 1820–1940* (Bloomington: Indiana University Press, 1988).

44. Tarr, "Note on Horse as Urban Power Source," p. 435; Hunter, *History of Industrial Power,* p. 38.

45. McShane and Tarr, *The Horse in the City,* chap. 6.

46. Reynold M. Wik, *Steam Power on the American Farm* (Philadelphia: University of Pennsylvania Press, 1953).

47. U.S. Bureau of the Census, *Historical Statistics of the United States,* Part

1 (Washington, D.C.: Government Printing Office, 1974), pp. 498, 499, 512; U.S. Department of Agriculture, Economic Resource Service, "A History of American Agriculture, 1776-1990," http://www.usda.gov.

48. Jeremy Atack and Fred Bateman, *To Their Own Soil: Agriculture in the Antebellum North* (Ames: Iowa State University Press, 1987), pp. 3, 6.

49. U.S. Bureau of the Census, *Historical Statistics of the United States*, Part 1, pp. 8, 105-106; ibid., Part 2 (Washington, D.C.: Government Printing Office, 1975), p. 818.

6. Studying Horses

1. Anna Sewell, *Black Beauty* (1877; reprint, New York: Signet Classic, 1986). Subsequent references to the novel itself are to chapters rather than to pages in a specific edition.

2. Rodney Engen, "Afterword," ibid., p. 214; Peter Hollindale, "Introduction," in Sewell, *Black Beauty* (New York: Oxford University Press, 1992), pp. xviii-xxi; Sewell, *Black Beauty*, chaps. 2, 3, 12, 15, 16, 18, 22, 24, 27, 28, 30, 36, 41, 45, 47.

3. Sewell, *Black Beauty*, chap. 9.

4. Ibid., chap. 29.

5. Ibid., chap. 3.

6. George T. Angell, *Autobiographical Sketches and Personal Recollections* (Boston: American Humane Education Society, 1892), pp. 11, 42, 46, 94-95; Angell, *Protection of Animals* (New York: American Social Science Association, Hurd and Houghton, 1874), pp. 14-16; Engen, "Afterword," p. 227; Hollindale, "Introduction," pp. xxi, xxv; James Turner, *Reckoning with the Beast: Animals, Pain, and Humanity in the Victorian Mind* (Baltimore: Johns Hopkins University Press, 1980), pp. 52-53, 75-76, 124.

7. Gordon Hendricks, *Eadweard Muybridge: The Father of the Motion Picture* (New York: Grossman, 1975), p. 46; Rebecca Solnit, *River of Shadows: Eadweard Muybridge and the Technological Wild West* (New York: Penguin, 2003), pp. 77-79.

8. Kevin MacDonnell, *Eadweard Muybridge: The Man Who Invented the Motion Picture* (Boston: Little, Brown, 1975), p. 89.

9. Etienne-Jules Marey, "The Paces of the Horse," *Popular Science Monthly* 6 (1874): 129-142.

10. Quoted in Hendricks, *Eadweard Muybridge*, p. 112; Solnit, *River of Shad-*

ows, pp. 183–191; Theodore A. Dodge, "The Horse's Motion as Revealed by Photography," *Dial* 2 (1882): 288–290.

11. Siegfried Giedion, *Mechanization Takes Command* (New York: Oxford University Press, 1948), pp. 24–25; Solnit, *River of Shadows,* pp. 209–212.

12. J. D. B. Stillman, *The Horse in Motion* (Boston: Osgood, 1882), p. 101.

13. W. Horace Hoskins, "A Nation's Loss: A Profession's Tribute to Fallen Leaders," in *Proceedings of the American Veterinarian Medical Association,* ed. Richard P. Lyman (Lansing, Mich., 1911), pp. 275–276.

14. Stillman, *The Horse in Motion,* pp. 100, 101.

15. Ibid., pp. 9–10, 15–21, 32–34, 46–47, 71.

16. Ibid., pp. 22, 29, 31, 55–56, 71.

17. Ibid., pp. 80, 86, 101–102, 109–119.

18. Samuel Haber, *The Quest for Authority and Honor in the American Professions, 1750–1900* (Chicago: University of Chicago Press, 1991), pp. xiii, 201; Magali S. Larson, *The Rise of Professionalism* (Berkeley: University of California Press, 1977), pp. 5–6; Arthur Stinchcombe, "Social Structure and Organizations," in *Handbook of Organizations,* ed. James G. March (New York: Rand McNally, 1965), pp. 153, 160, quoted in Larson, *The Rise of Professionalism,* p. 6; Burton J. Bledstein, *The Culture of Professionalism: The Middle Class and the Development of Higher Education in America* (New York: W. W. Norton, 1976), pp. 31, 84, 86–87; Donald A. Schon, *The Reflective Practitioner: How Professionals Think in Action* (New York: Basic Books, 1983), pp. 19–24, 31–34.

19. University of Pennsylvania, *Animal Locomotion: The Muybridge Work at the University of Pennsylvania* (1888; reprint, New York: Arno Press, 1973). This book contains three essays: "The Mechanics of Instantaneous Photography," by William D. Marks, Professor of Dynamical Engineering; "Materials for a Memoir on Animal Life," by Dr. Harrison Allen, Professor of Physiology; and "A Study of Some Normal and Abnormal Movements," by Dr. Francis X. Dercum, Instructor in Nervous Disease.

20. Raymond H. Merritt, *Engineering in American Society, 1850–1875* (Lexington: University of Kentucky Press, 1969), pp. 3, 40; Haber, *Quest for Authority and Honor,* pp. 295, 306.

21. Thomas H. Brigg, "Haulage by Horses," *Transactions of the American Society of Mechanical Engineers* 14 (1893): 1014, 1020.

22. Ibid., pp. 1015, 1017.

23. Ibid., pp. 1021–22, 1027.

24. Ibid., pp. 1014, 1044–47, 1064–65.

25. Samuel J. Berard, "Robert Henry Thurston—Brown 1859," *Brown University Engineer* 9 (August 1966): 12–19.

26. Brigg, "Haulage by Horses," p. 1059.

27. Robert H. Thurston, *The Animal as a Machine and a Prime Mover and the Laws of Energetics* (New York: John Wiley and Sons, 1894), p. 36; Louis C. Hunter, *A History of Industrial Power in the United States, 1780–1930,* vol. 1 (Charlottesville: University of Virginia Press, 1991), pp. xix–xx, 417.

28. Thurston, *The Animal as a Machine,* pp. 23–25, 30–32, 34–35.

29. Ibid., pp. 37, 41, 44–45, 50.

30. Ibid., pp. 51, 79, 81.

31. Ibid., pp. 3–4, 10–11, 24–25, 44–45, 97.

32. Brigg, "Haulage by Horses," pp. 84–85, 87, 89; George Basalla, "Energy and Civilization," in *Science, Technology, and the Human Prospect,* ed. Chauncey Starr and Philip C. Ritterbush (New York: Pergamon Press, 1979), p. 44.

33. F. H. King, *A Textbook of the Physics of Agriculture,* 5th ed. (Madison, Wis., 1910), pp. iii, 6–48; H. Copeland Greene, telephone conversation with author, 22 December 2002.

34. King, *Physics of Agriculture,* pp. 486–487.

35. Ibid., pp. 428–443, 487–502.

36. Department of Agriculture, "Feeding Standards," in *Yearbook of the Department of Agriculture, 1894* (Washington, D.C.: Government Printing Office, 1895), pp. 562–563.

37. Leslie E. MacLeod, "The National Horse of America," in *Report of the Commissioner of Agriculture, 1897* (Washington, D.C.: Government Printing Office, 1898), pp. 691–692.

38. Robert E. Kohler, *Lords of the Fly: Drosophila Genetics and the Experimental Life* (Chicago: University of Chicago Press, 1994), pp. 25–26; Liberty Hyde Bailey, *The Country Life Movement in the United States* (New York: Macmillan, 1913), pp. 1, 3.

39. George Rommel, *The Preservation of Our Native Types of Horses,* Department of Agriculture, Bureau of Animal Industry, Circular no. 137 (Washington, D.C.: Government Printing Office, 1908).

40. George Rommel, *The Regeneration of the Morgan Horse,* Department of Agriculture, Bureau of Animal Industry, Circular no. 163 (Washington, D.C.: Government Printing Office, 1910).

41. *American Breeders' Association Journal* 1 (1901): 12–13.

42. Captain Wilmot E. Ellis, "The American Cavalry Horse," *Munsey's Magazine* 33 (1905): 53; James Wilson, "Report of the Secretary," in Department of Agriculture, *Yearbook of the Department of Agriculture, 1910* (Washington, D.C.: Government Printing Office, 1911), pp. 44-45.

43. Nathaniel S. Shaler, *American Highways* (New York: Century, 1896), p. 242; Hal S. Barron, *Mixed Harvest: The Second Great Transformation in the Rural North, 1870-1930* (Chapel Hill: University of North Carolina Press, 1997), pp. 19-21, 23.

44. Department of Agriculture, Office of Public Roads, *Public-Road Mileage, Revenues and Expenditures in the United States in 1904,* Bulletin no. 32 (Washington, D.C.: Government Printing Office, 1907), table 1; Department of Agriculture, Office of Road Inquiry, *Historical and Technical Papers on Road Building in the United States,* Bulletin no. 17 (Washington, D.C.: Government Printing Office, 1898); Department of Agriculture, Office of Road Inquiry, *Proceedings of the Virginia Good Roads Convention,* Bulletin no. 11 (Washington, D.C.: Government Printing Office, 1895); *Prairie Farmer* 65 (January 1893): 4; Clayton S. Ellsworth, "Theodore Roosevelt's Country Life Commission," *Agricultural History* 34 (1960): 167; Barron, *Mixed Harvest,* pp. 11, 19.

45. Department of Agriculture, Office of Road Inquiry, *Proceedings of the National Road Conference,* Bulletin no. 10 (Washington, D.C.: Government Printing Office, 1894); Department of Agriculture, Office of Road Inquiry, *Proceedings of the Virginia Good Roads Convention.*

46. Department of Agriculture, Office of Road Inquiry, *Proceedings of the Virginia Good Roads Convention;* Department of Agriculture, Office of Road Inquiry, *Traffic of the Country Roads,* Circular no. 19 (Washington, D.C.: Government Printing Office, 1896).

47. King, *Physics of Agriculture,* pp. 431-433; Shaler, *American Highways,* p. 125.

48. Department of Agriculture, Office of Road Inquiry, *Wide Tires,* Bulletin no. 12 (Washington, D.C.: Government Printing Office, 1895); Shaler, *American Highways,* pp. 162-163.

49. Martin Dodge, "Steel-Track Wagon Roads," in Department of Agriculture, *Yearbook of the Department of Agriculture, 1898* (Washington, D.C.: Government Printing Office, 1899), pp. 291-296; Shaler, *American Highways,* p. 254.

50. Susan D. Jones, *Valuing Animals: Veterinarians and Their Patients in Modern America* (Baltimore: Johns Hopkins University Press, 2003),

pp. 12, 14, 40; "Importance of Veterinary Science," *American Veterinary Journal* 2 (May 1857): 155; Frederick A. Lyons, "The True Position of Veterinary Science," *American Veterinary Review* 3 (November 1879): 306, 315.

51. J. F. Smithcors, *The American Veterinary Profession: Its Background and Development* (Ames: Iowa State University Press, 1963), pp. 11, 95, 113, 351, and passim; Philip M. Teigen, "Nineteenth-Century Veterinary Medicine as an Urban Profession," *Veterinary Heritage* 23 (May 2000): 1–3; Teigen, "The Massachusetts Veterinary Profession, 1882–1904: A Case Study," *Historical Journal of Massachusetts* 25 (1997): 64.

52. O. H. V. Stalheim, *The Winning of Animal Health: 100 Years of Veterinary Medicine* (Ames: Iowa State University Press, 1994), p. 4; Jones, *Valuing Animals,* pp. 29, 31; "Alexander Liatuard's Letter," *New York Times,* 27 October 1872, p. 4; "Veterinary Sanitarians," *American Veterinary Review* 2 (January 1879): 430; James Law, American Veterinary College commencement address, ibid., 2 (April 1879): 5; "A National Veterinary Police," ibid., 3 (August 1879): 217; "Editorial," ibid. (October 1879): 271; E. Mink, "Medical Arts and Sanitary Science," ibid. (November 1879): 316; N. H. Paaren, "Necessity for Congressional Action in Relation to Contagious Diseases of Domestic Animals," ibid., pp. 320, 321; Daniel E. Salmon, "Scientific Investigations of the BAI," in *Proceedings of the United States Veterinary Medical Association, Session of 1891–92,* ed. W. Horace Hopkins (Philadelphia, 1893), p. 261; Rush Shippen Huidekoper, "The Identification of Animals," ibid., pp. 128–138.

53. Robert E. Kohler, *Landscapes and Labscapes: Exploring the Lab-Field Boundary in Biology* (Chicago: University of Chicago, 2002), pp. 7, 9.

54. Joanna Swabe, *Animals, Disease, and Human Social Life* (New York: Routledge, 1999), p. 78; Jones, *Valuing Animals,* pp. 11–12. Examples of hostility toward informal practitioners include "Influenza among Horses," *American Veterinary Journal* 1 (January 1856): 120–121; M. A. Cumming, "Veterinary Care and Farrier Care," ibid. (February 1856): 139; "Remarks on Influenza," ibid. (April 1856): 208; Robert Jennings, "Empiricism," ibid., 2 (April 1857): 102–103; Tait Butler, "Veterinary Education in America," *American Veterinary Review* 13 (1889–90): 440–449.

55. R. Kay, "Railroad Horses," *American Veterinary Review* 9 (August–September 1885): 207; C. B. Holmes, "Report on the Chicago City Railway," *Street Railway Review* 1 (1891): 14, 33.

56. Olaf Schwarkopf, "The Horse as a Producer of Antitoxins," *Journal of*

Comparative Medicine and Surgery 17 (1896): 13; "The Horse versus the Auto for the Physician," *American Veterinary Review* 32 (1907–08): 740–742.

57. "The Future of the Horse," *American Veterinary Review* 23 (1899–1900): 319–320; Jones, *Valuing Animals,* pp. 35–38; W. L. Williams, "Veterinary Inspection of Breeding Stallions," *American Veterinary Review* 23 (1899–1900): 408–415; "Conserving Horse Power," ibid., 32 (1907–08): 212; "Philadelphia Work Horse Parade," ibid., p. 290; "What Causes Horses to Run Away," ibid., 31 (1906–07): 153; "Horse and Human Keeping Step," ibid., p. 237.

58. J. H. Sanders, *Horse Breeding* (Chicago: J. H. Sanders, 1885), pp. 9, 11, 43–44, 78; Phillip Thurtle, "Harnessing Heredity in Gilded Age America: Middle-Class Mores and Industrial Breeding in a Cultural Context," *Journal of the History of Biology* 35 (2002): 48, 72; J. H. Reeves, *The Orange County Stud Book* (New York: Jason H. Tuttle, 1880), p. 31; James Douglas Anderson, *Making the American Thoroughbred* (Norwood, Mass.: Plimpton Press, 1916), pp. 3, 9; Margaret E. Derry, *Horses in Society: A Study of Animal Breeding and Marketing Culture, 1800–1920* (Toronto: University of Toronto Press: 2006), p. 15.

59. Frances Ware, *Driving* (Garden City, N.Y.: Doubleday, 1903), p. 107; John Kasson, *Rudeness and Civility: Manners in Nineteenth-Century Urban America* (New York: Hill and Wang, 1990), pp. 5–7. See also John Henry Walsh, *The Horse in the Stable and the Field* (Philadelphia: Porter, 1882); Edward Mayhew, *The Illustrated Horse Management* (Philadelphia: Lippincott, 1864); William Henry Herbert, *Frank Forester's Horse and Horsemanship of the United States,* rev. ed., ed. S. D. Bruce and B. G. Bruce (New York: Woodward, 1871).

60. Ware, *Driving,* pp. 129–130.

61. C. deHurst [pseud.], *How Women Should Ride* (New York: Harper and Brothers, 1892), pp. 9–10, 32–33, 34–35. See also Power O'Donoghue, *Ladies on Horseback* (London: Allen, 1881); H. O. de Bussigny, *Handbook for Horsewomen* (New York: D. Appleton, 1884).

62. William Youatt, *The Horse* (London: Charles Knight, 1849), p. 2; William Henry Flower, *The Horse: A Study in Natural History* (New York: D. Appleton, 1892), pp. 2–3; Sanders, *Horse Breeding,* p. 9.

63. Thomas P. Hughes, *Networks of Power* (Baltimore: Johns Hopkins University Press, 1983), p. 15.

64. G. W. Twitchell, *The Horse for Tomorrow*, Address delivered before the New Hampshire State Board of Agriculture, March 1895 (Concord, N.H.: Concord Republican Press Association, 1896), pp. 5–6; F. R. Marshall, *Breeding Farm Animals* (Chicago: Breeders' Gazette, 1911), p. 235.

65. Timothy F. Kruse, "Teamsters in the Gilded Age" (Master's thesis, University of Wisconsin, 1990), p. 12.

66. Turner, *Reckoning with the Beast*, p. 48; Pennsylvania Society for the Prevention of Cruelty to Animals, *Annual Report* (Philadelphia, 1869), p. 5. See also Pennsylvania Society for the Prevention of Cruelty to Animals, *Annual Reports*, 1869–1874.

67. Clay McShane, "Gelded Age Boston," *New England Quarterly* 74 (2001): 294–295; Harriet Ritvo, *The Animal Estate: The English and Other Creatures in the Victorian Age* (Cambridge, Mass.: Harvard University Press, 1987), chaps. 3 and 4.

68. Philadelphia Fountain Society, *Annual Reports, Addresses and Other Proceedings during the Years 1869 and 1870* (Philadelphia, 1871), p. 5; Philadelphia Fountain Society, *Annual Report, 1875* (Philadelphia, 1875).

69. Sewell, *Black Beauty*, chap. 49.

7. From Horse Powered to Horseless

1. Booth Tarkington, *The Magnificent Ambersons* (Grosset and Dunlap, 1918), chaps. 7–8.

2. U.S. Bureau of the Census, *Historical Statistics of the United States,* Part 2 (Washington, D.C.: Government Printing Office, 1975), p. 716.

3. Martin V. Melosi, *Effluent America: Cities, Industry, Energy and the Environment* (Pittsburgh: University of Pittsburgh Press, 2001), pp. 43, 59.

4. Naomi Rogers, "Germs with Legs: Flies, Disease, and the New Public Health," *Bulletin of the History of Medicine* 63 (1989): 600–615; W. E. Britton, "The Role of the House Fly and Certain Other Insects in the Spread of Human Diseases," *Popular Science Monthly* 81 (1912): 38–42; Nancy Tomes, *The Gospel of Germs* (Cambridge, Mass.: Harvard University Press, 1998).

5. Robin Doughty, *The English Sparrow in the American Landscape: A Paradox in Nineteenth Century Wildlife Conservation,* Research Paper 19, School of Geography (Oxford: Oxford University, 1973), p. 7; Jennifer Price, *Flight Maps* (New York: Basic Books, 1999), p. 84.

6. Clay McShane and Joel M. Tarr, *The Horse in the City: Living Machines in the Nineteenth Century* (Baltimore: Johns Hopkins University Press, 2007), chap. 2.

7. Paul Boyer, *Urban Masses and Moral Order in America, 1820–1920* (Cambridge, Mass.: Harvard University Press, 1978); Suellen Hoy, *Chasing Dirt: The American Pursuit of Cleanliness* (New York: Oxford University Press, 1995).

8. Vaclav Smil, *Energies* (Cambridge, Mass.: MIT Press, 1999), p. 117.

9. Z. R. Pettet, "The Farm Horse," in U.S. Bureau of the Census, *Fifteenth Census, Census of Agriculture* (Washington, D.C.: Government Printing Office, 1933), p. 60.

10. "The Future of the Horse," *American Veterinary Review* 23 (1899–1900): 318–320.

11. Isaac B. Potter, "The Gospel of Good Roads," *Good Roads* 1 (1892): 7, 15.

12. Ibid., pp. 22, 54, 57.

13. Walter Preston Brownlow, *Why Wagon Roads in the United States Are Bad and How They Can Be Improved* (N.p., 1904), p. 4.

14. L. F. Bates, "The Effect of the Bicycle upon Our Highway Laws," *The Wheelman* 1 (1882–83): 42–43.

15. Thomas Bender, *Toward an Urban Vision: Ideas and Institutions in Nineteenth Century America* (Lexington: University Press of Kentucky, 1975).

16. *Horseless Age* 4 (1899): 3.

17. Ibid., 1 (1895): 3, 8.

18. Ibid., 4 (1899): 19.

19. Ibid., 1 (1895): 8, 10, 2.

20. Ibid., 4 (1899): 6.

21. Ibid., 2 (1896): 2

22. Ibid., 4 (1899): 5–6.

23. Ibid., 3 (1899): 7; ibid., 5 (1901): 10.

24. Ibid., 11 (1903): 1.

25. Michael Kahan, "Pedestrian Matters: The Contested Meanings and Uses of Philadelphia's Streets, 1850s–1920s" (Ph.D. diss., University of Pennsylvania, 2002).

26. Henry Adams, *The Education of Henry Adams* (1907; reprint, New York: Random House Modern Library, 1931), p. 380.

27. Alfred W. Crosby, *Ecological Imperialism: The Biological Expansion of*

Europe, 900–1900 (Cambridge: Cambridge University Press, 1986), pp. 149–150.

28. Pettet, "The Farm Horse," p. 1.

EPILOGUE

1. Bob Ford, "A Stable of Horsepower," *Philadelphia Inquirer*, 20 May 2006, p. E1; Ford, "Barbaro, Broken," ibid., 21 May 2006, p. A1.

2. Sandy Bauers, "Amazing Animal, Stunning Injury," *Philadelphia Inquirer*, 23 May 2006, p. E5; William C. Rhoden, "The Anonymous Death of a Little-Known Filly," *New York Times*, 25 May 2006, pp. D1, D5.